The Ecology of Learning

The Ecology of Learning

Sustainability, Lifelong Learning and Everyday Life

John Blewitt

London • Sterling, VA

First published by Earthscan in the UK and USA in 2006

ISBN-10:   1-84407-204-5   paperback
ISBN-13:   978-1-84407-204-0   paperback
ISBN-10:   1-84407-203-7   hardback
ISBN-13:   978-1-84407-203-3   hardback

Typesetting by MapSet Ltd, Gateshead, UK
Printed and bound in the UK by Cromwell Press
Cover design by Danny Gillespie

For a full list of publications please contact:

Earthscan
8–12 Camden High Street
London, NW1 0JH, UK
Tel: +44 (0)20 7387 8558
Fax: +44 (0)20 7387 8998
Email: earthinfo@earthscan.co.uk
Web: **www.earthscan.co.uk**

22883 Quicksilver Drive, Sterling, VA 20166-2012, USA

Earthscan is an imprint of James and James (Science Publishers) Ltd and publishes in
association with the International Institute for Environment and Development

A catalogue record for this book is available from the British Library

Library of Congress Cataloging-in-Publication Data

Blewitt, John, 1957-
 The Ecology of Learning : sustainability, lifelong learning, and everyday life / John
Blewitt.
     p. cm.
 Includes bibliographical references.
 ISBN-13: 978-1-84407-203-3 (alk. paper)
 ISBN-10: 1-84407-203-7 (alk. paper)
 ISBN-13: 978-1-84407-204-0 (pbk. : alk. paper)
 ISBN-10: 1-84407-204-5 (pbk. : alk. paper)
 1. Environmental sciences—Popular works. 2. Environmental education—Popular
works. I. Title.
 GE110.B54 2006
 333.72—dc22

                                                                            2006012534

Contents

Acknowledgements

Many people have contributed to this book. Some appear in the text itself telling their stories and others have been influential through their writing and research. I thank them. But special thanks must go to two people. The first is Professor Cedric Cullingford of Huddersfield University, without whose support and encouragement this book would not exist. And the second is Lorna, my wife, whose deep commitment to an environmentally just and sustainable society impresses and motivates me like nothing else. This book is for her.

List of Boxes, Figures and Tables

BOXES

FIGURES

TABLES

Introduction

On a Personal Note –
The Story of the Flood

The afternoon was getting pretty dark. It had been raining heavily all day. In fact it had been raining hard for days. At times it seemed the downpour was more suited to the tropics than to North Yorkshire, such was its occasional ferocity. I had witnessed a wall of rain like this once before, but what we were all watching was not in Florida or Bali, or any other exotic location; it was in the gateway to the Dales.

My view of the rain and the low clouds was good. I was sitting in what masqueraded as my office or study at the top of the house, which was located, with a number of others, in a rather secluded and sheltered former quarry half-way up a hill on a busy road that linked Harrogate with the countryside. At around 4.00pm one late July afternoon the atmosphere suddenly became exceptionally thick and the rain came down so intensely that I thought it would go straight through the slate roof. My wife was in her studio in the basement, where she worked as an artist/designer and was dutifully completing assignments for a course she was taking at Leeds Metropolitan University. Most of her artwork, paintings, drawings, plans, books, lights, computers and assorted materials were there. From where she perched at her drawing board she could see clearly into the front garden, down the path and towards the entrance to our community.

A neighbour knocked on the door and informed us that the roads were like rivers and the surrounding fields were like lakes. And shortly after this warning, water started pouring down the quarry sides, off the road and into the close, down the path and slowly but relentlessly up the garden, and our neighbours' gardens, to the fronts of the houses, which comprised a small block of modern terraces, one detached house, a bungalow and our own Edwardian end-of-terrace home. The water was brown and there was a distinct smell of sewage in the air. We phoned the local council asking where we could secure sandbags and a burly neighbour went off in his truck to get some.

Soon after we were all placing sandbags around our doors, French windows and other vulnerable areas, but still the water continued to rise and the rain to fall. By about 4.30pm all of those who were at home that after-noon, and by some strange coincidence most of us seemed to be, wondered when the water would start to invade our dwellings. The weather was certainly getting odder, someone remarked. 'Climate change', said another by way of explanation and left it at that. The situation deteriorated further. My wife and I started to move stuff from the basement up the stairs to a place of safety. Then at about 5.00pm the murky floodwater reached the house, lapped up against the walls and, as water does, found it way in first as a dribble and then as a steady flow. Our immediate neighbours had only moved in the week before and the previous owners had lowered the floor of their basement to provide themselves with additional, more comfortable, living accommodation. They stood and watched as they recognized that their French windows and sandbags would be no real defence against the flood.

Within minutes of the house being breached, we had about a half a metre of water rushing through the basement, spouting from the external drains and our internal plumbing. The downstairs shower was a mini dirty fountain. I opened the back door of the basement to allow the water to move freely through and out of the house. We had rescued some of the most important artwork but not all and we completely failed to rescue the contents of the fridge-freezer, which was also housed in the studio. Next door the water was more than a metre deep and neighbours from all around stood thigh deep with plastic buckets in hand fruitlessly attempting to bale it out. We all felt immensely sorry for our new neighbours and interestingly we all bonded quickly through experiencing the common adversity. Like other suburban neighbourhoods we knew some people better than others. We had been on nodding terms with some and bosom friends with others but all this no longer mattered. The Dunkirk spirit, as the cliché has it, emerged spontaneously, but for a moment all I could think of was those old black and white submarine movies set during World War II – close all watertight doors. Except, of course, there weren't any.

Just after 5.30pm the rain started to ease off. By 6.00pm it had stopped and by about 7.30pm the water level in our house was just a few centimetres deep. Tremendous damage, however, had already been done. We later learnt the floodwater had been contaminated, as we suspected, because the local sewage works had overflowed. The tiled floor would have to come up and be replaced, the wall replastered up to a metre and a half. Everything that had been touched by the water had to be disposed of or destroyed but before any work could be done the basement had to be thoroughly dried out and disinfected. The insurance company sent us, eventually, an industrial drier and some people were called in to clean the place with what I imagine were disgracefully toxic chemicals. The long, complicated and hardly satisfactory process of claiming financial compensation soon started for a property that in its 90 years had never seen a flood before.

We read in the local paper two days later that over one inch of rain had fallen in less than an hour and that people were beginning to publicly express concern that the local council or highways authority or whoever was responsible had not properly maintained the drains. We looked around and noted that many were indeed blocked, that curbs were broken or sunken, enabling the water to maraud unimpeded where it liked. Paul, a semi-retired neighbour, was convinced the council had been negligent and was at least partially culpable for the destruction. God and climate change were assumed to be the other culprits. The question then was, what do we do about it? Would that Dunkirk spirit, that bonding, continue into the peace and translate itself into some form of collective community action? Would we all learn from our experiences and develop those skills and knowledge necessary to investigate not only whether the drains had been properly maintained but also whether in an age of increasing climatic uncertainty, unseasonable weather patterns, heavier than normal rainfall alternating with more frequent periods of drought or semi-drought, they were truly adequate to deal with this new reality? Indeed, the issue soon became whether there was really anyone, any household, community group, business or public sector organization doing anything other than look on with a bemused indifference and sense of powerlessness at these massive, seemingly abstract changes that had directly affected all of us and would continue to do so in the future. Undoubtedly, some people, groups and organizations were already active and vocal. My wife and I regularly attended local Friends of the Earth meetings and some, but by no means all, of our neighbours could be called 'green'. So we assumed there would be a good chance of our small community getting and staying together, lobbying the council, writing to the papers and in various other ways getting active.

For a moment we had all made the connections: the local with the global, the concrete with the abstract, the political with the environmental, the educational with the social, the scientific with the everyday. There seemed to a whole ecology of learning, a transformation of attitudes, values and conduct, just about to happen. But then next day I got in my car and drove to work, as did my neighbours. Paul convened a meeting for all affected households to organize the necessary action but only apologies turned up. A man from the council eventually came round, inspected the drains and pronounced that, more or less, they were all in good working order and that the flood was a freak and therefore unlikely to be repeated in anyone's lifetime. But of course that winter York was flooded and so was Malton, a few miles to the north of where I lived. Shrewsbury was similarly in the news and soon after so was the West Country, with images of the 'freak' rainfall and the flooding of the coastal town of Boscastle in Cornwall syndicated round the globe by the local TV station.

The experience taught me a lot, not least that although sustainable development, if it is to be in any way meaningful conceptually and practically, needs to be rooted in the experience of the everyday, it is also the everyday that is most likely to impede our understanding of sustainable development. We all certainly learnt a great deal about the insurance business, local government procedures, media representations and other people, but little action followed. The routine necessity of simply 'getting on with it' intervened and as usual took over. The people who were most affected, those who within a week of moving in were flooded out, were those who did the least and were the least interested in becoming part of any community response. They wanted, needed perhaps, to go out Friday and Saturday nights as usual. They wanted to 'do their own thing', go on holiday as planned and just 'get back to normal'. This troubled me but despite all my concern and commitment I also did relatively little because of course I was 'too busy'. I still regularly passed the protesters who literally banged the drum every Friday campaigning against animal testing and continued to read newspaper reports and academic articles about people who did do things, who persevered, whose learning and energy did not evaporate or become absorbed through chores, work or leisure. For some people what they had learned was obviously significant, did critically make a difference, was transformative and led to real changes in values and behaviour.

However, although I assumed this 'disorientating dilemma' would be a kind of blinding light on the road to enlightenment, deep down I realized that forms of political activism such as letter-writing or turning up to monthly Friends of the Earth meetings were minority, often middle-class, pursuits. Shopping was not, though, and neither was watching television or going on holiday or driving to work or going to the football match or drinking a cup of coffee or digging the garden or listening to the stereo. There were many things that were by no means minority interests or minority activities but which collectively made up the very fabric of our everyday 'lifeworlds', those worlds which in the first and final instance really matter and which go unnoticed until something happens, and even then maybe only briefly.

This is not to say that I, or my neighbours, didn't care or that we were wilfully indifferent; only that we had many other things to do. It was not as if we were environmentally naive or ignorant. We were probably more aware than most, but then an increasing number of people have a general idea that the global environment is changing, that the Amazon forests are being cut down, that there is a hole in the ozone layer (whatever that means exactly), that human rights abuses are not a thing of the past, that life in the competitive economic market can be nasty brutish and short, that while the big corporations provide the goods there is often a high cost to low prices. In 2001 the UK Government's Department of the Environment's *Survey of Public Attitudes to Quality of Life and to the Environment* (DEFRA, 2001) suggested that over three-quarters of people had heard of the term 'climate change', with most of those who had not having heard of either global warming or the greenhouse effect. Overall, 99 per cent of people had heard of at least one of these terms and two-thirds of respondents blamed the UK floods in the winter of 2000/01 on changing weather patterns, with nearly 75 per cent of 18–24 year olds and 64 per cent of those under 65 believing the floods were due to climate change.

Opinion polls and academic studies suggested that ignorance as such was not the big issue, even though the language of sustainability failed to resonate with most people's understanding of the everyday. In any case, impressions are what most people have and need to get by. Not everyone can be experts but everyone can develop a general knowledge and understanding of issues, activities, threats and opportunities. Some academics had counted the number of definitions of sustainable development circulating in public, policy and academic debates, noting the concept's imprecision while adding more precise definitions of their own. This is not really a problem as rarely do we hear of people having a 'sustainability' experience or saying that they believe development ought to be more sustainable. The problem with the concept was then, and remains, not so much that it lacks an agreed definition (neither, after all, has 'democracy', 'class' or 'community') but that 'sustainability' and 'sustainable development' fail to connect with our experiential understanding of the opacity of bureaucratic procedures, the filling of insurance claims, the need to go out and have a good time or shop for the week's groceries. Until now, perhaps, when we are becoming increasingly aware of the consequences of our unsustainable lifestyles, habits and routines – for example, the impact on global warming through increased CO_2 emissions emanating from cheap holiday flights, car travel, the importation of cut flowers from Africa and so on.

This book is an attempt at making that connection, of making those words resonate with the everyday, with the formal and informal learning experiences that enable us to navigate our way through the everyday every day – and, in so doing, hopefully to change it. It is an attempt to marry some important sociological and anthropological studies, academic theories and observations on the media, consumerism, work, community action and leisure with direct personal experiences, stories and voices (including my own) about engagement in a range of activities. My original intention was to travel far and wide and not intervene in the text at all, to write objectively in the third person, a disembodied voice without experience or engagement. However, I then realized it was also important to speak personally and subjectively, in other words to be objective but not neutral. I also felt it would be 'unsustainable' to travel far and wide particularly if I could successfully seek out examples and illustrations from close to where I live and work. And this proved easier than I anticipated, not just because I live in a fairly 'green' part of the country but also because a growing awareness and understanding of the need to be more sustainable is more common now than ever before. I believe if we look around us, learn about our communities, recognize the importance of place and that a little and a little soon adds up to a lot then most of us will be pleasantly surprised. It is possible to think globally and act (and write) locally. There is more going on than we realize and if we are able to reflect on this and on our own lifestyles then the process of learning from our social and cultural environment will itself become an ecology of learning. This book attempts to make some sense of sustainability and everyday life and in the process contribute a little to fashioning a better world.

1

Learning as Sustainability

This chapter offers a theoretical overview of learning and sustainability from a sociological and anthropological perspective and identifies a number of issues that will be explored more fully in later chapters. It comprises the following sections:

- On sustainability;
- On learning, lifelong;
- On eco-museums;
- On the everyday;
- On affordances and the everyday; and
- On education for sustainable development.

ON SUSTAINABILITY

There has been no shortage of academic and political critiques of the complementary concepts 'sustainable development' and 'sustainability'. Some academics play the game of counting the number of definitions, arguing about their inconsistency and then finally offering one of their own. Strict purveyors of disciplinary truth and rigour may view the concepts as utopian or incapable of being put into practice, while others see inherent and irreconcilable contradictions particularly in the tension between 'development' and 'sustainable'. But the idea that future social and economic development needs to take place within the limits of the Earth's ecosystem capacity and that it includes a proper consideration of social justice, poverty, political democracy and so forth is eminently sensible to many (Langhelle, 1999; Robinson, 2004). Robinson's commentary (2004) is concerned with the critical contradictions within the concept: there is a focus on growth and development, this much appreciated by governments and business, on the one hand and ecological sustainability, emphasized by many NGOs, academic environmentalists and activists, on the other. Robinson prefers the term sustainability, which 'focuses attention where it should be placed, on the ability of humans to continue to live within environmental constraints' (2004, p370). One of the main reasons why sustainable development and sustainability have generated such a vast number of definitions and criticisms is because they tend to reflect the political and philosophical value bases of those articulating a given definition. For those who want an unambiguous scientific, technical, discipline-specific and/or operationable definition this causes problems, but not for Robinson, who observes:

> *Diplomats are familiar with the need to leave key terms undefined in negotiation processes and in much the same way the term sustainable development may profit from what might be called constructive ambiguity.*
>
> *Certainly the plethora of competing definitions in the literature suggests that any attempt to define the concept precisely, even if it were possible, would have the effect of excluding those whose views were not expressed in that definition.* (Robinson, 2004, p374)

What is needed and what the constructive ambiguity surrounding the term sustainability can offer is the possibility of integration, synthesis and synergy – of a social learning process that bridges the gaps between the social and ecological, the scientific and spiritual, the economic and the political. Technical fixes are necessary but not sufficient if ecological, economic and social imperatives are to be reconciled. For Robinson, this cannot be done scientifically, only politically – in dialogue and in partnership with sustainability 'the emergent property of a conversation about what kind of world we collectively want to live in now and in the future.' Robinson concludes:

> *I would argue that the equivalent development in the field of sustainability is the recognition that multiple conflicting views of sustainability exist and cannot be reconciled in terms of each other. In other words, no single approach will, or indeed should be, seen as the correct one. This is not a matter of finding out what the truth of sustainability is by more sophisticated applications of expert understanding (the compass and ruler). Instead we are inescapably involved in a world in which there exist multiple conflicting values, moral positions and belief systems that speak to the issue of sustainability. While it is crucial to identify points of empirical disagreement and to resolve those with better research and analysis, the ultimate question is not susceptible to empirical confirmation or disconfirmation. What is needed, therefore, is a process by which these views can be expressed and evaluated, ultimately as a political act for any given community or jurisdiction.* (Robinson, 2004, p382)

In this way, sustainable development and sustainability may most productively function as a heuristic – that is, as a method or system of education or learning by which a person is enabled to find things out for him/herself and to fully appreciate the contested nature of knowledge, nature, the environment and sustainability (Macnaghten and Urry, 1998).

What is clear, then, is that sustainable development is multidimensional, encompassing social, ecological and economic goals. The notion of sustainable development being a 'dialogue of values' (Ratner, 2004) is another useful starting point. Ratner identifies three basic tendencies in sustainable development practice:

1 Sustainable development as technical consensus;
2 Sustainable development as ethical consensus;
3 Sustainable development as a dialogue of values.

Ratner argues (2004, p62) that the sustainability concept is meaningful because it is able to bring differences of belief and opinion, values and conviction into a common field of dialogue and so enhance the potential for agreement on collective action. He also finds it necessary to distinguish between trivial or populist conceptualizations and truly meaningful ones:

> *When advocates use the term [sustainable development] to mean 'sustained growth', 'sustained change' or simply 'successful' development, then it has little meaning, especially when development is considered as growth in material consumption. More meaningful interpretations are multidimensional, often distinguishing among social goals (including justice, participation, equality, empowerment, institutional sustainability, cultural integrity, etc.), ecological goals (including biodiversity preservation, ecosystem resilience, resource conservation, etc.), and economic goals (including growth, efficiency and material welfare). Such a multidimensional notion represents the mainstream in analysis and advocacy of sustainable development ... It recognizes ecosystem integrity as fundamental to the productive activities on which human society and economy depend, acknowledges ecological limits to growth in the consumption of resources, and assumes that the distinct goals of sustainability sometimes converge in practice and other times require difficult trade-offs. (Ratner, 2004, pp53–4)*

Understood as a dialogue and a heuristic, sustainable development is therefore process orientated. It is fashioned, promoted, communicated, created, learned, produced and reproduced through what we do, how we work, and what we make, trade and create, ranging from the micro, the immediate and the everyday, to the macro, the long term and the exceptional. Sustainable development and its objective, sustainability, will come about through learning and reflecting on everyday assumptions, habits of behaviour, structures of feeling and expectation. This learning will take place in schools, colleges and universities. More importantly it will take place in the home, on the high street, at the workplace, when on holiday, watching television, in the garden, putting the rubbish out for recycling, getting the train, talking with friends, surfing the net and so on.

ON LEARNING, LIFELONG

The concept of lifelong learning has been around for quite a time and throughout its existence has been subject to a number of debates, discussions and disputes. It is, to use a term loved by academics, a contested concept, harbouring within it a number of contradictions, approaches and potential applications. The international educator Ernesto Gelpi saw it as potentially both emancipatory and repressive, rooted in structures and experiences of production and consumption, focusing on the needs of marginalized groups and the reproduction of the market economy (Gelpi, 1979). Contemporary educators such as John Field (2000) and Frank Coffield (1999, 2000) have been highly critical of the economic and vocational focus of contemporary lifelong learning policy and practice that has emerged from governmental and international bodies such as the Organisation for Economic Co-operation and Development (OECD) and Britain's Department for Education and Skills (DfES). Richard Taylor, for many years the head of the School of Continuation at the University of Leeds (before it closed in 2005) and now at Cambridge, has called for a radical reform of higher education and the protection of a less instrumental, less vocationally orientated adult education (1996; Taylor et al, 2002). Despite all this, the significance of lifelong learning as a concept with a significant social side, a cultural resonance and a clear aim to empower as well as enlighten is far less instrumental and far broader than government-imposed funding and attainment targets that are narrowly conceived to be almost exclusively economistic. Learning is an inevitable aspect of all spheres of our lives from the everyday to the highly specialized and tightly prescribed. We cannot survive without being able to learn or without learning – how to cook, where to find the coffee in the local supermarket, how to get a job, what to put in to the new recycling bins, how to live more sustainably. The local authority may have just recently provided us all with colour-coded recycling bins in an attempt to reduce the amount of consumer waste going to landfill, but what goes where? Why not all plastics? Where to put the big brown monstrosity without it being an eyesore? Is it collected next Tuesday or is it Wednesday?

The EU has articulated the notion of lifelong learning as encompassing formal, non-formal and informal practices (CEC, 2000). Learning is recognized as taking place throughout society – not simply in the formal institutions of schools, colleges and universities, but also in community groups, in the supermarket, on the allotment, in front of the television, at the workplace, while plugged into the computer, when on holiday, while visiting a museum, city farm or community garden, or while enjoying a walk through the countryside. Informal learning in everyday life is perhaps a major key to unlocking the door to a more sustainable world. Computer games are fast becoming bigger business than Hollywood and computer simulations are an important part of the formal learning environment for many professions, from architects and planners to biologists and the US Marines. Games are also an important element in the everyday leisure and learning experiences of many children and young people. But you don't have to be a geek or ten to be into the new media technologies. Gee (2003) has persuasively demonstrated the learning potential of this emergent medium (discussed later in this book). Learning is also a key to how individuals manage the increasingly evident economic and ecological risks, uncertainties and complexities, which often seem beyond our control: it is not obviously our responsibility but they nonetheless shape our lives, hopes, expectations and anxieties. Most young adults today will have more than one career, many jobs will be short term, technology changes rapidly, weather patterns render idyllic holiday destinations less predictably idyllic, we may have to get our drinking water from standpipes in the summer and deal with floods in the winter, and what we eat may be slowly poisoning us. We need to learn to do different things, or the same things but differently. Learning is important if people are to care about themselves, about others and about the world as it is now and as it may be in the future.

Although not many people seem to be talking about it at the bus stop, in the pub or indeed in the universities, we have now entered the United Nations Decade of Education for Sustainable Development, 2005–2014. This global initiative establishes a broad context for learning about sustainability. It is being promoted internationally by the United Nations, to some extent also by national governments, and in many ways comes just at the right time as more people than ever before are currently attuned to the wider issues of climate change, renewable energy, free and fair trade, human rights, animal welfare, social exclusion, civil and political liberties, ethical consumption, and the 'risk society'. As weather patterns become increasingly severe or volatile, with spring appearing earlier and earlier, images of hurricanes filling the television news, the price of a barrel of oil reaching record highs, petrol and diesel becoming fuels of the past, and debates over the efficacy of renewable energy and the necessity of nuclear power resurrecting fears that had been buried years ago, the UN's initiative is more important than ever. There is a need for educational practitioners in the formal sectors to engage with the sustainability agenda but, as the framers of the Decade of Education for Sustainable Development make clear, that is not going to be enough:

> *Education for Sustainable Development (ESD) is for everyone, at whatever stage of life they are.* **It takes place, therefore, within a perspective of lifelong learning, engaging all possible learning spaces, formal, non-formal and informal, from early childhood to adult life.** *ESD calls for a re-orientation of educational approaches – curriculum and content, pedagogy and examinations. Spaces for learning include non-formal learning, community-based organizations and local civil society, the workplace, formal education, technical and vocational training, teacher training, higher education educational inspectorates, policy-making bodies, and beyond.* (UNESCO, 2005, p6; their emphasis)

Conceived in this way ESD embraces many spheres, approaches and arenas. It's not just about learning one discipline or one trade or knowing when to smile or be polite in public. It requires a holistic understanding of the world and the place of humans within it; it has a powerful ethical purpose; it is dialogic; it is about learning to learn how to make sense of the world around us and within us. The American educator Jack Mezirow has largely concerned himself with transformative aspects of learning. A 'meaning scheme', he writes, 'is the particular knowledge, beliefs, value judgements and feelings that become articulated in an interpretation' of an experience (Mezirow, 1991, p44). This schema is based on a 'meaning perspective', which is a broader structure of assumptions derived from previous experiences enabling us to assimilate, make sense of and transform our new experiences. These perspectives offer us criteria by which we can judge whether something is good or bad, ugly or beautiful, right or wrong, true or false, appropriate or inappropriate, sustainable or unsustainable. Mezirow does not like to separate the intellectual from the knowing, the cognitive from the intuitive, cultural or affective dimensions of learning and perception. For Mezirow, transformative learning is when our meaning schemes (specific attitudes, beliefs and attitudes) and meaning perspectives change as a result of experience and self-reflection. Perspective transformation is the process whereby people become critically aware of how and why their assumptions constrain the way they perceive, understand and feel about the world. It involves the changing of more or less habitual expectations, making possible more inclusive or integrative perspectives and the capability of making choices to act upon these new modes of understanding. Perspective transformation can occur slowly through gradual changes in attitudes and beliefs or through a shattering experience, a 'disorientating dilemma', which may be highly personal or be prompted by an eye-opening discussion, film, book or article that seriously contradicts previously held assumptions. These changes may be painful, involving the questioning of long-held beliefs and personal values; they may even challenge a person's sense of self and personal identity. Mezirow (1991, p193) notes:

> *Social movements can significantly facilitate critical self-reflection. They can precipitate or reinforce dilemmas and legitimate alternate meaning perspectives. Identifying with a cause larger than oneself is perhaps the most powerful motivator to learn. In turn, people who have undergone perspective transformations can bring great power to social movements.* (Mezirow, 1991, p193)

The importance of values and experience are evident in many environmental justice campaigns, illustrated graphically by Lois Gibbs, who founded the Love Canal Homeowners' Association of Niagara Falls in 1978. This small working-class community near Niagara Falls was the site of an unfinished canal, where between 1942 and 1952 the Hooker Electric Company dumped nearly 22,000 tonnes of chemicals. In the end, Hooker filled in the canal and sold the land to the town for US$1. An elementary school was built and opened in 1955 and a neighbourhood community established itself around it but by the mid 1970s over 200 toxic chemicals had begun appearing in the schoolyard and in the basements of people's homes. Residents of Love Canal experienced an extremely large number of sometimes fatal health problems, including cancer, epilepsy, asthma, birth defects and miscarriages. It was this experience, particularly as it impacted on her as a young mother, that transformed the attitudes, values and behaviour of Lois Gibbs. She initiated and led a campaign and has since become a very active environmental justice campaigner in the US. In an interview with Sharon Livesey (2003), she described her feelings thus:

> *I was worried about my kids. I just love them. I pride myself on being a really good mom. Especially after Missy developed the blood disorder, I was convinced that I would lose them. The tears and the anxiety. And I was so angry. And I think it was those two passions. To think that somebody had made that decision to allow us to move in to that house and live there! And then to have that report come out and say that we weren't worthy of being moved or helped in any way. They made a conscious decision that it was OK to make my child sick. This was on purpose, and that's the part that made me so angry and still does today when I go and sit with these folks in their living rooms, for example, in Hazelton, Pennsylvania. People know what is happening and they have chosen to let it happen. And people who know better.*

However, not everyone takes on a leadership role or feels sufficiently motivated, empowered or certain that they can make a difference, or even try to make a difference.

The Danish educator Knud Illeris sees learning as being made up of three fundamental dimensions, namely:

1   A cognitive process – *an acquisitive process comprising both intellectual and behavioural learning;*
2   An emotional or psychodynamic process *involving psychological energy, feelings, emotions, attitudes and motivations;*
3   A social process – *learning can only really take place as an interaction between an individual in his/her surroundings, ie the historical, societal and, one might add, environmental conditions of existence.* (Illeris, 2002)

Learning just doesn't take place on its own, in isolation, without someone doing the learning, although occasionally it can occur in quite mysterious ways. We do think about things, reflect on experience, search for answers or that fair trade coffee, which is inexplicably not on the shelf as it usually is. Learning often takes place following or during critical reflection that feeds back into ourselves, rearticulating our experiences and our understanding of those experiences. Some learning is simply an accumulation of facts or experiences easily assimilated into what is already there. On the other hand, a disturbing or disorientating experience may not be so easily assimilated. Some learning and conservation organizations intentionally offer a disorientating experience to their visitors, although this is by no means common. On a visit to Jersey Zoo (now known as the Durrell Wildlife Conservation Trust), just before viewing the great apes the visitor is invited to look at photographs and articles depicting and describing the 'bushmeat' trade: photographs of dismembered, decapitated or cooked apes and reports of menus in fashionable cosmopolitan restaurants serving this delicacy. Then the visitor walks round the perimeter of the large open enclosure where the gorillas lounge about eating their lettuces, picking their noses, grooming their young or simply yawning in the afternoon sunshine. Although this may sound rather unsubtle and obvious, when I experienced it I suddenly saw in those creatures aspects of ourselves. The effect of seeing the bushmeat images sickened me. It certainly was for me a disorientating dilemma which has stayed with me despite learning that other cultures view these apes in quite different ways – as competitors for food, as dangerous pests, as part of a traditional diet or as a good source of income. My knowledge has not compromised my emotional reaction, my emotional memory or my attitude that this trade – and indeed the practice of eating our nearest relatives – is wrong. But has it led me to do anything about it?

Alternative conceptions of the world, of rights and wrongs, emerge and become embedded in new conceptions and approaches to sense-making. They may not, however, always be clear. In fact, as the world is perceived as being rather more complex and interrelated than we might at first have assumed, our understanding may become less clear, our confidence less certain, our sense of powerlessness more acute. For those interested in what may be referred to as a systems-based 'meta learning', the work of Gregory Bateson (1972) is worth exploring and forms a significant part of Sterling's theory of sustainable education (Sterling, 2001). But my experience of the gorillas, and even more so perhaps of the orang-utans, is what Mezirow describes as a 'transformative learning' experience leading to the restructuring of cognitive and emotional meaning schemes and perspectives. Of course, it is possible that other individuals will take away something completely different from what I have described. I might be too squeamish, too irrational or plain emotional. I might even be denying myself the possibility of eating something quite delicious, and if I was a rich gastronome I might very well think differently. It is possible not only to interpret an experience in different ways but also to reject interpretations or refuse to interpret experiences at all. I might think I already know all I need to know, or I might take note of these new experiences but simply not relate to them in any way. Or I might, at a conscious level, deny what I see and refuse to learn anything more about it, dismissing it as too abhorrent, too boring, too liberal. In my refusal, denial or rejection I might therefore reinforce a disposition to block out similar experiences or I might simply select elements from experiences I feel comfortable with so distorting any intended learning outcome on the part of the conversation organization, campaign group, film-maker, neighbour, community group, etc. So the reason the bushmeat pictures were pinned on the wall was to show and condemn the awful nature of the practice. That's the way I saw it.

And this is where formal education comes in. By just sitting at home watching the TV, going to a museum or a zoo, being active in a community group, I have the opportunity and capacity to ignore, resist, distort and reject. I may find it hard to motivate myself, or think things through on my own. There are always pressing reasons, experiences, values, assumptions, prejudices, knowledge and necessary time-consuming, energy-sapping chores that prevent me, and others, from reflecting creatively and critically on experiences in a pro-sustainable or pro-environmental manner. The story of the flood I outlined in the introduction told me that most of us, despite our green knowledge and awareness, simply deal with the consequences of the destruction as best we can because we have to get on with things. I can also reject, dismiss or evade particular learning experiences as well as any college or university student, but within a formal setting it is at least theoretically possible for time and space to be productively used for this resistance or rejection to be explored, reflected upon, questioned, reviewed, written about, assessed and graded. As Illeris writes, 'It should not be forgotten that in many cases education forms the only context where participants have a realistic opportunity to allow their resistance to unfold and to adapt it in a constructive and progressive manner, and this can be the source of the most far reaching potential for learning.' (Illeris, 2002, p103) This important role of nurturing a predisposition to think and reflect critically on one's life experiences is essential to creating a learning mindset, an attitude to on-going lived experience that shapes an individual's readiness, in interaction with others, to change things, to apprehend and comprehend changes in the global environment and believe in, and to be able to initiate, changes in one's self after formal education. John Foster suggests this learning mindset is really:

> *A readiness to understand and undertake living as learning – not just a matter of accepting the old platitude that we live and (often somewhat reluctantly) learn, but a positive, eager commitment to the heuristic creativity of intelligence in encountering each emergent tomorrow. Such a commitment reflects the consciousness that tomorrow is always doubly indeterminate; it is not just 'open' in the classic sense that the truth-value of claims about it may not yet be determined ... it is also in principle indeterminable, in the sense that our epistemic and evaluative frameworks for establishing the significance and indeed the nature and identity of future events are themselves at issue in prediction or action. We have always to be open to the prospect that the newly emergent might, in challenging these frameworks, force us to revise them (and thus further revise itself in the process).* (Foster, 2001, p161)

Learning, as Scott and Gough (2003) argue, therefore becomes an element of the sustainable development process rather than simply an instrument or means towards realizing the dynamic goal of sustainability.

Learning, conceived as a mindset, should also be seen as lifelong and life-wide, in other words occurring in every area of our lives and occurring in a range of places within and beyond the formal contexts offered by educational institutions. All learning really becomes meaningful when there is some resonance with the everyday lifeworld of the learner. We tend to translate abstractions into concrete examples before they are felt and make any sense – global warming with baling out the basement, for example. Resonance is therefore essential if learning is to become a key constitutive element of any transformative process leading to a more sustainable future. The learning strategy informing the design of the Eden Project in Cornwall, for example, attempts to make a difference to visitors' attitudes, values and behaviour because what is seen, read, touched, heard, tasted or smelt has the power to reach out, to connect the everyday to the wider world. The approach adopted at the Eden Project derives largely from the notion of 'free choice learning', offering space and opportunity for visitors to make connections, thus encouraging future changes in values and conduct that are hopefully real, genuine and desired even if not immediate or direct. The experience of seeing the raw and unprocessed elements of finished or processed products – the cotton of shirts, coffee beans rather than instant granules, cork bark rather than the manufactured cylinders that keep the wine from spilling out of the bottle – connects with the everyday lifeworlds of shopping, consumption and pleasure. Few disorientating dilemmas here, instead gentle associations and calls, without emotional coercion, to reflect and to change. To this end, the learner may activate both the capacity and the capability to make connections intellectually, emotionally, imaginatively and ethically with other, perhaps unfamiliar, lifeworlds, experiences and values, for example fair trade, the experiences of growers in developing countries and our choice of eating Nestlé or Green and Black's confectionary. Thus, and supported by the work on consciousness by Damasio (2000) and Edelman and Tononi (2000), learning should be viewed as essentially social, contextual and interactive in nature. The human mind works in complex and dynamic interaction with the wider environment. Meaning is fluid rather than fixed and information is integrated with experience in processes that involve the continual construction, deconstruction and reconstruction of knowledge (Vanderstraeten, 2002).

If learning therefore is life-wide and lifelong, meaning is fluid, and people are active in making meaning and making something of their experiences, then perhaps it would be useful to apply an ecological perspective to this process. Sterling (2004) has written of the value of adopting systems thinking to our understanding of learning for sustainability (or ESD) and this ties in very closely with seeing learning as part of a wider social ecology of everyday life experience that, as Felix Guattari argues, encompasses the interrelationship existing between 'three ecologies' – (capitalist) social relations, human subjectivity and the natural world or environment. Guattari writes:

The increasing deterioration of human relations with the socius, the psyche and 'nature' is due not only to environmental and objective pollution but is also the result of a certain incomprehension and fatalistic passivity towards these issues as a whole, among both individuals and governments. Catastrophic or not, negative developments are simply accepted without question. Structuralism, and subsequently postmodernism, has accustomed us to a vision of the world drained of the significance of human interventions, embodied as they are in concrete politics and micropolitics. The explanations offered for this decline of social praxes – the death of ideologies and the return to universal values – seem to me unsatisfactory. Rather, it appears to be the result of the failure of social and psychological praxes to adapt, as well as a certain blindness to the erroneousness of dividing the Real into a number of discrete domains. It is quite wrong to make a distinction between action on the psyche, the socius and the environment. Refusal to face up to the erosion of these three areas, as the media would have us do, verges on a strategic infantalization of opinion and a destructive neutralization of democracy. We need to 'kick the habit' of seductive discourse, particularly the 'fix' of television, in order to be able to apprehend the world through the interchangeable lenses or points of view of the three ecologies. (Guattari, 2000, pp41–2)

Television is part of most people's lifeworld, and just as we can explore an ecology of learning, its essential connectedness, we may also wish to explore the possibilities for a media ecology as it is by no means clear, as we will see later, whether television or any other (new) media has such a negative effect as suggested by critics like Guattari (2000), Mander (2002), Postman (1987) and Putnam (2000). The media certainly shapes us, but then we may also in turn be shaping it given that it is undoubtedly part of the world of daily life, as Alfred Schutz (1970) might have put it, a world that is the scene and also the object of our actions and interactions. The natural attitude to this world is intersubjective, one that is common to all of us in its fundamentals. We have to dominate it, respect it and change it in order to realize the purposes we follow in cooperation with all our fellow creatures. We need to overcome certain obstacles and we may need to yield to certain pressures but what Schutz says invariably governs our natural attitude to the everyday world is a pragmatism. The world is both something we have to modify by our actions and something that modifies our actions in return. What we do therefore matters just as much as what we think or believe or learn. Our practical or theoretical knowledge of the world may not necessarily lead to more pro-environmental action, but our actions and how we apply the everyday technologies of work and leisure, in other words our doing, will influence our learning, attitudes, values and knowledge. And their meaning will develop or emerge through processes of engagement, of interpretation and reflection.

ON ECO-MUSEUMS

The potential and patterns of life offered to human beings by nature and ecological limits are things that we are not always fully cognizant of despite the popular interest in natural history journals and television programmes, heritage centres and areas of outstanding natural beauty. Indeed, museums, far from being the stuffy depositories for various cabinets of curiosities, are important venues for formal and informal learning, individual engagement and community involvement. Nilsson and Rosen discuss the Spread of Ecological Knowledge project, which aimed to integrate ecologically orientating activities with the more cultural- and arts-based work of many Swedish regional museums (Nilsson and Rosen, 2001). One such museum, the Skansen Open Air Museum in Stockholm has, since opening in 1891, trodden an ecological path, offering folk, zoological and environmental learning activities. By linking local situations with everyday life experience, cultural with economic themes, with traditional museum concerns of professional scholarship and curatorial conservation to direct community involvement, a new approach to the work of museums has developed. Complementing folk museums like Skansen there have emerged since the 1960s a number of eco-museums and cultural heritage centres directly involving local people in their design, construction, maintenance and more familiar curatorial work. First Nation peoples in Canada, Native Americans in the USA, Aboriginals in Australasia and working-class people in rural and former industrial areas of France, Wales, Norway, Italy and other European countries have seen close working relationships between local people and museum professionals forming. These museums are sites of research, conservation and communication of local, regional and national cultures, often nurturing or restoring through formal and informal learning a community's sense of worth and cultural identity. They are, to use the jargon of the present, invariably 'community led', place-based but socially, geographically, historically and environmentally relational. They are not necessarily enclosed spaces and frequently not confined to one building or site. Eco-museums articulate the idea that 'to inhabit a place is to dwell there in a practiced way, in a way which relies upon certain regular, trusted habits of behaviour' and habits of the heart (Kemmis, 1990, p69). For Howard and Ashworth (1999), it is the whole environment that sets the context for buildings, architecture, paths, rural landscapes, technologies, tools, clothing, human activities, objects and cultural practices including religious, spiritual and magical beliefs. The eco-museum is a museum of time and space linking past and present, human and natural ecologies, material and non-material cultures. The Troms Regional Ecomuseum of the Lapp population in Norway demonstrates the way of living of the Sami people, who until the onset of modernization were able to responsibly use the ecological resources around them. By documenting and preserving their craft traditions, landscapes, cultures and buildings, the local population 'has played a very important role in enabling people to "communicate with the past, the present and the future" and to increase the economic opportunities, re-establishing traditional processes and using natural resources to develop various forms of tourism and cottage industries' (Howard and Ashworth, 1999, p106). The eco-museum in Fresne, France was designed and created for such purposes and to be as socially inclusive as possible, telling the stories and relating the experiences of washer-women, prisoners, immigrants, ethnic minorities, young people and those who struggled hard to secure decent housing (Delgado, 2001). Apart from formal training programmes and the development of specific and identifiable skills, people involved in these developments learn about their own history, their own environment and their own futures by actively engaging in creative activity, participating or managing community projects, and building social trust and relationships of reciprocal responsibility. Eco-museums build social and human capital and are certainly not self-indulgent exercises in sentimental nostalgia. They are not exclusively designed with the economic aim of attracting tourists and other visitors – although this certainly may figure prominently in some business plans (Howard, 2002) – but are frequently instruments of individual and collective self-knowledge, vehicles for community problem-solving with outcomes dependent on what the motivating issue is, whether urban renewal or factory closure, and what action is agreed to and what acted upon. Fuller, discussing the experience of the Ak-Chin Indian community in Arizona, writes as follows:

> *Inherent in the operation of an eco-museum is a process that teaches people how to investigate an issue and speak out. An eco-museum not only provides a place in which to hold discussions and create exhibitions about issues of common concern, but also gives community members actual practice in asking new questions, researching facts, communicating ideas, defending positions, and coming to new understandings in ways that are culturally appropriate... The need to hear about the concerns of newly emerging groups – women who work outside the home, migrant labourers, latchkey children, elderly people isolated from their extended families – must be met if a community is to make the transition to a better life.* (Fuller, 1992, p332)

Eco-museums are therefore not necessarily about the natural world or the environment, although part of a community's story may certainly involve its destruction or restoration through industrialization or de-industrialization, and inevitably they reveal the consequences of human beings' relationship with the world. They are more about the everyday, concerned with learning about the past and, in so doing, understanding life in the present and our needs for the future.

ON THE EVERYDAY

Additional lessons may be learnt from the sociology of Henri Lefebvre (1991a; 2002) and the social anthropology of Tim Ingold (2000). Lefebvre argues that the everyday is where we are in terms of our direct relationship with the social and natural worlds and where our desires, capabilities, identities and potential are, in the first instance, formulated, developed and made real. Everyday life is also the site from which we can fashion a critique of dominant, alienating and exploitive ideas and practices and start to create new or alternative ways of doing things, of thinking and acting, of producing and consuming, combining to develop a new *art of living*:

> *Everyday life is profoundly related to* all *activities, and encompasses them with all their differences and their conflicts; it is in their meeting place, their bond, their common ground. And it is in everyday life that the sum total of relations which make the human – and every human being – a whole takes its shape and its form. In it are expressed and fulfilled those relations which bring into play the totality of the real, albeit in a certain manner which is always partial and incomplete: friendship, comradeship, love, the need to communicate, play, etc.* (Lefebvre, 1991a, p97)

For Lefebvre, the modern world has led us to take a privatized (thus deprived) and instrumental approach to life and living, the natural and social worlds, work and leisure, the ideal and the mundane. Dominant modes of communication, of information gathering and storage, often seem separated from everyday social relationships and social experience. Everything seems to have been commodified, packaged in images or oven-ready experiences that have their own peculiar meaning and purpose and which function to keep the economic wheels turning. We buy and consume processed foods, processed holidays and processed entertainments divorced from what we are actually capable of creating by and for ourselves. Our being is increasingly divorced from what ultimately our existence depends upon – the natural world. Lefebvre, in other words, is no fan of the consumer society but nonetheless recognizes a certain degree of ambiguity:

> *'Consumer society' manipulates needs; the masters of production are also the masters of consumption, and they also produce the demands for which and according to which they are supposed to be producing. Deliberately or not, they leave other equally valid needs and other equally objective demands to one side. It is not very often that a voice makes itself heard to criticize this illusion which is not entirely an illusion, this appearance which is not entirely an appearance, since needs – even if they are provoked and prefabricated – can not all be equally phoney and artificial.*

> *Ambiguity between individual and social needs and desires papers*
> *over unperceived contradictions, blunting them and coinciding*
> *with the three dimensional 'realness' of the everyday. Only when*
> *there is this ambiguity can the illusion and appearance be*
> *sustained.* (Lefebvre, 2002, p223)

From a personal point of view, I certainly need to get about, to be mobile, to have access to places of work and leisure, to get to the shops and occasional holiday destinations. I certainly need to eat, preferably fresh food, and I certainly like to fit in and be part of things. But do I really need to replace my car every couple of years, eat strawberries all year round, wear clothes which display a tick or a whoosh? If I do and act accordingly then I am my own worst enemy, contributing personally and directly to a system that offers me less by promising and delivering more. Everyday life is therefore a mix of what is seemingly repressive and functional (in terms of reproducing capitalist social relations) and what is potentially emancipatory, better and different. Consumerism and advertising also nurture authentic needs and desires that may remain unfulfilled – food that looks good but is nutritious and not packed with salt, sugar, saturated fats and E-numbers. Mobility and access should not be subject to traffic gridlock, pollution, poor public transportation, nor should it degrade the countryside. Urban environments can and should provide cultural and economic opportunities and pleasantly social, green spaces. Lefebvre argues for an urban revolution – a transformation of urban spaces manifesting 'a creative capacity in its effects on daily life' (Lefebvre, 1991b, p54), the starting point for a metamorphosis of the everyday which in many cases is closely associated with the city as poly- or trans-functional, as play as well as work:

> *In social life, play has a use. What is it? Relaxation and enter-*
> *tainment, yes, but more than that, it is rediscovered spontaneity,*
> *and, even more, it is activity which is not subjected to the division*
> *of labour and the social hierarchies. At first sight, humanly and*
> *socially speaking, play seems to be a minor, marginal activity,*
> *sidelined and tolerated by the important functions of industrial*
> *society. Compared with the reality of practical life and the truth*
> *of representations, it seems to be an illusion, a lie, something*
> *phoney. On closer scrutiny, the reverse is true. Play recalls forgot-*
> *ten depths and summons them up to the light of day. By making*
> *them stay within the everyday, it encompasses art and many other*
> *things as well. It uses appearances and illusions which – for one*
> *marvellous moment – become more real than real. And with play*
> *another reality is born, not a separate one, but one which is 'lived'*
> *in the everyday, alongside the functional.* (Lefebvre, 2002, p203)

Play enlivens experience, renders people more active and less passive, substitutes quality for quantity, and intensifies material and non-material exchange, ensuring that human creativity is nurtured and expressed. It is this creative quality that ensures productive human learning, and agency can push us beyond the quotidian, beyond business as usual. A new play ethic could well be a theme of a more sustainable and liveable world (Kane, 2004), and this resonates well with those theorists of the everyday who see beyond the routine and the mundane to the vital, 'puissance' (the will to live) and the creative (Maffesoli, 1996; Crook, 1998).

The environmental impact of our present highly materialistic consumer lifestyles has been well documented, well measured and graphically illustrated. The ecological footprint of the average European or North American is huge compared with that of the Indian or African, but the footprints of other peoples are increasing rapidly as China, Indonesia and other countries emulate Western modes of capitalist development (Wackernagel and Rees, 1996). Lifestyles are frequently associated with class, culture, ethnicity and values of progress, sophistication, success and wealth and can be defined as patterns of action that differentiate people, identifying and perhaps explaining social and personal identity, cultural affiliation and political awareness in a range of complex ways (Chaney, 1996). Consequently, lifestyles involve much more than the products and services we consume, though it is certainly the case that frequently our solutions to realizing wants and needs are met through the consumption of more commodities. For Giddens (1991) commodities are a primary means by which we express our values and desires as well as the way we are often judged by others. Bedford, Jones and Walker (2004, p4) define a sustainable lifestyle as a pattern of action and consumption, used by people to affiliate and differentiate themselves from other people, which:

- *meets basic needs;*
- *provides a better quality of life;*
- *minimizes the use of natural resources and emissions of waste and pollutants over the lifecycle; and*
- *does not jeopardize the needs of future generations.*

The authors discuss a range of indicators that illustrate sustainable lifestyles, identifying issues and challenges relating to data collection and analysis. In this way, the environmental, social and economic aspects of sustainability are addressed through a detailed examination of how we live our lives and how we might change the way we do things. All this will effect what we consider to be both our standard of living and our quality of life – the foods we eat, the clothes we wear, the holidays we take, the work we do, the cars we drive, the way we look, the way others see us and perhaps the way we want others to see us. We don't have to wear four thick woolly jumpers and live on turnips in the winter to be green, though that is of course an option. So what does it mean to be green?

The need for action is generally recognized and Bedford, Jones and Walker identify two key motivators affecting an individual's willingness to do something: first, knowing that everyone is equally engaged in taking responsibility for environmental activities; second, receiving feedback on the positive effects resulting from these actions. Cost and convenience are also important as 'any sustainable alternative that is cheaper, more efficient and convenient to undertake may encourage use, regardless of the individual's social or environmental concerns' (Bedford, Jones and Walker, 2004, p20). The focus groups the authors used told them that on balance people were satisfied with their existing standard and quality of life, and they accept that once people possess goods that make them feel content, they rarely wish to do without them. However, they also note that people place value on goods and services in different ways. Those with who are fairly materialistic will derive a lot of satisfaction from their possessions, whereas other groups with 'post-material' values may derive satisfaction just from feeling that they have made a difference through changing their lifestyles. A more sustainable lifestyle would almost by definition entail reducing wasteful consumption and lifestyle practices, creating alternative patterns of consumption and addressing overall patterns of disposal.

Christmas time in the UK is a wonderful example of how our materialist ethos generates unnecessary consumption and waste. Britons generate 10 per cent of their annual rubbish during the festive period, with only about 25 per cent of discarded goods, packaging and uneaten food going for recycling. In 2005 most of the eight million real Christmas trees purchased were as usual simply thrown out rather than composted or recycled, generating around 12,000 tonnes of additional rubbish. New technology purchases, including iPods, MP3 players, DVD recorders and plasma TVs, lead many people to discard their obsolete Walkmans, stereo systems and video recorders. The problem of rapid obsolescence is a serious one with modish hi-tech products since not only do they quickly become technologically redundant, but the user may also feel culturally redundant if he or she does not acquire the new model or product and talk about, use and be seen using it. Possibly the key to sustainable living is feeling good and satisfied through being green.

Consumption and lifestyle therefore serve a communicative and cultural function, binding and/or separating groups, communities, organizations and individuals. But purchasing behaviour also has a more personal domestic motivation – certain products may help us reorganize or rationalize activities in the home. For Douglas and Isherwood (1996) the desire to liberate ourselves from domestic chores, so we can spend more time going out with friends or pursuing other leisure interests, is a significant factor. Many of our domestic activities require us to use valuable time at particular times of the day or week – doing the washing, feeding the children or driving to work. The higher up the social scale you are or want others to perceive you as being, the less constrained by the necessary chores and activities you must be. Many labour-saving devices, from the vacuum cleaner to the personal computer, have been marketed using just this notion. We launder our clothes not just to clean them but to make them look, smell and feel fresh. Most households no longer do a weekly wash but three or four washes a week. If greener goods and activities do not match these expectations then it is quite likely that many consumers will ignore them. The same goes for other important things in our

---

BOX 1.1 ELEMENTS OF A SUSTAINABLE LIFESTYLE

- Living in multiple-person households
- Modal shift or reducing air travel
- Modal shift from cars to public transport
- Walking short distances
- Using smaller, fuel-efficient cars and car share
- Switching from fossil fuels to renewable energy
- Switching from electric to gas cookers and condensing boilers
- Insulating homes and fitting double glazing
- Reducing the temperature of the home environment
- Purchasing energy-efficient appliances and not leaving appliances in standby mode
- Reducing the temperature of wash cycles to 40°C
- Recycling household waste
- Composting organic matter
- Disposing of toxic materials safely
- Fitting water-saving devices for toilets
- Installing low-flow taps and showers
- Collecting rain water for garden watering
- Reducing meat and dairy consumption
- Reducing fish consumption and purchasing fish from sustainable stocks
- Purchasing locally grown produce
- Purchasing food grown using more sustainable methods of production
- Reducing levels of highly processed food
- Purchasing certified sustainable wood and paper

Source: Bedford, Jones and Walker (2004)

---

everyday lives that enable us to live without thinking too much about the consequences of what we are doing, consequences either for energy or resource use or for what we now understand to be comfort, convenience or cleanliness. I'll drive to work today, people say, rather than walk to the station or cycle because if I don't I could get soaking wet and could look a real mess when I meet my colleagues. Decent people have a bath or shower everyday to maintain a culturally acceptable level of cleanliness and hygiene. I'll keep the thermostat at about 21 or 22°C because I like to wear a comfortable T-shirt indoors. If I wish to maintain an acceptable level of comfort or cleanliness and lead a greener lifestyle then the technology, the architecture, the plumbing and the transport system must allow or enable that – the social expectations, resources and infrastructure services have all got to interrelate. The culture of everyday life, attitudes and behaviour, and associated social practices are inextricably bound up with any and every attempt, or movement, to fashion a more sustainable world. Bedford, Jones and Walker put this clearly:

> *One of the primary motivators for individuals who live in a society which values the acquisition of commodities is to increase consumption in order to achieve the highest possible quality of life. Hence, as environmentalism has become entwined with images of denial such as not driving a car and using less water, it is out of line with what society considers to be normal. Moreover, those who do willingly undertake environmental actions are perceived as 'pious, hair-shirted, sandal-wearing hippies'. These negative connotations ensure that people continue to distance themselves from 'abnormal' environmental stereotypes. If environmental attitudes are to be converted into action there needs to be a programme of normalization and an attempt to engage all members of society in more resource-efficient behaviours.* (Bedford et al, 2004, p23)

UK Government policy has attempted to promote more sustainable lifestyles. The public communication campaign 'Are You Doing Your Bit?' enlisted a range of celebrities to feature in short television spots exhorting viewers to turn off taps and lights, drive less and generally tread more lightly on the earth. The charity Global Action Plan (GAP) campaigns actively to change people's behaviour and for a while published a magazine, *ERGO*, with the explicit intention of showing that a sustainable lifestyle could be cool and attractive. Unfortunately the magazine, failing to reach a sufficiently large readership or sell sufficient advertising, folded. It failed to marry form with content, failed to combine the glossy with its ethical stance. Generally, though, media and other public information campaigns in themselves are insufficient to effect the necessary changes to the practices of everyday life. As we'll see later, GAP's other projects such as its Eco Teams and Action at Home or Work initiatives have had some positive influence on participants' understanding and behaviour (Burgess, 2003; Hobson, 2003).

Many practices and behaviours are an integral element of everyday life, learnt from childhood and continuously reinforced from then on. We do things without really thinking about them – turning (or not turning) off the TV at the switch, driving to work, eating a pizza and leaving the tap running. They are part of what Giddens (1984) terms our 'practical consciousness' – things and actions not brought to deliberate conscious reasoning because, quite simply, to get by and get on with the routines of everyday life we must do many things without continuous conscious reflection. However, when we do start to think about our taken-for-granted habits, routines, attitudes and practices we become more aware of them. There is a need to harness elements of knowledge and information that enable us to make these wider connections. Giddens calls this our 'discursive consciousness', an example being that when I get in my car and drive to work I may start to think about energy consumption, CO_2 emissions, climate change, pollution and so on because I have read an article in the *New Scientist* or talked with a colleague at work over lunch about a programme last night on global warming, or simply recognized that it is not

clever to spend over an hour driving the twelve miles to work. I might therefore ask myself, Why do I this? Or, Can I go by train? Or, I want to go by train
(and so do others) so why have 'they' cut the service? By enabling participants
to focus consciously on particular behaviours that form part of our practical
consciousness and providing information about deleterious environmental and
other effects, GAP's emphasis on action and conscious reflection enables this
new knowledge and information to speak to us. After reviewing two GAP
projects Hobson (2003, pp107–8) concludes that 'practices change not
through exposure to scientific knowledge *per se* but through individuals
making connections between forms of knowledge that link their own, everyday and experiential environments to broader environmental concerns ... thus
enabling them to see old practices in new ways that make intuitive "common
sense".' Knowledge, understanding and even desire may not, however, always
be enough to stimulate pro-sustainability or pro-environmental conduct. As
Kollmuss and Agyeman note, 'We might be perfectly willing to change our
behaviour but still not do so, because we do not persist enough in practising
the new behaviour until it has become a habit' (Kollmuss and Agyeman, 2002,
p256). One of the things we need to do is stick with it. Just do it, then just do
it again, and again.

ON AFFORDANCES AND THE EVERYDAY

Ingold (2000) notes that although the universal reason of Western science tends
to be placed above and beyond the world of everyday material reality and our
own vernacular or indigenous knowledge and understanding of it, science is
still rooted in our lived experience of it. Following Bateson (1972), Ingold
attempts to outline not so much an ecology of learning or an ecology of mind
but something more fundamental – a (sentient) ecology of life. There is, he
argues, no hard and fast boundary between mind and the world. As Bateson
(1972, p460) stated in his lecture 'Form, Substance and Difference', 'The
mental world – the mind – the world of information processing – is not limited
by the skin.' Rather, as Ingold explains (2000, p18), the mind should be envis-
aged as extending outwards towards the environment along multiple sensory
pathways leading to the unfolding of the whole system of relations constituted
by a multifarious involvement of the perceiver in his or her environment.
Information only exists by our moving in and through the world. Ingold
writes:

> *Organic life, as I envisage it, is active rather than reactive, the*
> *creative unfolding of an entire field of relations within which*
> *beings emerge and take on the particular forms they do, each in*
> *relation to the others. Life in this view is not the realization of*
> *pre-specified forms but the very process wherein forms are gener-*
> *ated and held in place. Every being, as it is caught up in the*
> *process and carries it forward, arises as a singular centre of*

awareness and agency; an enfoldment, at some particular nexus within it, of the generative potential that is life itself...

'Organism plus environment' should denote not a compound of two things, but one indivisible totality. The totality is, in effect, a developmental system, and an ecology of life – in my terms – is one that would deal with the dynamics of such systems. Now if this view is accepted – if, that is, we are prepared to treat form as emergent *within the life-process* – *then, I contend, we have no need to appeal to a distinct domain of mind, to* creatura *rather than* pleroma *[terms derived from Jung and used by Bateson (1972) to distinguish mind from substance], to account for pattern and meaning in the world. We do not, in other words, have to think of mind or consciousness as a layer of being over and above that of the life of organisms, in order to account for their creative involvement in the world.* (Ingold, 2000, p19)

Ingold also discusses how information does not turn into knowledge simply by one piece of data being added to another. Data only becomes information when it is put into some context and information only becomes knowledge once we have begun to understand its meaning within a context of direct perceptual engagement with our various environments – the three ecologies. We develop this capacity to understand and to know by being shown things, which act as clues to the world as it is and as it could be. We are shown things by family, friends, elders, teachers, television programmes, internet sites, travel agencies, books, films, adverts, material artefacts, consumer goods, animals, and images in magazines, on billboards, in newspapers, and so on. These elements inform our view of the world and help constitute the way in which we fashion our meaning schemes and perspectives. Formal and informal learning can be understood to be an education of attention involving science, logic, rationality, skills and capacities of various descriptions and also intuition derived from and underpinning the constant unfolding of our creative relationships with the wider environmental contexts of meaning-making. The next thing is to be clear about what is meant by 'our environments'. Here again Ingold's work on affordances, owing much to the psychological discussions of Gibson (1979), is of value.

Gibson suggested an alternative to the Western notion that there is the mind and there is the world and we can only act on the world through our cultural representations or constructions of it. Gibson discussed the 'affordances' of the environment, which exist as inherent potentials of the objects within the world, independent of any use made of them by individuals or other sentient creatures. Different people may share different perceptions of a shared environment, of what it affords, and people themselves are capable of designing and constructing their environment, putting to use what is there in various ways and in various combinations. Termites construct their world in one way because they are termites. Humans can choose one of many possible options, if they have the brain and will to, and create a few more through learning, leading to the development of knowledge, reflexive capabilities and greater understanding. Importantly, Ingold distinguishes nature from environment, with the former consisting of essentially neutral objects apparent only to detached or 'indifferent' observers and the latter constituted in relation to the person whose environment it is. He recognizes that humans may have the capacity to engage or disengage with the world, to effect outer-directed actions and inner-directed thoughts, but life, he emphasizes, is 'given in engagement, not in disengagement' Ingold (1992, p44). More important to the themes in this book, Ingold continues:

> *Although humans undoubtedly have the capacity to adopt such a 'designer orientation' towards the environment, I do not think this is the way it is normally perceived in everyday life. No more than other animals can human beings* live *in a permanently suspended condition of contemplative detachment. If the animal is always and immediately 'one with its life activity', so is the human for much (if not all) of the time. Thus with Gibson, I believe that our immediate perception of the environment is in terms of what it affords for the pursuit of the action in which we are currently engaged. The man throwing the stone did not, we suppose, first 'construct' the stone as a missile by attaching a meaning or 'throw-quality' to impressions of it received through the senses. Nor was the act of throwing merely the bodily execution of a command subsequently issued by the mind of the basis of this construct. Rather, it was the very involvement of the man in his environment, in the practical context of throwing, that led him to attend to the 'throwability' of the object, by virtue of which it was perceived as a missile. Such direct perception of the environment is a mode of engagement with the world, not a mode of construction of it.* (Ingold, 1992, p44)

Gibson's concept of affordances can be productively used to outline a theory of how technology, including the materiality of artefacts, shapes everyday social life, enabling as well as constraining action (Hutchby, 2001). Although Gibson himself says little beyond the notion that 'behaviour affords behaviour', this rather undeveloped notion is picked up by Reed (1988), who suggests that social agents directly perceive their mutual affordances and share with others their direct perceptions of the environment. Being socialized into the same culture, having had similar experiences through living in the world, individuals will become familiar with the same information. Everyday social life is therefore a consequence of our direct perceptual involvement in the world. Objects take on their meaning and significance by being part of the routine pattern and social relationships of day-to-day activities – doing the washing, driving to work, eating a burger, painting the cupboard, cutting the grass, shopping to fill the freezer, looking good, having fun, watching a DVD.

Without falling into the trap of eradicating agency, the anthropologist Clifford Geertz proposes (1973, p44) that culture should be viewed as a 'set of control mechanisms – plans, recipes, rules, instructions … for the governing of behaviour'. Without culture human action would be chaotic, meaningless, shapeless but our great capacity to learn offers us options, possibilities, plasticity, agency. For Geertz, what is most important is our capacity for developing and applying concepts, 'the apprehension and application of specific systems of symbolic meaning' (1973, p49). He writes:

> *The 'control mechanism' view of culture begins with the assumption that human thought is basically both social and public – that its natural habitat is the house yard, the marketplace and the town square. Thinking consists not of 'happenings in the head' (though happenings there and elsewhere are necessary for it to occur) but of a traffic in what have been called, by G. H. Mead and others, significant symbols – words for the most part but also gestures, drawings, musical sounds, mechanical devices like clocks, or natural objects like jewels, anything, in fact, that is disengaged from its mere actuality and used to impose meaning upon experience. From the point of view of any particular individual, such symbols are largely given. He finds them already current in the community when he is born, and they remain, with some additions, subtractions and partial alterations he may or may not have had a hand in, in circulation after he dies. While he lives he uses them, or some of them, sometimes deliberately and with care, most often spontaneously and with ease, but always with the same end in view: to put a construction upon events through which he lives, to orient himself within 'the ongoing course of experiences things', to adopt a vivid phrase of John Dewey's.* (Geertz, 1973, p45)

A person's development, then, is also the development of a person's environment enfolded within which is the history of that person's activities. So, just as perception is involved in action, so consumption is involved in production and in both perception and consumption 'meanings embodied in environmental objects are "drawn into" the experience of the individual subject. These meanings are affordances or use-values.' (Ingold, 1992, p51). If there is a distinction to be made between persons and environments it is to be understood as being between effectivities and affordances – between the action and capabilities of subjects and the possibilities for action offered by objects (Ingold, 1992, pp51–2). Perception is therefore about discovering meanings in the environment through exploratory action, and through language and symbolic thought people are able to know the world and describe and explain it discursively to themselves and to others in society. The knowledge they create through language, number and image renders knowledge explicit and is sometimes created through a disengagement with the world as in the ivory tower of academe, for instance, or at least through achieving some critical distance by meditating in the bath or listening to some music on the radio. Culture is therefore our framework for interpreting the world rather than simply perceiving it. Systems of cultural classification are not so much precon- ditions for practical action in the world but 'invoked to recover the meaning that is lost when that action turns reflexively inwards on the self' (Ingold, 1992, p53). It may not be easy to be green but then what does being green mean? Think about it.

Knowledge can also be tacit, and this ties into our understanding of every- day practical consciousness and informal learning. Illeris (2002) writes of everyday life consisting of a succession of separate situations which each seem to have their own specific meaning and are perhaps unconnected because we are frequently unable to, or do not bother to, make the connections. Everyday consciousness likewise is characterized by fragmentation, unmediated contra- dictions and stereotypes, which may be routinely interpreted by means of 'theme–horizon–schemes'. Through these schemes we apparently reject, define away or not adopt experiences or events that offer disturbances to our way of just getting on with things, of not thinking about things too much. Alternatively, we may distort the event, perception or experience in order to make it fit with our pre-existing 'theme–horizon–schemes'. We do this so as not to be overwhelmed, but this also impairs learning that can transcend every- day understanding or 'practical consciousness'. Only through thematization, in other words an accommodation transcending everyday consciousness, can this take place. So for Illeris, thematizations enable the individual to make sense of our extremely complex everyday world, with its opaque financial and power structures, scientific uncertainties, ecological risks and rapidly changing technologies. Consequently, in this conception everyday consciousness consists of generalized means of defence, which have positive and negative, and defen- sive and offensive, aspects. It is positive because without defence mechanisms we simply would not, or could not, cope; negative because our lives are filled and fulfilled with and through routines, intellectual short-cuts, labels, preju- dices and so forth. We are defensive and so distort to get by, to survive, but there is an offensive aspect within us which means that when demands become too great, too disturbing or too insistent we can mobilize our energy and will and do something about the situation internally for ourselves or collectively with, and for, others. Parallel to everyday consciousness, says Illeris, is every- day learning, which occurs informally and/or incidentally as we navigate our way through life. This learning is not necessarily intentional or even conscious but it is usually absorbed and more or less understood, perhaps intuitively, so that we can relate to and make sense of the complexities of everyday living. It becomes part of our practical consciousness. We can learn to get up and switch off the TV or turn the thermostat down by talking to others about rises in our fuel bills or the environment, thinking about it a bit, and learning to live in a slightly cooler environment. It can soon become a way of life, part of our life, an element of our practical consciousness, routine and habit. This is what you do to be a little more sustainable. It becomes simple. To do otherwise would be unthinkable, odd, unnatural, unreasonable, irresponsible, stupid... unsustainable. But what is also important is not to compartmentalize too rigidly, to separate explicit from tacit learning, explicit from tacit knowledge. We need to think about things, read about things, and watch programmes on the TV that enhance our understanding. Illeris (2002, p178) writes:

> *It is not that the tacit dimension is clearly attached to everyday learning, but rather the contrary, that a very large part of everyday experience is converted into tacit learning. However, even in more goal-orientated learning contexts within various learning spaces, the acquisition of tacit knowledge will occur in parallel with explicit knowledge – and 'knowledge' is actually an imprecise word in this whole context, for understanding, insight, emotions, values, opinions, etc. are all involved.* (Illeris, 2002, p178)

I can make sense of the everyday in various ways – of my car and the use I put it to when the train doesn't arrive, of the money I pour into the tank when I fill up. All this will also have its effects, affects and meanings: my annoyance with the rail network, traffic congestion, so-and-so on the car radio, what I read in the paper, the flooded fields I saw on my way to work. Combined with the experiences of others, this is part of your and my cultural baggage – our cultural inheritance, the structure of our feelings and the routine predispositions and proclivities that together help constitute the *habitus*, that is the subjective internalized structures, schemes of perception, conception and action, the objective co-ordination of practices common to a group or culture, systems of durable dispositions, and cultural proclivities (Bourdieu, 1977). Thus, in building a more sustainable world what is important is the articulation of learning and experience in social behaviour, culture, consciousness and habit and the way critical reflection enables people to create meaning, identify alternative possibilities and make connections. As Maiteny indicates, thinking, knowing in the abstract, is not enough. There needs to be an inner change too. There needs to a clear relationship between the psyche, the *socius* and the environment:

> *The less experiential and more individualistic the sense of connectedness with the environment, the more tenuous or fragile seems to be the commitment to behaviour change. This would support the view that intellectual information about environmental problems is inadequate on its own to stimulate behaviour change. It is not a great surprise... Experience of relationship is more likely to generate feelings of being part and parcel of ecological processes, rather than separate and somehow insulated from it. Damage to the whole by the parts is, in a sense, 'experienced' as also damaging the parts, including oneself. Experience is more likely to motivate imperatives to break environmentally damaging behaviours (or 'bad habits') in everyday life that arise from*

within *persons. Intellectual activity alone is less likely to trigger this.* (Maiteny, 2002, pp303–4)

ON EDUCATION FOR SUSTAINABLE DEVELOPMENT

Higher, further and adult education can contribute to the shaping of various macro and micro contexts and socio-cultural frameworks that enable individuals and groups to fashion and perceive new opportunities for value-based action (conduct) and sustainable ways of living and being (van Oers, 1998; Edwards, 2001). The experience of sustainable design, green buildings, open space, modes of transportation, environmental mediascapes, campus greening projects, transdisciplinary approaches to learning, problem identification and creativity are potentially of great significance to fashioning alternative lifeworlds and conduct. Western education and Western attitudes to learning more generally could learn by reappraising the social, educative and cultural practices of pre-modern and indigenous peoples (Latour, 1993). Aboriginal ways of knowing offer an alternative, a counterpoint, to the established verities and appetites characterizing so much formal, institutionalized, rational-technocratic discipline-focused learning, teaching and research in higher education at least. Globalization has unarguably adversely affected the lives and cultures of indigenous peoples and for a broadly encompassing education for sustainable development to emerge, people creating and operating within systems of Western knowledge, and of knowledge transfer within universities, governments and corporations, should learn to listen to other voices and respect other cultures, however distant.

Deborah McGregor, member of the Whitefish River First Nation and Assistant Professor at the University of Toronto in the Aboriginal Studies Program, writes:

Aboriginal people define TEK [Traditional Ecological Knowledge] as much more than just a body of knowledge. While this is a part of it, TEK also encompasses such aspects as spiritual experience and relationships with the land. It is also noted that TEK is a 'way of life'; rather than being just the knowledge of how to live, it is the actual living of that life. One way of looking at the differences between Aboriginal and non-Aboriginal views of TEK is to state that Aboriginal views of TEK are 'verb-based' – that is, action-oriented. TEK is not limited, in the Aboriginal view, to a 'body of knowledge'. It is expressed as a 'way of life'; it is conceived as being something that you do. Non-Aboriginal views of TEK are 'noun-' or 'product-based'. That is, they tend to focus on physical characteristics. TEK is viewed as a thing rather than something that you do. Aboriginal views of TEK are inclusive of non-Aboriginal views, but tend to be broader in scope and holistic. The focus is not solely on the physical aspects, such as the natural

> *environment. TEK is also viewed by Aboriginal people to be*
> *inherently sustainable and spiritual.* (McGregor, 2004, p79)

A problem will exist if we in the West simply attempt to incorporate elements of TEK into our own data sets, technocratic and utilitarian modes of policy formulation and implementation (Morito, 2002). TEK or, more broadly, indigenous knowledge (IK) offers an alternative way of thinking, valuing and being (Booth and Jacobs, 1990). However, as Agrawal (1995) notes, like Western knowledge IK is not necessarily static or immune from being influenced from either changing socio-cultural and environmental contexts or from an engagement with Western methodologies. Values help fashion the substance of thoughts and feeling and if elements of indigenous world-views are recognized by those articulating and implementing dominant Western conceptions of growth and development, then not only will there be some elements of accommodation but quite possibly changes will mean new possibilities can be envisioned and realized which enable us to escape 'the "flatland" of pure materialism' that characterizes and resonates with our everyday life experiences (Groenfeldt, 2003). A lesson may be learned from indigenous education, in which, as Cajete (1994, p220) writes, 'there is a way of learning, communicating and working in relationship that mirrors those ways found in nature.' Consequently our relationship with nature – our sense of belonging, care of place and space, and respect for local knowledge – in all its various guises requires the fashioning of experiences, of learning, knowing and doing that enable a certain degree of re- and de-schooling. Without this, the concrete and immanent everyday experience of globalization, risk, uncertainty and complexity at home, in the workplace, in the shopping mall or in the car may remain uncontextualised (and separable) from the dominant learning experience in schools, colleges and universities. The increasing significance of new communication technology, biotech products, genetically modified foods, water purity, and car and air travel offer opportunities and threats that may enhance or diminish our lives together with our understanding of, and commitment to, fashioning a more sustainable world. Change, inner and outer, is extremely difficult, but the meanings, actions, behaviours and artefacts we produce may offer or afford other possibilities than those presently on offer.

We can learn, like many indigenous people still do, by listening to the stories of our elders, of worlds and loves we have lost, of improvements we have gained or fought for, of the significance of little things which are frequently drowned out by the social and technological imperatives of contemporary living. I spoke with Hilda, a woman in her 102nd year, increasingly frail but still living independently in her own home thanks to daily visits from a nurse. She is as mentally agile as a person half or a quarter of her age; at 99 she repainted her garage; at 100 she could still be seen gently turning over the soil in her beloved garden; at 101 she could vividly recall a world of nearly a century past and could still worry and wonder what the future holds for the generations who will follow her. She once employed a young man to undertake some heavy work in the garden. She noticed that while he worked he kept his Walkman plugged into his ears. 'What a pity', she told him, 'you have missed the birds sing.' He took the phones out, put his ears to the wind and worked for the rest of the day listening to music of another kind.

Hilda's family was well off. Her father owned a furniture factory, a telephone and a car before World War I. Timber was sourced locally and local crafts people were employed. Although fully realizing that others were by no means as materially fortunate as herself – 'there was poverty, terrible poverty, dear' – what came through to me from our discussion was that, despite her family's wealth, business success, privileged lifestyle and life chances, there was a simplicity and a satisfaction that seems missing today. Competitive and aspirant consumption was well known in the world of Hilda's childhood and youth but there are still lessons to be learnt. People travelled less, often went on holiday (if they could) near to where they lived, ate largely locally-produced foods and seemed to gain pleasure from small things – from creative and social activities, which Hilda still can and does engage in. There is a danger in romanticizing the past or looking back nostalgically on a world that never truly was, but whatever the case it is possible to learn from people stories, whether they be of hardship and privation or the opposite:

> When I was five my father had a furniture factory and we lived in a house on the premises and as a little girl I used to see long trailers being pulled by great big lovely horses. The trailers held trees – beech, oak, ash, elm: English trees – that were brought into the factory from local woodlands. They went through a circular saw and were made into planks of a certain thickness and then put out in a drying yard. There were piles of these planks with little bits in between them to season. The sanding was done by hand, although my father bought a machine about six feet wide which could use more than one plank at a time. On a Saturday afternoon we would go round and look at the finished bedroom suites, many of them my father had designed. The complete operation was done under the one roof. You wouldn't get that nowadays, would you?
>
> We had a very happy childhood, a very simple childhood. You know Hinkley Point, the power place. It is near a village called Stogursey and there was a little hamlet called Stolford, sort of on the coast, which was next door to Hinkley Point. A very simple village. I remember we had well water. Our maid had relatives in Stolford. The first time we stayed there we had rooms in quite a nice big house. There was no promenade – just a pebble beach and the commons behind it where we used to get wonderful mushrooms. The men were fishermen and there was a big long wide stretch of mud when the tide was out. These fishermen would roll their trousers up and they had a sledge, which they used so they didn't sink when pushing out to the line of nets just at the sea's edge. They used to collect shrimps and various things,

bring them back to the cottages and boil them and of course we always had lovely fresh shrimps and other fish. But I remember the shrimps more than anything else. They were lovely, beautiful. We used to do them ourselves, pick off the tails – that was part of the fun.

However, the world was changing, with trade and technology allowing new and different possibilities that clearly enhanced and improved life:

My father had a car and then another, both French cars. One of them was quite big because we were four children you see. Stolford was about ten miles from Bridgwater and the last bit of lane was just wide enough for us. The car brushed the verges in the summer burgeoning with herbs, weeds and wild flowers. We used to spend our school holidays by the sea; all of August. My dad went back to business. He didn't have the whole month off like we did, just a few days. You know, children today want so much. They cost so much when they are on holiday but we never wanted anything, we made our own fun, we paddled and bathed, explored the sunken forest... One day when the weather was nice we camped out at Hinkley Point where the power station is now. Mother made a cover of some sort. It was just a wild woody area and such a lovely place for picking blackberries. My father painted quite a few pictures of Hinkley Point before there was this nuclear power station. Things have changed now.

To fashion a less grasping and more sustainable world we do need to listen and to learn from a wide range of people and things. Maybe it is time for us all to listen to the birds sing, to listen and talk to our elders, and reflect on the meaning they make of past, present and future lifeworlds. Maybe we need to recapture what is simple, particularly in our complex hi-tech world. We need balance and the ability to see the long view. We need to learn, and to start learning from where we are in our everyday lives.

Turn off the computer and go for a walk.

2

Sustainability and the
Practice of Everyday Life

This chapter focuses largely on the sociology of everyday life, looking particularly at consumption issues and how changes to our everyday habits may lead to more sustainable lifestyles and development that is both desirable and fulfilling because it is human scale. Our need for and capability of learning from our environment and using this learning to change informs the discussion. The chapter comprises sections on:

- The practice of everyday life;
- Going slow;
- Consumerism;
- Car culture and ethical consumerism;
- Eco-localism; and
- Human-scale development.

THE PRACTICE OF EVERYDAY LIFE

In his justly famous but not always accessible book, *The Practice of Everyday Life*, the French philosopher Michel de Certeau wrote, 'We never write on a blank page, but always one that has already been written on' (de Certeau, 1984, p43). We always find everyday life in process, going on with or without us. It is dominated by social relationships, which ensures that, while everything seems to be commodified, everywhere we can find traces of and opportunities for people resisting, reworking or re-appropriating ideas, practices, objects and consumables. de Certeau stresses the possibility of agency rather than subjection, viewing most of us as living, if only perhaps most of the time, within the margins of a dominating consumerist society. Together with this society's myths and symbols, a range of different practices and logics exist which seemingly contest and contradict other more powerful ones. This constitutes society, and green consumerism may be an example. It is, for example, through various tactics of consumption that the weak make use of the strong, thereby rendering the practices of everyday life fundamentally political. The choice of trainer may therefore become a political act – it is possible to buy a product not made by a ten-year-old child in Vietnam. Consequently, de Certeau does not see people as cultural dupes (or dopes) or as suffering from 'false consciousness' or as strictly controlled, disciplined and punished, as Foucault suggested, through various microphysics, discourses and technologies of power. We may not always like or agree with what life in contemporary society offers, or what we read in the papers, see on the television or even buy in the supermarket. Dissent is always there even if it is sometimes inarticulate and unarticulated:

> *Thus, once the images broadcast by television and the time spent in front of the TV set have been analysed, it remains to be asked what the consumer makes of these images and during these hours. The thousands of people who buy a health magazine, the customers in a supermarket, the practitioners of urban space, the consumers of newspaper stories and legends – what do they make of what they 'absorb', receive and pay for? What do they do with it?...*
>
> *In reality, a rationalized, expansionist, centralized, spectacular and clamorous production is confronted by an entirely different kind of production, called 'consumption' and characterized by its ruses, its fragmentation (the result of the circumstances), its poaching, its clandestine nature, its tireless but quiet activity, in short by its quasi-invisibility, since it shows itself not in its own products ... but in an art of using those imposed on it.* (de Certeau, 1984, p31)

For de Certeau, a model form of silent production is reading. We make sense of what we read, not necessarily in the way the author intended. We also may not read the same text in the same way every time. We continuously make sense of what we learn at school, college or university, throughout everyday life at work, on holiday, in the supermarket or wholefood shop, in museums, at the club, at home in the kitchen, walking in the city, telling stories, or at the cinema and may make different meanings at different times. The film *The Day After Tomorrow* – a melodrama focusing on the search of a father for his son after rapid and devastating climate change has buried much of New York and North America under tons of ice and snow – may at first viewing seem pure Hollywood sensationalism, but after experiencing a particularly cold winter, people may consider it to have a little more going for it than its detractors claimed. These readings or interpretations are 'utopian spaces' that may resist incorporation and assimilation, where power relationships may be challenged symbolically and ultimately in more material ways too.

de Certeau draws on the ideas of the nineteenth-century Prussian military figure von Clauswitz to help make a distinction between *strategies* and *tactics*. A strategy is defined as the calculation of power relationships that becomes possible as soon as a business or other organization 'with will and power' can be isolated. It assumes a place that can be secured for itself and from which others' threats or actions can be handled. This place provides the organization or individual with some security, autonomy and capacity to observe what is happening, who is doing what, when and where. This provides a little power from which a certain knowledge of events, things, persons and processes can be constructed. On the other hand, a tactic is defined as a 'calculated action' determined by the lack of an appropriate place and has to deal with whatever is going on from a position that may not necessarily be controllable. A tactic allows for a certain flexibility, pragmatism or opportunism with which to make the best of things in an attempt perhaps to make a difference to oneself and maybe to others. Because it does not have a place, a tactic depends on time. de Certeau writes:

> *Many everyday practices (talking, reading, moving about, shopping, cooking, etc.) are tactical in character. And so are, more generally, many 'ways of operating': victories of the weak over the 'strong' (whether the strength be that of powerful people or the violence of things or of an imposed order, etc.), clever tricks, knowing how to get away with things, 'hunter's cunning', manoeuvres, polymorphic simulations, joyful discoveries, poetic as well as warlike.* (de Certeau, 1984, xix)

We, perhaps the weak, develop an art of manipulating and enjoying, of changing our worlds or life experiences. Through conversation we develop the art of manipulating 'commonplaces', in the process making them 'habitable'. We re-appropriate through our consumption, through our everyday life practices that have as their goal a 'therapeutics for deteriorating social relations' from which a 'politics of such ploys should be developed' (de Certeau, 1984, pxxiv). We can reduce, reuse and recycle, jam as well as consume culture, build as well as buy. Kalle Lasn (2000), founder of *Adbusters* and latterday Situationist, has developed a strategic approach to contesting, challenging and rearticulating media messages, advertising slogans, corporate marketing and PR campaigns. The aim is to turn around, reclaim these images, to make people think, to switch on their critical freedom, to offer a learning experience that may be transforming. The consumer becomes a producer, the viewer a political activist, a guerrilla fighter using techniques and methods available to any individual or group. Turn off your TV for a week, buy nothing for a day, create your own pro-sustainability message, song, poster, poem, movie, still image, webcast, blog or newspaper article. If BP can go beyond petroleum, then others, societies even, can as well. This may be a defence but it is also a way in which certain cultural spaces can be created for different types of activities, social relationships, products, values, attitudes and ways of living. It is a way of doing different things, being proactive and even pre-figurative.

Practices are social and historical. As Reckwitz writes:

> *A practice represents a pattern which can be filled out by a multi-tude of single and often unique actions reproducing the practice...*

> *The single individual – as a bodily and mental agent – then acts as the 'carrier' of a practice – and, in fact, of many different practices which need not be coordinated with one another. Thus, she or he is not only a carrier of patterns of bodily behaviour, but also of certain routinized ways of understanding, knowing how and desiring. These conventionalized 'mental' activities of understanding, knowing how and desiring are necessary elements and qualities of a practice in which the single individual participates, not qualities of the individual.* (Reckwitz, 2002, pp249–50)

It is important to understand how everyday social practices are connected to wider social structures, processes, modes of awareness, knowledge, values, organizations, activities, spatial location, affiliations and experiences; these are influenced by gender, race, class, the media, politics, philosophical values, nature and history.

GOING SLOW

In recent years the speed as well as the uncertainty of everyday life has increasingly become an issue for many people. For decades, centuries even, commentators have noted that urban life particularly has meant a speeding up in virtually every aspect of our lived experience. From trains, boats and planes to so-called labour-saving devices, fast food, broadband connections, just-in-time production methods to fast-moving television series like *Crime Scene Investigation*, whose aesthetic seems more in line with the fast elliptical edits of music videos than with traditional Poirot-type crime dramas. Speed is increasingly characterizing everyday life. I'm very busy. I haven't the time. I have to work faster, harder and smarter to stay where I am. Of course, this is nothing new. In the nineteenth century it was once believed that if trains travelled faster than sixty miles an hour passengers and carriages would simply burn up like a twentieth-century rocket re-entering the atmosphere. There exist both a love for and a fear of speed, rapid change and loss of the human scale. Silent film comics such as Harold Lloyd in *Speedy* and Charles Chaplin in *Modern Times* offered their own satirical takes on the relentless pace of modern living, working and being. Apart from more choice and lower prices, what supermarkets offer is speed – pick what you want from the shelf, go to the checkout, pay and drive off. In a few stores you may even be trusted to check out and pay for your shopping without overt scrutiny from a member of staff.

Speed has become an integral part of our lived experience. The more and the faster we accumulate goods and chattels the more successful we can pretend we are. However, there has been a reaction to this, which like so many things that impact upon everyday life has wide connections beyond the immediately apparent. Barbara Adam (1998) has noted that our very understanding of time has changed. Time is now no longer so easily equated with distance, place or season. Some fruits have been redesigned to stay fresh for months because harvesting occurs before the fruit is ripened. It is then transported from one part of the globe to another and stored in specially controlled conditions before being purchased in the local out-of-town supermarket. Chickens are bred faster in industrial conditions to satisfy increasing consumer demand for cheaper and 'healthier' white meat. In 1800 pigs took between two and five years to reach slaughter weight. In the early twentieth century it was about a year. In the early twenty-first century it is about six months – pigs sometimes still have their milk teeth when they go to the abattoir. Industrial dairy production means that a cow very rarely sees its fifth birthday, rarely its second, even though over its now vastly shortened lifespan it gives slightly more milk than it would do if it were left to live out its years naturally, normally to an age of around 20.

A combination of government subsidies, international trade regulations, the externalization of energy costs, cheap labour and economies of scale often means that lamb from New Zealand or apples from South Africa are cheaper than those produced locally in the UK. Perhaps it is worth considering that the high street delicatessen is more likely to have expensive 'speciality foods' from ten miles away than from ten thousand. Produce in the supermarket is more than likely to have been selected for its long shelf-life and aesthetic appearance – the perfectly round firm and unblemished tomato – than for its taste, which is often almost non-existent. And despite all the extremely rigorous health and hygiene standards embalming modern all-year-round foods, we still cannot be sure how safe they actually are. And a concern for food security, even if we exclude issues relating to GM, antibiotics or growth hormones, is an important one that has to do with our approach to time, to instant satisfaction, to unseasonality, to lifestyle, to cultural expectation, to wanting to consume not so much the fruits of the Earth but the Earth itself – without thinking about it too much:

> *Safety ... is difficult to establish in a context of time-distanciation and time lags, where damage and harm are being produced out of sight, below the surface, for often unknown periods of time and where the symptoms do not necessarily allow for a backwards reconstruction to originating sources and causes.*
> (Adam, 1998, p155)

It doesn't matter whether we are talking about irradiation, pesticide, herbicide, insecticide use or post-harvest preservation treatments, governments tend to assume processes are safe until they are proven harmful. As Adam notes, historically it is the poor who have tended to be treated as 'the canaries of the food system':

> *By ensuring that new industrial alternatives to traditional foods are cheaper, the promoters of these foods are guaranteed a captive consumer group, keen to try the latest innovation. Tinned meat and vegetables, refined foods from across the world that have*

been chemically treated for beauty and storage, irradiated food, hormonally treated milk, baby milk contaminated with Chernobyl radiation – all are foods that have duly been tested by the poor, with and without their knowledge and/or consent. Choice does not come into it when the cheaper option is the only *alternative to starvation.* (Adam, 1998, p157)

There is an alternative, not necessarily cheap or fast, but one which foregrounds everyday life as politically and symbolically important, as a tactic, as a way of learning to live and to be different. Perhaps it is in the sphere of everyday social relationships that collective, strategic, political change emerges, but there can be no collective change which is not rooted in individual experience. Carlos Petrini is familiar to many as the originator of the Slow Food movement, which has now spread throughout the world, generating a number of related initiatives including slow shopping and the Slow City idea. Slow food is about spending the time to prepare and eat food that is wholesome, tasty, local and, wherever possible, organic. It is about retrieving food and mealtimes more generally as a site for social interaction, discussion, companionship, rest and relaxation. Not scoffing some pre-packaged, processed, possibly genetically modified and microwaved food bought from Asda/Wal-Mart (Figure 2.1) and spooned from a tray while sitting, in isolation, in front of the television or computer screen.

Joanna Blythman's *The Food We Eat* (1996), Eric Schlosser's *Fast Food Nation* (2001), Greg Critser's *Fat Land* (2003) and numerous press reports and documentaries, including the excoriating *Supersize Me* by Morgan Spurlock, have identified that where food is concerned speed and convenience may seriously damage your health. It doesn't have to be this way. It is possible to significantly re-orientate our expectations, learn different habits and cultivate alternative assumptions. Carlos Petrini explains that the Slow Food movement in Italy was born:

[a]s a gastronomical association, paying attention to the traditional pleasures of the table and wine, in order to oppose in some way the crazy speed of the 'fast life' – the way of life and food production that leads to the homogenization of flavour and the erosion of culture.

However, we quickly realized that the flavours we wanted to save were closely connected to the work of people – of farmers, who with their ancient knowledge are the true custodians of biodiversity and the land. We had this fundamental realization of the connection between sustainable agriculture and gastronomic culture. Anyone who thinks of themselves as a food lover but does not have any environmental awareness is naïve. Whereas an ecologist who does not enjoy the pleasures of culture certainly has a sadder life. (Petrini, 2004, p51)

Figure 2.1 *Asda/Wal-Mart, near Leeds: Low prices, but at what cost?*

Petrini explains that once we have lost a traditional recipe we have lost the knowledge and use of a product. When everything is standardized for mass consumption and supermarket purchase, our choice of local and seasonal foods actually diminishes. Slow food is therefore about relearning local food traditions, or learning sometimes with the assistance of popular TV chefs, a new culture of cooking that may rebuild a more intimate and direct relationship between consumers and producers and maybe even members of the same household. Many families it seems have dispensed with the kitchen table and the important social, familial ritual of eating and talking together at set times. There may not be a slow food brand but it may be possible to brand an associated lifestyle – slow, pleasurable and sustainable.

> *There will never be a Slow Food brand on any product. There are already too many brands around and they create confusion. It is up to people to apply their ideas, their knowledge, their learning. The producer's duty is to teach and communicate what they do, while the consumer has the duty to get informed and to use their consumer power. It is only with education and with a return to a more human dimension of production that this 'virtuous circle' can be created.* (Petrini, 2004, p53)

You can buy bread freshly baked in the supermarket but the dough is likely to be of the frozen variety prepared in a factory and 'baked off' on the premises (Blythman, 2003, pp99–103). On the other hand if you are lucky, as I am, there may still be a local family bakery producing a wide range of breads, rolls and cakes from organic flour sourced from a local mill. Each day I'm offered a different combination from a repertoire of over 40 products and, just as it may

Box 2.1 The Edible Schoolyard

Michael K. Stone

The Edible Schoolyard (ESY) is a non-profit programme located on the campus of Martin Luther King Middle School in Berkeley. Its mission is to create and sustain an organic garden, landscape and kitchen classroom that are wholly integrated into the school's curriculum and lunch programme. The garden is designed and maintained using sound ecological practices. ESY involves every student at King School in all aspects of farming the garden, from the way food is grown and harvested to the recycling of waste back into the earth. Through the program's kitchen classroom, each student also participates in preparing, serving, and eating the food. ESY is designed to awaken children's senses and to encourage awareness and appreciation of the transformative values of nourishment, community and stewardship of the land. Aesthetically, ESY's goal is creation of a beautiful environment that will inspire social, personal, and social responsibility.

Students in the garden cooperate without being asked. The changed context breaks assumptions about how teachers and students relate. Phoebe tells a story: 'I was working with one of my students. We noticed that the wood chips we were spreading were steaming. "Why is that?" I asked. "Because of bacteria in the wood," the student answered. Then he said, "Miss Tanner, let's have a conversation." I had thought we were having a conversation, but for him it was still a lesson. "Who's your hero in life?" he asked. I told him Rachel Carson and asked who his was. A couple of others joined us. Everyone shared, and really listened to each other. That doesn't happen in a classroom.'

Most King School classes incorporate the kitchen in their schedule. Esther Cook has been The ESY kitchen teacher and manager since the kitchen opened. At first, she says, teachers looked at the kitchen and garden sessions as 'time away from the curriculum. Now they're seeing ways to make the lessons part of the curriculum.'

A Spanish class tries Venezuelan cooking, speaking in Spanish while cooking. A maths class costs out the ingredients of a meal, learning that good food can be served on a limited budget (literally, a take-home lesson). For a drama class, Esther gives groups of students the same ingredients and invites them to 'improve' different recipes.

Setting the table with a tablecloth and flowers, and sitting down to eat together, even for twenty minutes, creates a different model of eating and relating for children used to taking meals on the run. Classes teach about fresh, nutritious food, not with 'eat this because it's good for you', but with 'try this and see if it doesn't taste better'.

Source: Adapted from http://www.ecoliteracy.org/publications/edibleyard.html

be surprising to learn that there are more apples than Granny Smith's, Braeburns or Golden Delicious, the customer soon learns that there are more breads than white or brown, sliced or unsliced. Customers not only learn about new and intriguing tastes, smells and shapes, but also learn about themselves and the rather impoverished experiences that characterize so much of our food consumption. Unfortunately, this type of shop is becoming increasingly rare, but Steve B's bakery competes successfully with a nearby Tesco Metro, Costcutters and Somerfield on taste, variety and price while maintaining a loyal and committed customer base who seem quite happy to walk to the end of the high street to make their purchase. And Steve's customers are not all middle-class greenies. Slow food is not just a fad for the affluent. Small retailers might not be able to compete with supermarket loss-leaders but you can be certain of buying a head of lettuce from a local greengrocer for less than a prepared bag of the average supermarket salad. These leaves, prepared by poor migrant workers, washed in a chlorine solution up to twenty times stronger than that found in swimming pools, inserted into a modified atmosphere packaging used to raise levels of carbon dioxide and reduce levels of oxygen allow 'freshness' to last up to ten days. Some US bagged salads are supposed to stay fresh for a month. This processed salad has a much reduced nutritional value (Lawrence, 2004), but bagged salads are big business worth over £256m in the UK and about US\$1.2bn in the US. Today, 69 per cent of British households buy a bag of salad at least once a month (Bennett, 2005). We can learn a lot by going slow and may even modestly change some supermarket practice in the process. For example, Sainsbury's have recently introduced bagged salad washed only in spring water.

As Carl Honore (2005, p241) concludes, the Slow Movement 'certainly implies a questioning of the untrammelled materialism that drives the global economy' but is not in itself inimical to capitalism – 'a Slow alternative could make the economy work for us, rather than vice versa'. Slow is often marketed as a means to intensify pleasure and that most precious of commodities, time. It also has a direct link to improved human health through improved diets and lifestyles, a better environment, and closer relationships with food producers creating more cohesive communities. Going Slow may be viewed as one of those tactics de Certeau wrote of – a learning opportunity and lifestyle option for people of all ages and backgrounds. It is also a term that may be applied to the formal education system – the clearing away of junk food served up for school dinners as Jamie Oliver did so successfully with his influential UK television series *Jamie's School Dinners*. In the US, Alice Waters campaigned for healthier food by promoting 'edible schoolyards' and school gardens to facilitate children's understanding of food, food production and natural ecology. The Slow metaphor could conceivably have a wider application as it is an aspect of what the American philosopher Albert Borgmann describes as a 'focal practice' – a way living, doing and being that focuses on what really matters, like skills, satisfactions, relationships and other experiences which enrich our lives. The culture of the table is but one such focal practice; Borgmann writes:

> *In the preparation of the meal we have enjoyed the simple tasks of washing leaves and cutting bread; we have felt the force and generosity of being served a good wine and homemade bread.*

Such experiences have been particularly vivid when we came upon them after much sitting and watching indoors, after a surfeit of readily available snacks and drinks. (Borgmann, 1984, p200)

A focal practice requires 'resoluteness'. It requires effort and learning and doesn't necessarily come easily or quickly; and so much the better given that many technologies, devices and conveniences offer spurious rather than real benefits to health and well-being. Convenience food is a clear example here, but we also need to be able to clearly see this, to clearly reflect upon and to learn of detrimental effects on the capacities of local food producers to produce for, and satisfy, local markets and ultimately ourselves.

CONSUMERISM

Consumerism is a troubling issue for many sustainability practitioners. The view that we consume too much but still want to consume more is frequently heard. But the question perhaps is not really how much is enough, as Alan Durning (1992) asked, but why we buy, buy and buy in the first place. It is almost a truism that mass-produced material goods have symbolic value. As advertisers might say, when you buy this car you are not just purchasing a means to move around, you are buying cool, you are buying sophistication, speed, sex appeal or fun. The early 21st century has become a shoppers' paradise. There are opportunities everywhere – from your local corner shop (if you have one) to the internet, television shopping channels and the mall. But shopping involves more than just whipping out the credit card. Window-shopping or walking in a mall are also aesthetic, recreational and social experiences not unlike being a tourist (Lehtonen and Maenpaa, 1997). Going to the market, mall or high street shopping centre frequently involves meeting others, conversing, interacting, being sociable. It may involve being entertained by street musicians, artists and performers. Shoppers may adopt a particular role or persona – the bargain hunter, the browser, the retail therapist, the giver of gifts, the housekeeper, the ethical consumer. These essentially shared identities and practices offer a type of bond or association, and in some areas shopping malls and big stores have turned themselves into de facto community centres (Cohen, 1996). Consumption then is an element of many social practices – eating, travelling, going to work and so forth Warde writes:

Practices, rather than individual desires, we might say, create wants. For example, the paraphernalia of the soccer supporter – team shirts, match tickets, newspaper reports, memorabilia, etc. – are more directly the consequence of engagement in the practice of supporting a football team than they are of individual taste or choice. It is the fact of engagement in the practice, rather than any personal decision about a course of conduct, that explains the nature and process of consumption.

> *Practices steer the process of consumption. They steer the manner of appropriation of items, the processes of learning about, identifying, appreciating and putting to use; they identify which items are to be preferred, and also often which suppliers are to be preferred; and they prescribe modes of enjoyment.* (Warde, 2004, pp5–6)

Shopping seems to be as natural as breathing, but people had to learn to be shoppers and consumers even though it is a practice easily acquired and possibly addictive. The habit can be a difficult one to break. As the industry expanded and more goods were produced so new needs had to be created. People had to want, or need, the new products being manufactured. As Susan Strasser (1989, p5) has written, 'People who had never heard of toothpaste had to be told that they needed it; the very ideas of chewing gum and flashlights had to be introduced.' Today the same may be said for digital video, mobile phones, iPods, high-definition televisions and many other electronic goods. And bargains are there to be had. The biggest retail success story of modern times is undoubtedly Wal-Mart – a massive chain of huge functional cut-price discount stores spreading across America and now into Europe. Wal-Mart's main motivation, like that of any other store, is simple – sales per square metre. But that is not the end of the story:

> *Paradoxically, the flood of high-quality, even luxury, goods at cheap prices has helped the American middle class standard of consumption seem within reach, even while the mass of Americans' income and chances have been eroded. This is the most important ideological effect of the discounters. They are delivering the consumer entitlements of middle class life to people whose very class identity is precarious.* (Davis, 2001, p175)

There are ethical dimensions to this consumer paradise. With the sourcing of cheap produce comes environmental degradation, destruction of small businesses and the economic vibrancy of many local high streets and town centres, the exploitation of foreign (often child and female) labour, and the emergence of *maquiladoras* on the US-Mexican border and sweatshops in New York. Campaigns and boycotts of some big corporations have dovetailed into widespread anti-globalization protests, knowledge of which has spread thanks to the accessibility of books like Naomi Klein's *No Logo* (2000). Documentary films like Mark Achbar and Joel Bakan's *The Corporation* or Robert Greenwald's *Wal-Mart: the High Cost of Low Prices* combine with sharp investigative journalism to change the zeitgeist, though what is less well known perhaps is that many stores want to know their customers totally. Loyalty cards, 'market basket analysis', CCTV and new software programs are able to profile and predict customer preferences and behaviour with tremendous accuracy. Shoppers are known both as individuals and as market types. Companies like Paco Underhill's Envirosell offer a significant service to big retailers enabling them to shift more merchandise by making layout more customer-friendly and enticing. Believing that the store itself is a medium of communication, it is important to get the aesthetic, the lighting, colours, shelving design, layout, sounds and smells just right. Without knowing it, consumer preference is being subtly, or subliminally, 'educated'. This is not obvious and apparent magazine or television advertising, aimed at either a general or niche market, but something far more fine-grained and almost totally integrated into the daily, quotidian, shopping routine. It involves such things as moving treats for the dog from a high to a lower shelf because the elderly or children think most about buying pets a little something. It means scenting baby product aisles with baby perfume. It means providing shaded parking places for 'drive thru' customers at fast-food outlets, as they frequently own newer cars than sit-down customers and wish to consume their produce in the comfort, privacy and luxury of their beloved vehicles. This finding, writes Underhill (2000, p91), 'affirms the overall trend among fast-food restaurants to shrink the size of the building and increase the size of the drive thru and the parking lot, thereby allowing customers to have it their way – which, in nearly every case, is as it should be.' In other words, it means encouraging and facilitating the desire to make a purchase and perhaps on reflection to act purposely in response. For Davis:

> *Imagining a different world means imagining a world based on values other than consumption... Information collection and surveillance need to be seen not only as threats to individual privacy, but as the linchpins of a process of social engineering. Market research needs to be exposed as a pseudoscience and a source of social distortion, especially when it is a basis for community development decisions.* (Davis, 2001, p189)

A world based on values other than consumption is one sustainability theorists and practitioners have been trying to communicate for years. The nineteenth-century artist and utopian thinker William Morris had similar thoughts. Arguments for a simple life that 'treads lightly on the earth' and down-shifting to secure time, happiness and focus are strong (counter-) currents in the consumer society, but consumption is also a necessary part of production and a decent (whatever that means) material standard of living and quality of life. Being a consumer is therefore inevitable, though it is also possible, as many campaigners argue, to be ethical at the same time. This may mean buying locally, buying organics, buying fairly traded. It also means fully integrating ethical consumption into the everyday patterns, practices and motivations of everyday social learning and behaviour.

Shopping can be a pleasurable activity. It can also be a chore, if a necessary one – a means whereby individuals create an identity or image or simply buy stuff to get by rather than get on. Most of us buy clothes because we need to be warm as well as look OK, buy furniture to relax on as well as to say something about our taste, buy groceries in order to live, buy gifts to make other people, as well as ourselves, happy. As the anthropologist Daniel Miller

(1998) shows, shopping is not by any means all hedonistic materialism. In fact it has a lot to do with building and objectifying social and personal relationships. Brands such as Kellogg's and Heinz, says Miller, have lasted for over a century because they represent or articulate in some way stability, history and family tradition. This is not retail therapy but it may be a form of individually and collectively making a point. We experience alienation in many areas of our lives and it is sometimes through consumption, through shopping, that we may express some creativity or attempt to transcend aspects of this alienation:

> *Consumption, far from being the continuation of the projects of production and distribution, whether in capitalist or socialist systems, is actually the point of negation, where the particularity of goods is used to create fluid relationships in direct opposition to the vastness of markets and states. So the intricacies of our relationships expressed through consumption reassure us that we are not merely the creatures and categories of capitalism or the state – this is the very opposite of the effect of commodities upon us that we usually assume, when we take goods to be merely symbols of capitalism or the state.* (Miller, 1998, p147)

The purpose of shopping is not so much to buy things that people want but to attempt to be in a relationship with people who may want those things. In our society the only things that may stand as inalienable, writes Miller (1998, p152), are 'human subjects and relationships'. If Miller is right, then what becomes important is not so much curtailing consumption but re-orientating it towards more sustainable and ethical purposes. And this may be achieved by combining brand advertising and appeals with the development of informal learning opportunities that articulate self-regarding *and* other-regarding qualities, that connect with the everyday values of care and concern that already exist in much day-to-day activity, including shopping, parenting, supporting the local football club, helping out a neighbour, supporting or running a local business or charity and so on. Maybe through consumption, which may in itself be neither moral nor immoral, people can learn to cultivate a range of competences and capabilities needed to be more sustainable: participating in public or civic activities, caring for both self and others close to home and those slaving away in sweatshops out of sight and far away. This requires us to think about what we consume and how we consume, recognizing that what frequently appears on the market initially as a luxury good or a naughty treat very soon becomes a needy essential – a car, two cars, air-conditioning in the car, fridge-freezer, two fridge-freezers, a microwave, a cell phone, a new cell phone, a computer, a laptop, a Blackberry, a Thai holiday, regular Thai holidays, plasma television, a Dyson, a new Dyson, a bigger plasma television and so on. Societies construct objects and in the process construct people. As novelties become normal, meanings change too; even when product designs seem fairly fixed, their social significance or purpose may continue to change as advertisers and users retune their cultural resonances. The gas-guzzling SUV found in many urban areas offers convenience and status – both necessities – and a sense of security and empowerment. However, with increases in the price of oil and the acceptance that Western lifestyles are in many ways responsible for the rapidity of climate change, the meaning of the SUV is beginning to shift from being a mark of social superiority to being a symbol of social and environmental irresponsibility.

CAR CULTURE AND ETHICAL CONSUMERISM

As Paterson (2000) shows, car culture is intimately bound up with the global political economy and has been for decades. Cars themselves symbolize modernity, growth, success and development as the massive expansion of car use and ownership in China testifies. Although many motor manufacturers, including Mercedes, Toyota and Ford, are now designing and marketing more eco-efficient cars and the concept of the hyper-car is now a well-known element of what could be termed the 'natural capitalism movement' (Hawken, Lovins and Lovins, 1999), environmental campaigners argue strongly for the need to reduce private car travel, increase and improve public transport options, and impose congestion charging in towns and cities to reduce pollution, improve the quality of urban living, and stem the tide of road building and environmental degradation. Efforts to establish contexts for informal (and formal) learning and cultural change, including the development of new green or ethical habits – car pools, car-free housing – will always confront serious structural barriers, vested commercial interests and the perceived immutability of social and personal needs. Cars are important to people for many reasons, and, as Maxwell (2001) shows, a whole range of social ethics, including thriftiness, saving time and work, and looking after and caring for friends, family and neighbours, are interwoven with everyday car use. The school run is a clear example, but for many people going for a drive is a pleasurable experience and taking an elderly neighbour to the shops is just being a good neighbour, a valuable and quantifiable instance of informal volunteering. Nevertheless, people often experience guilt feelings about their car use, particularly when the social and environmental consequences are considered. Many of Maxwell's interviewees dispelled their anxieties by stating that in practical terms they just *had* to use the car – there was no practical alternative. And there often isn't, particularly in rural areas where public transport is non-existent. This led to a gap between what people said they would like to do and what they actually did unless they were able to devise and implement highly disciplined types of behaviour – preplanning and timing activities to coincide with specific journeys, car sharing, bus times and so on. For Maxwell, it is therefore a mistake to think of consumer behaviour, and especially car use, as largely individualistic or plain selfish:

> *The meanings of car use are fundamentally embedded in social*
> *relations of everyday life, and that in an understanding of the*

interrelationships between the plural ethical discourses associated with car use provides an alternative means of understanding the gap between attitudes and behaviour. (Maxwell, 2001, p215)

It isn't easy being a green consumer, green student, green citizen or green anything else for that matter. There doesn't seem to be enough physical or cultural affordances to make it so. Seyfang, writing on ecological citizenship and shopping, notes:

A major criticism of the mainstream model of sustainable consumption through market transformation, from an ecological citizenship perspective, is that it is a citizenship of the market, and purchases are the only votes that count. Individuals may not be able to act on their ecological citizenship preferences for a variety of reasons, and therefore are unable to influence the market. These barriers include the affordability, availability and convenience of sustainable products, as well as feelings of power-lessness generated by the thought that individual action will not make any difference, disenchantment with corporate green marketing and preference for products that are not available, such as an efficient, clean and safe public transport system... Patterns of material consumption exercised through the market-place embody multi-layered meanings above simple provisioning, for example, aspirational consumption, retail therapy, self-expression, a need for belongingness, self-esteem, self-validation, a political statement, an ethical choice, status display, loyalty to social groups, identity, and so forth... Accordingly, these motiva-tions may be incompatible with ecological citizenship desires for sustainable consumption. (Seyfang, 2005, pp296–7)

Although information and environmental awareness may not necessarily trans-late into action (Barr, 2003), Berry and McEachern (2005) show that a prior awareness of ethical issues does affect how a potential customer responds to product information like a table of ingredients or a brand image. The main outcome of a product label is often to confirm a decision made outside the shop or supermarket – a decision in large part influenced by marketing, the media or the experience of everyday life. Labels may also serve as an accessible and preliminary introduction to some wider issues like fair trade or local organic production. Governments have used media advertising, regulation as well as labelling, to influence consumer choice – the SMOKING KILLS label on cigarette packets is an obvious example – but this is not always enough to alter behaviour, particularly if the source of the information is not completely trusted or socially welcome. Government and scientific wavering over BSE and CJD did little for the trust and authority ratings of either the UK Government or the scientific establishment, even if the Environment Minister did feed his daughter a beefburger in front of the press and TV cameras. More significantly, governments have tended to define sustainable consumption as the consumption of more sustainable products rather than a wider cultural reframing of the nature of consumption itself to promote more sustainable ways of living and being. The UK's National Consumer Council has argued that the government should promote lifelong learning skills that enable individuals to be more acute and critical consumers. Alternative Trading Organizations (ATOs) like Café Direct invest a significant amount of their profits in a market communication strategy aimed at consumers and producers to press for the adoption of fair trade principles. There also seem to be developing fair-trade 'brand communities', with Nestlé, Starbucks and Costa Coffee taking note by establishing their own fair-trade sub-brands. The global sale of fair-trade products reached £300m a year in 2003 (Lury, 2004). The Co-op Bank vigorously promotes its ethical policy, since if a person is to change his or her primary bank it is frequently for ethical reasons – 98 per cent of Co-op customers do not want their money invested in arms for oppressive regimes, 98 per cent do want their money invested in renewable energy and 96 per cent want business to be responsible for labour rights in developing countries. And although other companies may promote their products on the basis of low price rather than quality, downplaying or ignoring fair trade, ethics or issues of environmental sustainability, things are changing as high-profile campaigns, exposés or boycotts shift attitudes and behaviour. People may learn about the ethical or the unethical nature of a product incidentally, accidentally or informally via a campaign group's stall in the high street or an ad for fair trade in the paper. For some this may be more effective and more welcome than going back to school, being preached at, or being seen as, or seeing oneself, as a do-gooder greenie.

I remember speaking to Laura after a community development meeting about her ethical purchases. She told me she wanted to buy a coffee table but could not easily find one that was fairly traded. She first went to a local shop and found something she liked and that was quite reasonably priced, but the wood was not from a sustainable source. Although beautifully crafted and 'exactly what I wanted', it was suspiciously half the price of a similar product imported from France. The oak table in question was from China, and the shop couldn't say whether it was a fairly traded product or not and was slightly surprised that this ethical issue was preventing Laura from completing the purchase. She then went on the internet and looked at the online catalogue of a big store with a reputation for both quality and ethical trading. But the problems continued – she found an attractive table made from rubber tree wood at a fifth of the price of the Chinese oak table. It isn't always simple being green or ethical. Like many other things you either have to work at it, compromise or perhaps even face disappointment:

> *I was looking on the website for a coffee table and I thought that*
> *store would do good quality, that they'd be ethical and they'd*
> *know who their sources are, which they did I suppose, but as it*
> *turned out they couldn't guarantee that it was from a fairly traded*

organization. The timber – I suppose they replace rubber planta-
tions, but I don't know how quickly rubber trees grow. But it was
so cheap, I couldn't imagine anyone making it would have been
paid anything more than a pittance. I think everything should be
fairly traded. No one should be classed as a slave anymore, which
is in effect what some are. No one should be working ridiculous
hours and be paid nothing to do it. People should expect a fair
wage for what they do, and we should expect to pay a suitable
amount that enables people to have that. We wouldn't do it
ourselves or expect our families to do it. Why should we expect
other people in Third World countries to have a lesser standard
of life, so we can have luxury items at their expense? Fairly traded
goods promote the right work ethic and right work relations.

I don't know how the company reacted to me cancelling the
order. You don't know whether you are a lone voice in the wind,
but if more people took notice, I guess, and cared about where
their products came from, then they would cease to trade with
that particular organization or make certain they could reassure
their customers like me that where they were from and the people
making the goods were treated with respect, had a fair wage and
had a reasonable standard of life, which we all expect. (interview
with author)

Laura eventually found what she wanted with the help of an ethical consumer
guide in *The Ecologist*. It is perhaps the use of the web that indicates how new
processes of communication and information can work to promote and
reinforce more sustainable practices. When I asked why she went to so much
trouble, she had problems answering. It was simply the right thing to do, she
said, adding that she could not really recall when she started to think and
behave ethically. It just seemed to have developed as she learnt more about the
world from what she read, surfed and observed. Her meaning schemes and
perspectives gradually altered as the profligate and ephemeral aspects of our
consumer culture seemed increasingly unjustified and apparent. Did you see in
The Independent the other day...

Gabriel and Lang (1995) have shown how citizenship debates and struggles have frequently taken either an anti-consumerist or a pro-consumer angle.
Many consumer campaigns, particularly boycotts, have raised general public
awareness and changed people's values and behaviour – including that of the
big corporations themselves (Clouder and Harrison, 2005). This may influence all manner of behavioural changes, from a deliberate decision to purchase
products on ethical grounds to boycotting other products, brands or companies completely. Even corporate giants like Nestlé and Shell have felt the pinch
at times. And boycotts are interesting not only because they may be morally
transformative for some people, a way of 'reclaiming capitalism' through doing
something; they may also be, like consumption itself to some extent, self-realiz-
ing and a genuine, critical and significant learning experience:

Contradicting our expectation that boycotters would interpret their boycotting action as a consequence of their identification with particular interest groups or communities, we found that boycotts also act as expressions of individual uniqueness. Rather than pursuing 'consumer resistance' solely as a means to enact the goal of widespread social change, many boycotters seem to also view boycotting behavior as an intrinsically satisfying activity, an end in itself. On a deeper level this self-expression seems to be motivated by a drive for moral self-realization. (Kozinets and Handelman, 1998, p476)

ECO-LOCALISM

The economics of eco-localism offers an alternative paradigm to utilitarian growth-orientated economic theory and the habits of mass standardized consumption. Many of these ideas have been developed from Fritz Schumacher's *Small Is Beautiful* (1974), a seminal text for many sustainability practitioners.

In an article published in *Ecological Economics*, Fred Curtis (2003) clearly outlines its key characteristics and its specific criticisms of the dominant economic ideology and of globalization. What is perhaps key to eco-localism is that 'place matters' in the sense that local ecosystems provide multifarious resources and constraints to localized economies. Eco-localism has much in common with Max-Neef's (1991; 1992) understanding of human-scale development and of bioregionalism as well as articulating a necessary interrelationship of physical, financial, social, human and natural capitals. Globalization creates long supply chains, increases material consumption, and has deleterious consequences for the natural world. It is therefore necessary to '(re)localize the economy':

The eco-local economy is not defined solely by the production (for profit), market exchange and consumption of commercial goods and services.

Instead, it is equally constituted by collectives and cooperatives, buying clubs, community enterprises, not-for-profits, barters and skills exchanges, mutual aid, volunteer activity, household and subsistence production, and what is variously termed the informal sector or the underground economy. This broader definition flows both from the community orientation of eco-localism and its focus on quality of life values. It is a broadly defined social economy.

Though broadly defined in 'sectoral' terms, the eco-local economy is more narrowly drawn in its geography. It is a place-specific, bounded economy. Where 'the economy' is a national or global construct in conventional theory, in eco-localism it is

> *bounded in space by limits of community, geography and the*
> *stewardship of nature.*
>   *Natural limits to the eco-local economy are frequently*
> *expressed in terms of environmental geographies.* (Curtis, 2003,
> p86)

For eco-localists, it is possibly more important to consume less, to reduce the material throughputs within local and national economies, than to be more eco-efficient, although obviously that is important too. Sourcing and trading locally, reducing financial and environmental transport costs and challenging the (capitalist) ethos of material consumption and cultural consumerism are further key principles. It is quality not quantity that counts. Goods should be made to last, to be shared, to be reparable rather than disposable, to be simple rather than complex, and so offer an alternative and more fulfilling lifestyle based on the need to reduce our ecological footprint. However, it is possible to argue that green and/or ethical consumption still reproduces a consumerist ethos of a sort. Curtis writes:

> *For eco-localist theory, the reduction of human environmental*
> *impact requires both throughput-reducing technological change*
> *and lower average material standards of living... Such reductions*
> *in consumption will be borne primarily by those in wealthier*
> *societies, particularly as the material standards of living of those*
> *in poor economies are brought up to subsistence levels. The brunt*
> *of such reductions will be borne by the currently high-consuming*
> *economies not only for ethical reasons of fairness but also*
> *because limiting consumption to eco-local resources reduces a*
> *community's ecological footprint to its local geographic borders.*
> *Wealthy areas under eco-localism would no longer support their*
> *high lifestyles by using their financial wealth to purchase the*
> *resources of other places or to discard their wastes there.*
> *Reducing material-per-capita consumption may be the most diffi-*
> *cult aspect of eco-localism for many to accept as it contravenes*
> *the culture of consumerism, the more is-better assumptions of*
> *conventional economic theory, existing settlement patterns*
> *(cities), and the goals of globalization.* (Curtis, 2003, p92)

Farmers' markets may be seen as a specific example of the convergence of localism, quality, authenticity, community and sustainability, changing relationships between local food producers and local consumers and nurturing the growth of more sustainable, slower lifestyles. These have grown rapidly in recent years in urban and rural areas (Holloway and Kneafsey, 2000) and have discernable economic benefits (Bullock, 2000), including more money being spent and circulated in the local economy, producing increased expenditure in other shops on market days and thus providing outlets for local produce and a reinforcement of local job and business networks. The roads leading to

Figure 2.2 *Farmers' Market, Crediton, Devon: Voted best farmers'*
market in the south-west of England, this market meets on the
first Saturday of every month

farmers' markets have not, however, always been smooth. Local traders
frequently protested about having them on too regular a basis and in the 1990s
often objected to farmers' markets in principle. Having chaired a Local Agenda
21 committee attempting to introduce a farmers' market to a small northern
town, I clearly remember that the slogan 'think globally and act locally' meant
very little when livelihoods were felt threatened – even if they were not. La
Trobe (2001) shows that, with the expansion of farmers' markets, their market
share in the US, Canada and the UK is still miniscule compared with that of
the big supermarket chains, and what is important is that more and more
customers meet with, talk to and sample the produce of local growers and
producers. Farmers' market produce is fresh, unadulterated by additives or
preservatives (though not necessarily organic), tastier and has a higher nutritional value than produce shipped longer distances, stored for months and
artificially ripened. Farmers' markets invariably offer consumers an enjoyable
and sociable learning experience. They are places to meet friends, discuss local
issues, compare and contrast experiences, get to know producers, get to know
where the food comes from, how the beasts are reared, how the vegetables are
grown, when they are ready to eat and how to cook them (Bentley, Hallsworth
and Bryan, 2003). Producers are invariably the sellers too and the personal
contact, the customer care, becomes an important aspect of sustainable

Figure 2.3 *Linscombe Farm, Devon: Pesticide-free organic food, grown and sold locally, enabling a slower, more sustainable quality of life (left: squash store; right: polytunnel)*

marketing communication and renewed localized sociability. As Phil, an organic farmer with a successful business just a few miles from me, said at the local monthly market, 'one of us tends to be out deliberately chatting to people because it's our local base.' Through this chatting he learns about the potential markets for his produce, likely future production requirements and the habits, tastes and peculiarities of his local customers. In fact, Linscombe Farm, which he runs with his wife Helen, is a model of sustainable agriculture. All the food he sells at markets or through his veg box scheme is grown on the farm. His polytunnels provide vegetables all year round and the compost used on the land, of which there are mountains of the stuff, contains no manure, just plant material.

Farmers' markets put people back in touch with seasonality, non-standardized, non-atmospherically-modified, chlorine-rinsed produce and indeed other non-human creatures – the origin of our cling-film wrapped pork chops. When my wife first put our name down for some locally reared organic pork, being still a bit of a city boy, I felt decidedly odd when the farmer told us a pig was about to be slaughtered and how much of it did we want. It was all a bit too basic, a bit too close, a bit too real. In my local farmers' market I once noticed a trader offering English heritage apples with a sign informing customers that blackbirds like apples too. The apples tasted wonderful, even if one or two exhibited an earlier appreciation by a blackbird. Farmers' markets and consumer-producer cooperatives operate in many rural areas, on the outskirts of and within many large towns and cities, and, although they may not offer everything Asda/Wal-Mart or Tesco do, they offer an example of, and site for, learning about sustainability and the development of good sustainability practice. On the subject of one successful community-supported agricultural (CSA) initiative in the US, Sigrid Stagl writes:

> *While tastes and preferences usually do not change rapidly, they do change over time as people interact and as social institutions that surround them evolve ('endogenous preferences'). Such changes may be observed in CSA markets as consumers interact with the farmer/s and other members. During the membership at Roxbury Farm CSA the analysis of household survey data showed that social motivations (like supporting local farms, concern for the environment, eating vegetables in season and reducing packaging) were enhanced. While 'doing something for my health' drew people into CSAs, this factor decreased over time in importance, while 'eating vegetables in season' and 'reducing packaging' gained importance. These findings provide an example that preferences are not only changed by political measures but also in markets. The direction and extent this change takes depends on the personal history of the consumers, the institutional settings and also the degree of direct interaction and feedback markets allow. CSAs are making a contribution to changing preferences to more sustainable behaviour within their limited realm.* (Stagl, 2002, p154)

Stagl also notes that some members reported that changes in eating and shopping habits carried over into the off-season, saying they were buying more organic vegetables at the store and a greater variety of vegetables than they had done before their CSA membership. Many participants in the scheme said their involvement in CSA had obliged them to start questioning aspects of the larger food system, which could possibly in turn render people more willing to consider ethical consumption in other spheres or more likely to seek information about sustainable consumption from the press and broadcasting media.

LEARNING AND CHANGING

Consumer behaviour is a complex business, influenced by moral, normative, emotional and social habits, sometimes even rational thought, democratic deliberation and clearly green intentions. However, people are often stuck with behaviours that do not seem to change. Owning new technologies like mobile phones and iPods, ferrying children regularly to school and holidaying abroad are relatively new phenomena, partly resulting from changes in cost, availability, attitudes, technological affordances and culture. Humans are social beings with the capacity to learn, often through trial and error, persuasion or forms

BOX 2.2 ECO-LOCALISM

Eco-localism concludes that environmental sustainability requires small-scale, local or regional, self-reliant community economies on the basis of specific analytical propositions and concepts and with a clear set of assumptions. These eco-local propositions include:

- The environment, natural capital, varies by locality and region;
- Sustainable use and preservation of such locally varied eco-systems requires locally adapted knowledge, communities, products, cultures and practices;
- Globalization and long-distance trade and investment undermine the place-specific knowledge, communities, cultures and economies necessary to sustainability;
- Sustainability requires locally adapted and symbiotic forms of social, physical, human and financial capital. Business enterprises, networks, education, money, banking and investment all need to be locally oriented;
- Not all people have insatiable preferences. Not all needs are individual. Humans have non-material as well as material needs. Human nature is broader than *homo economicus*. Thus, a broad goal of economic activity is quality of life, only part of which rests on individual purchase and consumption of commodities;
- Sustainability requires the subordination of financial capital to social and natural capital preservation. Economic decision-making must be subordinated to society and nature;
- By uniting production and consumption within eco-local boundaries, both positive and negative externalities of the production and use of goods and services are localized. This creates pressure to reduce pollution and resource use and to increase positive externalities such as ecological restoration and community building;
- The relatively small scale of production in decentralized local economies may be efficient as the goal is not simply to maximize a single output relative to its inputs, but to do so in a particular social context with multiple goals. Efficiency is thus redefined;
- By producing goods and services with local needs and consumer desires in mind, local economies may produce higher quality, longer lasting and more locally appropriate and useful products. Consumers may meet their needs by sharing, social or collective consumption, individual purchases and producing some of what they consume;
- Reduction of environmental impact to levels within sustainable limits is the joint result of both lowered average material standards of living and lowered throughput per unit of output via the use of locally appropriate technologies and the shortening of the economic distances separating production and consumption; and
- The values, vision, analyses and conclusions of eco-localism are not merely theoretical. They are in use in many communities, institutions and localities. They are the deliberate and positive choice of many consumers, investors, businesses, home-owners, workers, farmers and eaters. Eco-localism is thus a positive economic paradigm; it describes the reality of many people's lives as well as the desires of many others.

Source: Curtis, 2003, pp98–9

of social modelling. As Bandura (1977) argued many years ago, we learn by observing what others do – peers, parents, friends, neighbours and characters and celebrities on television – and from marketing and advertising publications. We imitate others, particularly if we like, admire or find these others attractive in some way. Modelling is an important way of learning physical behaviours, new routines and new social practices situated within the fabric of everyday living. Jackson writes:

> *The potential applications of social learning theory for pro-environmental behaviours are legion. We have already remarked on some of them in the course of earlier discussions. Modelling plays a key role in the establishment and maintenance of social norms. For example, I learn and remember how, where and when to put out the recycling as much from observations of those around me as by information from the council. My identity-related buying behaviours (clothes, cars, appliances, etc) are influenced by those on whom my identity is modelled and by those from whom I am hoping to distinguish myself.* (Jackson, 2005, p111)

There is also a need to unfreeze existing habits and routines before new ones can be learnt and embedded in a person's practical, conscious and social routine. I might learn about a new fair-trade coffee from seeing a television advert or a promotion in a local supermarket or at a farmers' market. Having seen this more than once, I might decide to try it. I might like what I taste, but if I have been buying another brand for a long time that habit will need to be broken. Drinking more of the fair-trade coffee and having it readily available will help break my old habits of drinking unfair but cheaper coffee, particularly if in what I'm doing my caring and considerate values are also engaged. The social psychologist Kurt Lewin (1951) suggested that change involves analysing and challenging existing meaning schemes and perspectives before different or new actions become part of a new social routine. He also argued that this 'unfreezing' of existing routines best takes place in socially supportive environments. Jackson adds to this:

> *Perhaps more importantly, [the unfreezing] appears to be well-supported by empirical evidence. For instance, the conceptual model of discursive social change forms the intellectual basis for the Global Action Plan's 'Action at Home' programme, which has been amongst the most successful of the attempts to encourage and support pro-environmental behaviour changes at the household level. In fact, community-based approaches to social change are becoming an increasingly important part of the landscape of sustainable development.* (Jackson, 2005, p116)

Apprehending and internalizing new lifestyle or consumer alternatives requires significant unfreezing, which may take the form of a personal transformative experience (Cherrier, 2005). It may also be the result of much wider social and economic circumstances, a slow process but one that is experienced both collectively and individually. Referring to the devastating foot-and-mouth epidemic in the UK in 2001, our local organic vegetable grower and box scheme provider, Phil, observed:

> *Here in the West Country there was a massive shift in public perception over the course of the foot-and-mouth epidemic. Suddenly people went from buying vegetables that had no pesticide residues for what I'd call 'selfish' reasons (to do largely with personal health) to understanding the wider picture – environmental sustainability, etc. It was really a fundamental step. People realized that a food purchasing decision just wasn't something isolated. It had wider ramifications – the farmed countryside was connected to what was on your plate and the situation in Africa and Asia and that connection was being made by a significantly wider audience and very, very quickly, so it was very noticeable. We've always had this core group of deep green, very switched-on consumers, but suddenly the message 'buy local' became, very largely I've got to say thanks to the input of the editor of the* Western Morning News, *very important.* (interview with author)

Phil went on to say that not only are farmers' markets and buying local becoming part of many people's lifestyles, but increasing numbers of local people now want greater access to more frequent markets, which still tend to be once a week at best. Producers and consumers have a joint responsibility to learn how to change values and behaviour and in so doing to learn how to change society:

> *The biggest single issue is for consumers to take responsibility for their own impact, for what they are doing. They have got to relate the famine in Africa to their teabag or their bunch of flowers. The consumers have got to understand what they are doing and that is the key to it, but it is going to be a long process and the media have got to be onside, which they are at the moment. If you put the blame elsewhere as conventional farmers tend to do, you are taking away your own sense of responsibility. We've got to be responsible for our own markets and at the end of the day we've got to be responsible for educating our own customers. Though we accept help from the media. Of course, some customers don't want to think about it. Some don't want to be fed information – they just want the vegetables. The quality of the produce will do it – affect the biochemistry of their brains!* (interview with author)

Social agency can be understood in a variety of ways. Sociologists tend to think in terms of external circumstances and structures, although Giddens's (1984) theory of 'structuration' recognizes that human beings are not simply subject to forces beyond their control or understanding but can actively work and think on them and in the processes transform both the world and themselves. Institutions, social rules and context (ie time–space boundaries, co-presence of other actors, processes of reflexivity, etc.) fashion human social life, conduct and agency. One's life space, life situation or lifeworld is structured by ideas, values, social habits and routines, discourses and technologies that both enable and constrain human action. Ingold (2000) and Hutchby (2001) both write about social and other technologies, physical artefacts, producing 'affordances' allowing certain behaviours and actions to flourish and denying possibilities to others. Psychologists tend to think in terms of internal drivers or personality traits. Harre (1984) suggests people achieve agency by having intentions, knowledge of social rules and something he refers to as 'activation'. Sometimes we can intend to do something and have sufficient knowledge to act but not do so. We tend to obey our own inner commands just as we may obey those of others or be influenced by status or the 'credibility' of significant others:

> *By being forced to listen to the exhortation of others, I learnt to exhort myself, and by watching others push each other into action, I learn to bestir myself. It is my grasp of the theory that I am a unified being that enables me to understand that I am the recipient both of exhortations and kicks and shoves, that I can exhort and shove others and, finally, putting all this together, that I can so treat myself.* (Harre, 1984, p193)

Harre writes that there is a difference between being stimulated to act and having a constraint removed, thereby enabling action to occur. Sometimes a critical incident, a significant learning experience, a disorientating dilemma or major change in life experience may lead to a transformation of values, attitudes and behaviour; this may constitute either a release or a stimulus. Agency may therefore be seen as involving a constellation of things – life space, affordances, intentions, knowledge and 'activation' meaning:

> *It is a complex of beliefs about my own nature with a repertoire of speech acts to go with them. There is no more (and no less) mystery in coming to understand how I can obey myself than in coming to understand how I can obey you. In general, my obedi-ence to your commands is explicable in terms of our relative location in one or more moral orders... Precisely the same must be said of personal agency. There is a moral order in which I stand in various relations to myself, expressed in remarks like 'you owe it to yourself', 'don't let yourself down' and so on. To understand agency (and its sibling* akrasia *[moral weakness]) is to have a grasp of this moral order as it is differently realized in various cultures.* (Harre, 1984, p195)

HUMAN-SCALE DEVELOPMENT

A more satisfying life on Earth should perhaps tend towards the local and human scale than the automated mass society, as Borgmann suggested over 20 years ago. But this is a matter of opinion and discussion. Manfred Max-Neef (1992) has argued that neo-liberal capitalist development does not necessarily satisfy genuine human wants and needs, and neither does it offer development attuned to the 'human scale' needed for empowerment, participation, decision-making, cultural diversity, social autonomy, learning and community economic activity. All human needs are interrelated and interactive and development needs to be based on the construction of 'organic articulations of people with nature and technology'.

Max-Neef organizes human needs into two categories, each of which has various 'satisfiers':

1   Being, having, doing and interacting; and
2   Subsistence, protection, affection, understanding, participation, creation, leisure identity and freedom.

Thus food and shelter are not needs as such but satisfiers of the need for shelter and sustenance; education is the satisfier for the need for understanding. There is no one-to-one correlation of needs and satisfiers; indeed, a need may attract many satisfiers and one satisfier may serve a number of needs.

For Max-Neef fundamental human needs are finite, few and classifiable. It is the same for all cultures and times. Only the means by which needs are satisfied may change according to time or place. He further suggests that poverty is not a purely economic phenomenon, but should be understood more broadly – that there are many poverties of subsistence (starvation, homelessness), of protection (violence, poor health care), of affection (oppression, environmental degradation), of understanding (poor education), of participation (marginalization and discrimination), of identity (exile, diaspora), and so on. These poverties, if left to fester, lead to social and human pathologies – social and political violence, involuntary unemployment, and so forth.

What is also important is the relationship between human needs and human potential and the degree to which socio-economic and political arrangements enable opportunities to emerge and be realized. Satisfiers are not just the available economic goods, so it is imperative that economies are organized in such a way that goods 'empower satisfiers to meet fully and consistently fundamental human needs'. Max-Neef writes:

> *While a satisfier is in an ultimate sense the way in which a need is expressed, goods are in a* strict sense *the means by which individuals will empower the satisfiers to meet their needs. When, however, the form of production and consumption of goods makes goods an end in themselves, then the alleged satisfaction*

Table 2.1 *Matrix of Needs and Satisfiers*

Needs according to axiological categories	Needs according to **existential** categories			
	Being (personal and collective attributes expressed as nouns)	**Having** (institutions, mechanisms, laws, tools expressed in one word or more)	**Doing** (personal and collective actions expressed as verbs)	**Interacting** (locations and milieus; times and spaces)
Subsistence	Physical and mental health, sense of humour, adaptability, equilibrium	Food, shelter, work	Feed, procreate, rest, work	Living environment, social setting
Protection	Care, adaptability, autonomy, equilibrium, solidarity	Insurance systems, savings, social security, health systems, rights, family, work	Cooperate, prevent, plan, take care of, cure, help	Living space, social environment, dwelling
Affection	Self-esteem, solidarity, respect, tolerance, generosity, receptiveness, passion, determination, sensuality, sense of humour	Friendships, family, partnerships, relationships with nature	Make love, caress, express emotions, share, take care of, cultivate, appreciate	Privacy, intimacy, home, space of togetherness
Understanding	Critical conscience, receptiveness, curiosity, astonishment, discipline, intuition, rationality	Literature, teachers, method, educational policies communication policies	Investigate, study, experiment, educate, analyse, mediate	Settings of formative interaction, schools, universities, academies, groups, communities, family

	Being	Having	Doing	Interacting
Participation	Adaptability, receptiveness, solidarity, willingness, determination, dedication, respect, passion, sense of humour	Rights, responsibilities, duties, privileges, work	Become affiliated, cooperate, propose, share, dissent, obey, interact, agree on, express opinions	Settings of participative interaction, parties, associations, churches, communities, neighbourhoods, family
Leisure/ Idleness	Curiosity, receptiveness, imagination, recklessness, sense of humour, tranquility, sensuality	Games, spectacles, clubs, parties, peace of mind	Daydream, brood, dream, recall old times, give way to fantasies, remember, relax, have fun, play	Privacy, intimacy, spaces of closeness, free time, surroundings, landscapes
Creation	Passion, determination, intuition, imagination, boldness, rationality, autonomy, inventiveness, curiosity	Abilities, skills, methods, work	Work, invent, build, design, compose, interpret	Productive and feedback settings, workshops, cultural groups, audiences, spaces for expression, temporal freedom
Identity	Sense of belonging, consistency, differentiation, self-esteem, assertiveness	Symbols, language, religion, habits, customs, reference groups, sexuality, values, norms, historical memory, work	Commit oneself, integrate oneself, confront, decide on, get to know oneself, actualize oneself, grow	Social rhythms, everyday settings, settings which one belongs to maturation stages
Freedom	Autonomy, self-esteem, determination, passion, assertiveness, open-mindedness, rebelliousness, tolerance	Equal rights, commit oneself,	Dissent, choose, be different from, run risks, develop awareness, disobey	Temporal/spatial plasticity

Source: Max-Neef (1991)

> *of a need impairs its capacity to create potential. This creates the conditions for entrenching an alienated society engaged in a productivity race lacking any sense at all. Life, then, is placed at the service of artefacts, rather than artefacts at the service of life. The question of the quality of life is overshadowed by our obsession to increase productivity.* (Max-Neef, 1992, p202)

There is a dynamic relationship between needs, satisfiers and economic goods. Max-Neef offers a matrix – though not an exhaustive one – to illustrate his ideas. He suggests that satisfiers themselves fall into various categories, namely violators or destroyers, pseudo-satisfiers, inhibiting satisfiers, singular satisfiers and synergistic satisfiers. Fundamental human needs are conceived systemically where hierarchical linearities have no purchase – no satisfier is more important than another and there is no fixed order of precedence. However, there is a pre-system threshold below which the experience of deprivation, for example of subsistence or affection, is so great that the need to satisfy paralyses or otherwise disables any other activity.

Inevitably new categories could be added or substituted for the ones above as our life experiences, values and social worlds change. Referencing Borgmann (1984) once more, there seems to be an evident need for an economic sector that has a two-tier structure: one that is local and labour-intensive and another that is more automated, mass-producing goods and services necessary to maintain and reproduce life, health and economic security. Together they enable us to enjoy and engage in various focal practices that genuinely constitute wealth rather than just material affluence, a good life that is at once intentionally sustainable, manageable and conducive to a more satisfying life on Earth. As Gilg, Barr and Ford (2004) show from their large household survey in the south-west of England, pro-environmental, pro-social and essentially caring attitudes and values are strongly associated with green consumption and green lifestyles – buying products with reduced environmental impacts, purchasing recycled paper, buying organic, buying local, and so on. Complementing this, Kollmuss and Aygeman review a wide range of internal (personality traits, knowledge, emotions, values) and external (economics, culture, social infrastructure) factors influencing the development of pro-environmental behaviour, concluding, unsurprisingly, that 'many conflicting and competing factors shape our daily decisions and actions' (Kollmuss and Aygeman, 2002, p256). Maybe some of the competition and conflict can be reduced if we concentrate more on those focal practices and satisfiers needed for a more human-scale sustainable development, with everyday life experiences looking forward to, prefiguring, a freer, more ecologically sensitive and healthier world. Going slow and checking out the local farmers' market is both a start and a satisfier or two.

3

Learning through Leisure

This chapter explores the value of learning and the growth of leisure, tourism and edutainment. The Eden Project, the Earth Centre and the Centre for Alternative Technology are used as examples of institutions that offer a range of informal and formal learning opportunities relating to sustainability and everyday life. The chapter comprises sections on:

- The Eden Project;
- Eden's medium and message;
- Stories, interpretations and learning;
- A whole learning thing;
- The Earth Centre and the Centre for Alternative Technology; and
- Lessons?

THE EDEN PROJECT

The Eden Project is both a major tourist attraction and a stunning learning environment communicating a modulated series of pro-sustainability principles. In 2004 1,223,959 people visited Eden; of these 85 per cent were on holiday, 70 per cent were travelling to Cornwall from beyond the South-West region and 44 per cent were visiting Cornwall because of Eden (Jasper, 2005). Outside school term time the average visitor age is 53, and Eden's visitors are more likely to read the 'quality' newspapers *The Independent*, *The Guardian* and *The Daily Telegraph* than the popular tabloids *The News of the World*, *The Express* or *The Sun*. The quality papers tend to publish more articles on the environment and sustainable development than the higher circulation tabloids, so Eden's largely informal learning experiences, intended to offer pleasure, meaning and ecological significance, resonate quite loudly with these visitors. It does this by combining what Greenblatt (1991, p42) has termed 'resonance' and 'wonder'. If Eden makes a difference to visitors' attitudes, values and behaviour through what is seen or in other ways experienced there, it does so by reaching 'out beyond its formal boundaries to a larger world, to

This chapter is an extended version of an article titled 'The Eden Project – making a connection', first published in *Museum and Society*, vol 2, no 3, November 2004, www.le.ac.uk/ms/museumsociety.html

evoke in the viewer the complex, dynamic cultural forces from which it has emerged and for which it may be taken by a viewer to stand'. Eden engenders 'wonder', stopping the viewer 'in his or her tracks, to convey an arresting sense of uniqueness'. Eden is not a theme park like Disneyland, although certain elements of the Eden experience – the land-train ride, the ice-skating rink in the winter, performer-guides and so on – are similar. Neither is it an open-air museum like Beamish in County Durham or St Fagans, the heritage village in Wales, or a botanical garden like Kew, although again there are similarities with its staffing structure of curators and plantspeople. It is difficult to find exact comparators for Eden. Its edutainment mission is similar to that of Sea World in Florida (Davis, 1997), to attempts to democratize high art at MOMA (Goldfarb, 2002) and popularize science at London's Science Museum (Macdonald, 2002) and earlier approaches of mixing amusement with edification in the world fairs of a century ago (Bennett, 1995) and more recent Expos also bear comparison. When asked by John Elkington of SustainAbility in the 'Liability' edition of *Radar* (October 2004) whether Eden would end up as a 'green Disneyland', Tim Smit was emphatic:

> WE WON'T – *or else we will have failed. The temptation to slide into corporate atrophy is always there, especially when times get tough. The only antidote is to close your eyes and take a risk. This makes you come to life. Seriously, if we became a theme park in the pejorative sense you imply, we would all have wasted the last seven years of our lives. As to lessons from Disney – none, save a profound respect for the way they have implemented the logistics of serving so many people and the way in which they have nurtured their brand without any significant dilution.* (Smit, 2004)

Eden strives to reach people in innovative, experimental ways and by providing visitors with an enjoyable and memorable experience. On average 87 per cent of visitors said they felt very or quite satisfied with the experience. Jasper (2005, pp34–5) writes in his visitor evaluation report, 'consistently, the humid-tropics biome, parking, overall enjoyment and staff were rated as being the closest to being "just wonderful". Visitors also rated Eden's performance in relation 'to its aim to be at the cutting edge of environmental and social best practice' as also 'very close to "just wonderful"'. Visitors love the Eden Project.

Eden opened fully on 17 March 2001. It was partly funded by a £43m grant from the Millennium Commission and its total cost was £86 million. It was the brainchild of Tim Smit, former music producer and founder of the highly successful Lost Gardens of Heligan, near St Austell, Cornwall. In *Eden*, Smit (2001) writes of the immense effort, perseverance, collaborative work, idealism, luck and sheer determination that enabled a disused china-clay quarry in an economically depressed part of Cornwall, Bodelva (also near St Austell) to be transformed into what tourist agencies call the 'eighth wonder of the world'. In its first year of operation it attracted nearly two million

Figure 3.1 *The Eden Project, Cornwall*
a) The 'Hemp Man' and the iconic biomes; b) The plant sphere at the
interactive learning and exhibition centre, the 'Core'

visitors and during its second just over one and half million. By August 2003
Eden Project: The Guide (Eden Project, 2003) was third in *The Daily Telegraph*'s non-fiction bestseller list and by the middle of 2004 The Eden Project had brought in an estimated £526 million of additional income to the Cornish economy, with over 50 per cent of Cornish businesses reporting Eden having a positive effect. Its iconic structures, two huge interrelated clusters of modified geodesic greenhouses, or 'biomes', have generated global fascination. Their architecture and engineering is undoubtedly a magnificent achievement (Pearman and Whalley, 2003). Each biome nurtures plants and tells stories: one of the humid tropics region and the other of the warm temperate zone. Together with the outside planting, both biomes, to quote Eden's Foundation Director, Tony Kendle, are 'used as a lens to focus in on the amazing worlds that each one represents; how the politics of the world, for example, lie within a cup of sweet tea' (Eden Project, 2003, p2). The construction of a third, dry tropics biome is currently being planned and funding sought.

A new learning centre designed and constructed to high environmental standards by Nicholas Grimshaw and Partners and McAlpine, is known as the Core and was opened in the late summer of 2005. Inspired initially by the Fibanacci spirals found in many natural forms, including the seeds of sunflower heads, pine cones and snail shells, it was later realized that this pattern did not offer the necessary structural solutions for designing a roof that could maximise the use of solar panels. Consequently, the roof's geometry was altered in such a way as to mimic a process called phyllotaxis, derived from nature's recurring ratio observable in nearly all plant growth. A Waste

Neutral Recycling Compound was started in 2003/4 thanks to further grants of £10m from the Millennium Commission, £10m from the South West Regional Development Agency and £13m from the European Union's Objective One programme. Eden's Waste Neutral programme involves an on-site recycling facility including dedicated public areas for workshops and exhibitions, enhancing the capability of its associated public education and awareness-raising activities to transform conduct among its business clients, suppliers and visitors. The project's success in this area will be a key criterion for judging its overall effectiveness. As Chris Hines, the leader of Waste Neutral, said at its launch in March 2004, it is about Eden being a trail blazer, modelling behaviour that other organizations can and should emulate:

> To buy products that are made from recycled as first choice. There's a tricky bit there in that most products made from recycled materials are of pretty poor quality and the design element is naff. All too often these things have been invented by people who haven't worked with designers. You take them off the shelf and then realize they've been made from recycled material. We weigh or measure the materials we send off to be recycled and make this pledge to buy in an equal or greater volume of materials made from recycled materials, and we sell them to the public or we use them on-site. Now that does mean they have to be of good quality. They've got to come off the shelves. And when we've done this we will be waste neutral. We think in the future there will be a consumer-led demonstration of the positive value of using waste materials matching market demand and performance requirements against appropriate recycled materials. They must be able to perform. There's no point buying something made from recycled materials and six months down the line it's failed to do its job. They've got to be good. (Hines, 2004)

Sometimes criticized in the past for the energy needed to regulate the temperature of the biomes, Eden secured £76,000 from the European Union Objective One Fund and £64,000 from the Department of Trade and Industry's Clear Skies initiative to install, in the spring of 2006, a state-of-the-art biomass boiler to be run on miscanthus (elephant grass) and woodchip, grown specifically for and sourced locally within Cornwall. This is another example of Eden modelling socially desirable behaviour and a corporate social/environmental responsibility.

EDEN'S MEDIUM AND MESSAGE

The overall site design exploits the biomes' spectacular visual impact by locking the visitors' gaze and focusing attention on a compelling image. Thanks to highly effective marketing and promotion, many visitors came to view the project while it was still being built – awe, wonder and interest were generated from the beginning. A large number became Friends of Eden, with their memories of the early days of the project firmly and lovingly imprinted in their minds. As Jo Readman, Eden's Director of Education and Messaging, says:

> *At Eden … we use a quite theatrical approach to engage the emotions straight away… In the first year there was this curiosity among the public, who wanted to see what we were doing, why we were trying to build the biggest greenhouse in the world in a hole full of water. They'd come to the site. People didn't see anything until they came right close and all of a sudden – bang! We put it in a hole deliberately because it was exciting. And we used film and theatre techniques to lead people along – dramatic suspense.* (interview with author)

Eden's evolving education, interpretation and communication strategies have been influenced by Smit's Heligan experience, where the restored gardens tell the stories of those who created them (Samuel,1998), and by advertising, commercial design, radical theatre, popular television and cinema narratives – *Eastenders*, *Harry Potter*, *The Simpsons*, natural history programmes and TV commercials. The message for the Eden team is 'they all connect', they all are able to engage people's interest and attention, and this is reinforced by the media backgrounds of the project's key staff, whose professional lives centred on influencing audience attitudes, values and behaviour – indeed still do, if in a slightly different way. Consequently the hope, intention and expectations are that Eden will make a difference. Jo Readman again:

> *So the message we are trying to put across is, 'You can make a difference. It is about celebrating and enjoying the environment you live in. Be positive about the future – you can do something.' A lot of other places, in their education policies, say, 'Look, everything is going wrong and it's all our fault. We've got climate change. We've got war and we've got famine and we've got poverty.' Yes, we have, and they are all dreadful things, but there is something you can do about it. So we look at what other people are doing and we look at what the individual can do by starting way, way, way back down the line by connecting to their environment, by connecting them to the rest of the world. Unless we connect people to that we can't take it forward.* (interview with author)

The Director of Communications, Bryher Scudamore, former editor of the BBC's consumer rights programme *That's Life* and of BBC Online, clearly outlines an approach that suggests conveying information in a moral way motivates an audience to action:

That's Life was a television programme that changed people's behaviour. That's Life assumed the audience had maximum intelligence and minimum information. We were able to help people understand all sorts of things in their lives and take actions that could help them. Not just about consumer stuff, about being defrauded by clever double-glazing salesmen, but about being an organ donor – the gift of life. The figures on how people decide to be organ donors changed dramatically after we did our Ben Hardwicke story, and many thousands of people are alive now because of the information they were given. So at the heart of what I believe in is informing the largest possible number of people so they can then make choices, informed choices. One of the reasons I love Eden is because it has exactly the same philosophy – giving people information so they can make informed choices. (interview with author)

Many public communication campaigns and television and radio dramas have certainly succeeded in doing just this (Singhal et al, 2004). In taking some of its cues from the mass media and popular culture, Eden is some conceptual and temporal distance from the moment when curatorial scholarship defined the cultural and educational purpose of a museum. However, the tradition of informal public education and social improvement clearly informs the project rationale and the desire to reach more than the environmentally committed individual informs much of the development work on learning, communication and interpretation. Tony Kendle explains the need to capture the interest of the general public:

We're interested in trying to get the other 50 million. We know that an awful lot of visitors come just because we have built a big spectacular thing, but that is exactly right, that's the strategy. That's why they are there. We are very conscious that a lot of other environmental, sustainability projects don't have that audience. They tend to be talking to the [environmentally] literate. What we are trying to do with the majority of our visitors, we are working very far down the scale for some of them, beginning to explore for them, make them reflect on, issues, particularly of connectedness, that they may not have ever thought much about. So we feel as though we are starting to foster the seeds of engagement or something so that a proportion of those people might later on start to think about joining Greenpeace or WWF or whatever. It's very much fostering the seeds. (interview with author)

Eden is also a major leisure and tourist attraction, but for Lefebvre (1991a, p33) leisure and tourism are not necessarily consonant with having meaningful learning experiences, given that leisure is really a break from the alienating grind of working for a living, a way of keeping body and soul together. Although Lefebvre has a point here, so does Eden in its aim to marry learning with leisure, rendering both a meaningful and authentic experience of the everyday. People learn all the time, and want to learn, but they do not necessarily want to be educated when they are on holiday:

> *Leisure must break with the everyday (or at least appear to do so) and not only as far as work is concerned but also for day-to-day family life. Thus there is an increasing emphasis on leisure characterized as distraction: rather than bringing any new worries, obligations and necessities, leisure should offer liberation from worry and necessity... [The public] mistrust anything which might appear to be educational and are more concerned with those aspects of leisure which might offer distractions, entertainment and repose and which might compensate for the difficulties of everyday life.* (Lefebvre, 1991a)

Constructivist theories of learning and the 'new museology' (Vergo, 1989) shun the didactic and the somewhat intimidating approach to learning that exhibitions often represent, providing additional insight into the development and purpose of Eden's learning ecology. Times have changed. Foley and McPherson (2000) suggest that commercial imperatives, funding conditions and managerialist pressures have rendered visitors, rather than exhibits or collections, the primary purpose of a museum's existence, leading museums 'to be reconceptualized as leisure resources and tourist attractions'. For Roberts (1997), a former manager of public programming at the Chicago Botanic Garden, the purpose of museums should be both education and entertainment. People use museums for many purposes – relaxation, leisure, socializing, discussion and learning. Museum educators see objects as eliciting multiple meanings and stories, and the task of museum education is to nurture reflexivity by empowering visitors to interpret objects, to engage in critical dialogue with the messages presented to construct meaning. Education Manager Sue Hill refers to a dynamic tension surrounding Eden's evolving education and interpretative practice:

> *We have this huge amount of material, ideas, information, facts. We have this stuff. You want to transmit it. We have guides who have learnt the telephone directory about humid tropics. We want to tell people but part of the tension in the project is actually restraining them from doing that and actually encouraging guides to enter into conversation with people where you are inviting the public to express their hopes, fears and questions about the future and their relationship to the natural world, about their relationship to their food, medicine, health. It's about engaging people in a participatory discussion rather than dolloping them with a load of stuff.* (interview with author)

Eden offers a multiplicity of discourses, stories, exhibits and perspectives that are in large part, but not totally, complementary – tourism, commercialism, environmental management, consumerism, enterprise, regeneration, globalization, conservation, entertainment, sustainability, public relations, education. Each unit team – from catering to horticulture – will give a different inflection to the core message, and the project's youth, size and continuing expansion means that a key management task is to ensure coherence without being autocratic or compromising the creative energies of its staff. The issue of car travel and parking has been seriously scrutinized, and although 17.5 per cent of visitors travel to the site by non-car modes, many critics perceive an apparent contradiction in the acres of car parking space provided and Eden's commitment to sustainability. But what, asked one senior member of the Eden team, is meant when people say they are anti-car? Do they oppose pollution, congestion, fossil-fuel consumption? Smit (2001) tackles the issue directly, noting that cars are an inevitable and, for many, a positive aspect of everyday life. Without a degree of pragmatism, the Eden Project, located as it is in a deeply rural part of England, would not have survived. Most tourists use cars because they are the most flexible and effective means of getting around Cornwall, though a £3 discount is offered to those travelling to the project by bike.

Eden's focus on offering information, choices, stories and alternatives enables the project to use hot issues like transport and GM, water shortage, climate change and ecological debt, if it chooses, as a tool for stimulating reflection and reflexivity. The project is in constant dialogue with pressure groups, local government, suppliers, and transport and planning authorities. However, there are problems, as Kendle explains:

> *One thing we often suffer from is what people project onto us –*
> *an expectation that something they have vaguely taken on board*
> *as a typically green message must be something that Eden*
> *believes. There is a widespread assumption that Eden must be*
> *anti GM crops. Now actually our position is we're not a lobby*
> *group, we're a project that is about debate and we want to give*
> *within Eden a chance to people, some of them highly honourable,*
> *with a lifetime in science, who've got their own passion for saying*
> *why their work is important, a chance to express that without us*
> *censoring it or saying right from the beginning we're not going to*
> *listen to that... There are some things we are completely deter-*
> *mined to say and carry on saying, for example I would not for a*
> *minute shy away from saying that GM is wrapped around too*
> *many unresolved issues.* (interview with author)

The project's interpretative and educative practice is therefore about intentionality, shaping conduct, altering cultural values and ways of thinking and perceiving. It adapts the narrative template offered by Anna Lewington's *Plants for the People* (2003), a book used by guides staffing the interpretation stations in the domes as source material for their extemporized interactions. Sue Minter, Director of Living Collections, notes:

> *Most botanic gardens would not address the social issues and the economic issues. Frequently they'd look at the history of the crop, cocoa for example, in the Empire, but they wouldn't so much look at issues to do with fair trade or pesticide abuse. And that is the type of thing you can do with performance and all those sort of interactive things. On the one hand we are trying to grow cocoa brilliantly and cocoa actually flowers and fruits better here than in virtually any other botanic garden. So, people are just engaged by seeing it. We can use that as a jumping-off point for talking about the issues.* (interview with author)

For Jo Readman, education is at the project's core and, although there is some unease with the didactic connotations of the word, education combined with entertainment pervades virtually every activity. Eden's media promotion, visitor experience, restaurant and retail consumption are all designed to reinforce and reproduce informal learning opportunities which emphasize connectivity and encourage people to reflect on their relationships with plants and each other. Creative approaches to learning have to be harnessed and learning itself must be effortless, which leads Readman to use, albeit somewhat reluctantly, the word 'edutainment'. In an internal evaluation document, 'Planting Stories', Eden's Research Manager Andrew Jasper (2002, p5) wrote, 'In a straightforward manner the interpretation presents stories relating to each plant collection in a showmanship manner.' Building on the pioneering work of Tilden (1957), and more recently Falk and Dierking (1992, 2000, 2002), Hein (1998) and Hooper-Greenhill (2000), interpretation, understood as the imparting of messages to visitors in a memorable way, is conceived as a dynamic relationship in which good stories find themselves repeated in various forms, like ripples in a pond, through planting, art installations, live guides, books and pamphlets, workshops, lectures, performances, signage and music. The meanings of these stories, following the constructivist perspectives adopted by other educators, are understood to be relational, plural, contingent and open to challenge, being negotiated through visitors' cognitive frameworks, interpretative communities and strategies. Knowledge is situated and provisional. Many planting stories and associated images, particularly those redolent with controversy like those of coffee, hemp, tobacco, cotton, and plants for fuel and perfume, are polysemic. What the visitor brings to the story completes the narrative, giving meaning and making things meaningful. As a former guide remarked, the hemp and cannabis story always attracts 'a certain kind of person', affirming Bruner's (1990) understanding of narrative as the primary way we organize, interpret and culturally articulate our lived experience. Thus the hope that visitors connect what they see with what they already know and feel, together with the notion of 'free-choice learning', associated by Falk and Dierking (2000, p13; 2002) as involving 'considerable choice on the part of the learner as to when, where and what to learn', underpins much of Eden's interpretation strategy. Unlike other cultural heritage organizations where interpretation is used to make sense of the displays or collections, at Eden, as Jasper has noted, the plants are used to interpret the message.

STORIES, INTERPRETATIONS AND LEARNING

The plant stories and displays integrate signage, art, sculpture, performance, cultural association and memory. Their design and implementation has been based on instinct and intuition as well as more rational internal evaluations and critical reviews of successes and failures elsewhere. The aim is frequently to engage the visitor on many levels – cognitive, emotional and sensory – serially and simultaneously. Internal staff development exercises have revealed that when Eden employees visit other museums, heritage sites or botanic gardens they relate to beauty, smell, colour and sound – a whole constellation of sensory experiences. I witnessed a group of adults with learning difficulties in the Mediterranean biome engaging through touch, smell and sight; they apprehended the difference between the natural and synthetic with little verbal explanation. I, along with other visitors who followed, did so too, although for us the guide's verbal messaging was more detailed and sophisticated. So the message is, touch a cocoa pod, smell it, recognize it as the origin of that bar of chocolate you have in your bag and, if you can speak to the growers, talk to them about their life, work and income, look them in the eye, make a connection. Sue Hill again:

> *For me, the challenge is – if you look at the workshops we do in Eden Live, the most powerful moments have been when we've brought over a coffee grower from Ghana, or a banana grower or cocoa grower, and they look the audience in the eye and they talk to them about their lives and what impact fair trade or sustainable farming or whatever has on them. And it is those moments when the audience finally connect and it's an emotional reaction – 'Oh, there's the woman that grows our chocolate' – and though intellectually people realize there are people growing the food that they eat and the clothes they wear, when they actually get to look at them face to face and hear their story and personally identify with them, that's when they go, 'Wow, so when I go and buy fair-trade chocolate, it actually makes a difference to you, someone else.' And it is trying to present that kind of authentic experience day in, day out … that is really hard to do.* (interview with author)

Emotional authenticity is the key, and because visitors encounter an artificially produced but architecturally stunning environment, the Eden team attempt to fashion an experiential understanding that is as emotional, visual, kinetic and spiritual as it is linguistic or intellectual. When engaged in conversation by guides or performers, visitors sometimes use Eden as a means of retrieving their own memories, of telling their own life stories or of narrating critical incidents from their personal lives. Certain spaces within and outside the domes offer opportunities for reflection, occasionally finding a more material manifestation through such activities as the 'Wishing Line', on which visitors are invited to hang their feelings, desires and hopes. Some of those recorded have been deeply personal, indicating that the project offers to some a sense of spiritual security akin to that of a sacred or contemplative garden. Consequently, the realization of Eden's interpretation strategy brings to mind Carr when he writes of museum learning requiring 'a moment when people redefine themselves and their roles, ... [when] they become individuals in the process of transforming experiences' (Carr, 1990, p11). People do not evaluate stories in isolation. To be memorable the stories need to resonate with the world-views, emotions and cultural contexts of self and others. To be compelling they need to have a (moral) point as well. Indeed, cultural anthropologists like Bird (2003, p40) affirm that 'from an audience's point of view, the best stories are those that leave room for speculation, for debate, and for a degree of audience participation'. Eden requires engagement, so exhibition makers must be sensitive to the nature of their audiences and popular culture. Adjacent to the citrus plants are displays of consumer products – tinned fruit, throat lozenges, juices and marmalades. Karp (1991, pp22–3) writes:

> *Almost by definition, audiences do not bring to exhibitions the full range of cultural resources necessary for comprehending them; otherwise there would be no point to exhibiting. Audiences are left with two choices: either they define their experience of the exhibition to fit with their existing categories of knowledge, or they reorganize their categories of knowledge or reorganize their categories to fit better with their experience. Ideally, it is the shock of non-recognition that enables the audiences to choose the latter alternative. The challenge for exhibition makers is to provide within exhibitions the contexts and resources that enable audiences to choose to reorganize their knowledge.*

This desire for authenticity allied with the capacity to touch people has made some of the Eden team suspicious of popular images of the environment and sustainability. Ironic as it may seem, they perceive a certain clichéd redundancy in the *National Geographic* or television images of indigenous peoples, the natural world, plants and gardens. These images can be overly familiar, saccharine or culturally too paternalistic to effectively provoke the 'shock of non-recognition' that Karp advocates. Their reality is the reality of the image. Eden does not, on the other hand, fully endorse the need to offer visitors the 'disorientating dilemmas' Mezirow (1991) considers important for perspective transformation in adult learning or the cognitive conflict that Ballantyne (1998) sees as necessary to develop 'environmental conceptions' and which may be witnessed in the 'bushmeat' stories and photographs informing the visitor experience of the higher primates at the Durrell Wildlife Conservation Trust in Jersey. Similarly the 'Wildwalk@Bristol', while telling the story of evolution, ends with a clear and forceful message about human culpability for the planet's ecological breakdown, using a collage of sounds, artefacts and moving images. Eden attempts to reach people less aggressively, although with the opening of the Core and the staging of the Africa concert as part of the much criticised Live 8 concert in 2005, Eden's environmental and sustainability messages are arguably becoming sharper, more challenging and politically more confident.

The relationship with the creative artists commissioned to design the exhibits is of crucial importance. Their effectiveness is dependent on whether the installation–planting story resonates with the everyday life experiences and prior learning and cultural repertoire of the visitor, who may resist being shocked into non-recognition or shamed into action. Holidays have other purposes, and this commonsense belief offers both a challenge and a dilemma. Peter Hempel, the Eden Brand Director, admitted in 2003:

> *What we decided very early on was that we didn't want to go the traditional, predictable approach to interpretation, which would be largely, as in botanic gardens, labels and signs. Most museums tend to focus on the touch-screen, multimedia, audio-visual graphics led interpretation, which we felt was wrong on a number of different levels really. It was about the transmission of infor-mation rather than the exploration of ideas or stories. The second reason was we thought it was dull just asking people to read text or look at imagery or whatever. It's not likely to really move people. Then moving on ... what types of media really engage people, engage the senses as much as the ears and the eyes, the emotions, but also understanding that if we have a site that has already been designed to deliver eighty-five different stories around crops, natural habitats or particular plants ... it's down to the role that Eden can usefully play in the broader educational and communication sphere, which is about exciting, engaging, hooking people, awakening interest rather than delivering the whole story.* (interview with author)

One of the most intriguing planting stories, and a good illustration of the creative process, focuses on wine production and consumption. The specific exhibit installation consists of grapevines and dancing mythical creatures (maenads), representing a scene of Dionysian pleasure whose full comprehen-sion obviously requires a degree of cultural knowledge and visual literacy. There is little signage, so without the help of a guide, who may or may not fully understand the cultural signs and symbols, the exhibit may remain opaque. As one member of a tour group casually noted, 'you don't pick up so much just walking around on your own'. The guide 'transmitted' information and offered an interpretation of a relationship between love, wine and happiness. In Classical times, he said, the Mediterranean was a pleasure garden. Little has changed except that today countless hotels and tourist leisure complexes have industrialized these pleasure gardens. Peter Hempel again:

> *The vines exhibit, for example, is where you had an artist [Tim Shaw] exploring the cultural significance of the association with mythology and human behaviour related to the vine – intoxication in particular. Responding to that, the artist, who was particularly interested in that relationship, came back with a creative proposal about how best to integrate sculptural form with vine form to create a truly integrated exhibit. That's where I think it probably works best, where you have the landscape, the horticulture and the artistic intervention working together... It was a very close working collaboration where the selection of the vines, the location of the vines and support was all done in collaboration with the artist. There is no text there at all. It's high interpretation.* (interview with author)

High interpretation relies on visitors making meaning from what is seen, smelt and touched and assimilating aspects of the dominant Eden message of human–plant connectivity. But while the keynote message does offer visitors a rudimentary framework for interpretation that can be built on during a visit and afterwards by activities, thoughts and reflections, still some of the symbolism, as Foundation Director Tony Kendle, citing the light of civilization motif in the olive exhibit, acknowledges, 'just looks pretty despite all the thought that went into it'. Peter Hempel adds:

> *The casting of artists has been quite considered in the sense that work, irrespective of whether you understand all of the thinking the artist has been through or would like to express, is accessible on different levels, whether you think, 'Christ, this is a mad raving party going on amongst the vines' or whether you are looking at the deeper symbolism of orgiastic or ritualistic behaviour or whatever. I think we cast the artists quite deliberately because we feel they do have a broad populist and accessible appeal... The tone is quite important. It is not taking itself too seriously, it's not too worthy, it's not too preachy, it does not tend to transmit lots of information. We are trying hard not to compromise the sensory physical experience of somebody walking though a naturalistic environment as well... If we think something is going straight over people's heads, we can always refine things.* (interview with author)

There is a considerable amount of evaluation work being undertaken at Eden on operational matters, with learners engaged in formal education projects or with non-formal family groups. A personal meaning-mapping methodology has been adopted to measure conceptual learning, but questions remain over the nature of non-cognitive and aesthetic learning. Tony Kendle suggests the artworks probably function primarily to draw visitors' attention by providing signs and additional visual interest to the plant displays. My initial observations tend to confirm this. Sue Minter:

> *Take the classic example of Robert Bradford's bee in the outdoor exhibit, which has ended up rather bigger than it was originally intended to be. There were supposed to have been other pollinating insects and they were supposed to connect with the flower. What people have tended to respond to is the size and the impressive nature of that... So we are learning all the time. The interesting thing is that most botanic gardens have engaged with art frequently on the basis of art lands from Mars. It's decoration, it's in a nice green environment and it's not integrally integrated into the interpretation process... We observed that people do appear to engage with different things and we are experimenting.* (interview with author)

Although there is some repeat messaging of underlying themes and assumptions broadly relating to sustainability, Eden consciously fashions a plurality of stories, interpretations, nuances and emphases and thereby of experiences, meanings and understandings. However, too many possible meanings invite the prospect of meaninglessness or confusion and a relativism that Eden does not endorse. The notion of a core message implies a defining principle, and this is frequently articulated in the form of a brand, even though some Eden team members question the assumed uniformity of this 'corporate' approach, which could compromise the aim to render concepts such as sustainability, biodiversity and cultural diversity personally meaningful. For these internal critics coherence is embedded in the overall *gestalt* of the site, which invites exploration, interest and investigation. Sue Hill:

> *We don't have an exhibit style in a sense. You walk around the site and you might see a fantastic slickly produced signage, but you might also see a handmade piece of stuff made by a local primary school and those things inhabit the same space. A lot of the interpretation is delivered by people, delivered by guides and storytellers, rather than necessarily big black boxes with television screens in.* (interview with author)

Guides' training has evolved over time and views differ as to how they should interact with visitors and visitors with the project. Initial training in presentation, delivered by a member of Cornwall's Knee High Theatre Group, has led guides staffing the mobile interpretation stations to refer to plant specimens as 'props' to engage visitor attention. Gill, a former guide and trained teacher, suggested that the tight schedules and scripted interactions favoured when

Eden first opened limited opportunities for spontaneity and creative participation. They now pursue a policy of 'kissing' – engaging visitors casually and openly as they walk round the site. Gill:

> *Yes, you do engage with people because they are interested or you catch them looking at something, but I think people learn just as much if they are wandering past and if they hear you shout that you are going to do a talk, out of curiosity they'll stand and listen. They have their visit enhanced. If I do a guided tour, the one thing I always used to say to them at the end of the tour, 'I haven't told you everything because I don't know everything, but I hope you've gone away with your head splitting with questions'... I don't try to indoctrinate them but what I think is if you are showing someone that a product that they use is destroying the rainforest then you owe it to them to show them an alternative. If we are talking about recycling, it's no point telling them recycling is good if you are not then going to tell them where the value is or what the problems are and why some areas don't do it. We all know constraints of it, the cost and whether it is really worth it or not. Fair trade is another one. It's opening people's eyes to choice.* (interview with author)

A WHOLE LEARNING THING

During the spring and summer months there are live workshops, world music, theatrical performances, dance and displays creating a festive atmosphere, producing a 'flow' (Csikszentmihalyi and Hermanson, 1995) that frees people of their cultural suspicions, nurtures an intrinsic motivation to learn or apprehend, and so draws them into the defining spirit of the project. The use of 'first person interpretation' often promotes reflexivity and liberation from everyday social reality (Jackson, 2000), but not every performance format, for example world music, will be familiar and this may offer some elements of non-recognition to visitors. However, the cultural memory and experience of play and anticipation of fun predisposes visitors to look, learn, listen and participate, with the 'ludic' element emerging for both adults and children in the workshops. Emma Barker, Eden's Events Manager:

> *One of the amazing things we have noticed – I think it is something about Eden that gets adults to start acting like children again. We've got photos of adults making paper kites, colouring in. You know, the child has sat down and the adults are also enjoying colouring in, playing the game just as much as the child. The adults back off if there are a lot of children in there because they don't want to be seen as taking the place of the children... When we have had workshops on quieter days, with fewer*

*children in there, we have had adults sitting down cutting, stick-
ing, gluing... and they love it. Like if you see a bouncy castle you
still want to take your shoes off and jump up and down on it.
Adults do it here.* (interview with author)

Play has long been recognized as a significant element in Western culture
(Huizinga, 1953) and a key aspect of learning in museums, although, as evaluation studies show, play, particularly playing with gadgets and buttons, may
become diversionary unless the context is conducive to constructive critical
engagement (Sachatello-Sawyer et al, 2002). So, although flow may make
people open to new experiences and to new learning, it also offers serious
challenges to advocates of edutainment. In many ways Eden shares a great
deal with shopping, shopping malls and what Bryman (1999) refers to as the
'Disneyization of society', which encompasses four key attributes:

1 Theming – gives coherence to attractions and differentiates one organization from another;
2 The dedifferentiation of consumption – the interlocking of different forms
   of consumption like shopping, play and eating;
3 Merchandising – the promotion of goods bearing a particular logo or
   brand; and
4 Emotional labour – scripted interactions or the guaranteed cheerfulness of
   site guides and workers.

The food in its restaurant is either locally sourced or organic. Eden's retail
outlet sells branded goods ranging from books on organic horticulture to
locally caught Eden pilchards, although one of the oldest surviving pilchard
works in Cornwall closed in 2005. Its plant catalogue, launched in February
2004, sells plants 'with stories to tell' about global conservation and species
protection. The project has its own publishing house and many products sold
in the shop display the Eden brand logo, though the project neither formally
endorses nor certifies merchandise. Many goods are clearly linked to environmental issues. Jo Readman:

> *We can just educate – these products are good for social issues,
> are good for the environment. And the other categories we've got
> are ones that are recycled and can be recycled. Ones that are
> produced without fossil fuels... So, by buying into any of those
> products, metaphorically, and in reality, you are actually helping
> to make a difference.* (interview with author)

Meaning-making and story-telling frequently translate into visitor purchasing.
Sue Hill:

> *We do know, in terms of indicators, we have had it documented
> on-site, that if we are telling an organic story, if we're telling a fair*

trade story, the sales go up in the retail shop on that particular product. So if we are doing fair trade, sales, or organic sales, will go up that particular week. When they get up to retail they have still got it on board, but we don't know whether that's almost like a gimmick, just at the Eden shop, or whether they then go into a supermarket and still make that choice, that decision. That's what we don't necessarily know. (interview with author)

Shopping is a form of play, a social activity, and malls are places 'to be with things', where visitors have an aesthetic relation to their environment and gain pleasure from new or exotic displays and experiences attempting to assimilate them into the known and the familiar (Lehtonen and Maenpaa, 1997). The Eden site-plan and pathways through the biomes are reminiscent of IKEA, and visitors consume images of Eden on- and off-site – on television, in the Bond movie *Die Another Day*, on posters, in holiday brochures, websites, garden magazines, local, regional and national newspapers. The Eden Communication and Marketing team maintain a very high profile with the broadcast media, with the site having being used to host *Question Time* and featuring in programmes like *3 Non-Blondes* and key staff appearing on *University Challenge*, *Countryfile*, BBC radio's *Desert Island Discs* and *You and Yours* and even featuring in a warts and all two-part documentary, *The Gardeners of Eden*, for BBC television in 2005. Combined with its own media productions, including two lengthy in-house documentaries for sale at the project and a DVD of the Live 8 concert on sale more widely, Eden is a significant part of the environmental 'mediascape' and a vibrant cultural symbol. For many first-time visitors the project is already familiar because of this extensive and regular media coverage, most of which is sympathetic. In fact in some ways the media profile is beginning to establish a brand, whereby people are attracted to the site for a particular learning–entertainment–consumption experience. When interviewing visitors, Friends of Eden and staff, I sometimes felt I was listening to an Eden media release.

Eden is a marketplace for ideas, experiences and commodities. Visitors buy things – their entry, pleasure, learning, food, pictures and souvenirs – that extend their free-choice learning into the palpable realm of everyday living; this is very important if Eden is to go 'Beyond Bodelva'. To this end the Eden Foundation encourages and undertakes research and acts as a hub for a growing network of organizations working for a sustainable future. It coordinates a Friends' organization, has established a Global Centre for Post-Mining Regeneration in association with Rio Tinto, English Nature, MIRO and Anglo American, and contributes significantly to sub-regional economic development. Dave Meneer, the Marketing Director, told me:

We have a desire both in terms of the effect of our messaging and our money-making to go beyond Bodelva. If you don't go beyond Bodelva you've got a green theme park and so what, really... If you set yourself up as a theme park, that's fine, but we always

---

BOX 3.1 WANT TO CHANGE THE WORLD? JOIN THE CLIMATE REVOLUTION!

Climate change is a threat to our civilization. Society's metabolism, based on fossil fuels since the Industrial Revolution, needs a radical rethink.

How should we supply energy, water, food, housing and information in a carbon-constrained world?

How can we re-engineer international policy, the financial system and the law to help?

The changes required are profound. This is the Climate Revolution.

Understanding what the public think about climate change and carbon emissions is crucial to help make the transition to a low-carbon world as smooth as possible. We are working with Consumers for Change, who have commissioned an independent survey. We would really appreciate you taking about 10 minutes to fill it in: www.surveymonkey.com/s.asp?u=913491646740

Also, supported by BT, we are running a digital media competition about the ideas of the Climate Revolution. There is £6000 in prizes to be won. See: www.edenproject.com/climaterevolution

Source: Eden Email 7.3.06

---

had higher ambitions. There are an awful lot of people we employ here we wouldn't employ if we were just a green theme park. A green theme park would not have a huge research department. You wouldn't have various Foundation people. You wouldn't have people working with local farmers to grow things and sell them... An ideal example of Beyond Bodelva at the moment would be books. We publish books that we sell in our shop and in WH Smith and elsewhere. They make us money and tell our story. (interview with author)

There is also an intention, when time and funding permit, to create a virtual Eden acting as both a learning and a trading environment. For the present, the project is increasingly using its email list and internet site to encourage participation in and commitment to actions promoting sustainability.

The Eden Project is in a continual state of rapid co-evolution with the world around it, with the intention of becoming a hub of an international network for people who want to work collaboratively to create a more sustainable future. One example is the bigSMALL Community Ecosystem Partnership, which is an Eden Foundation co-venture with World Steward in the US. bigSMALL is seen as a conditional co-operative of thousands of small donors, acting jointly to protect biological and cultural diversity alongside villages developed according to ecological principles. The Gardens for Life programme is another where areas of school grounds across the world, in both developed and developing countries, are set aside for the production and consumption of home-produced produce. Andrew Jasper has commented that he has 'never known an organization move so fast – too fast sometimes', and Eden is certainly a kaleidoscope of constantly evolving, constantly developing images, voices, stories, performances, smells, emotions, thoughts, transactions and activities. Its own story and core message offer an overall framework for visitor interpretation despite the tensions, recognized inconsistencies and apparent contradictions. For some critics, for example, the failure to condemn GM rather than simply acknowledge the unresolved issues is incompatible with its support for sustainable agriculture. Eden's commitment to and advocacy of environmental sustainability may not be as clear or as distinct to the casual visitor as to a formal study group focusing directly on recycling or area regeneration, but there are certainly opportunities to develop this if the visitor has a mind to. Eden addresses many audiences and, as Tony Kendle explains:

> One of the things we didn't see coming in a lot of the planning of the project was the degree of visitor interest in us and what we are doing as opposed to us being a window on all sorts of stuff. As time goes by and as the two things become less and less easily divisible and as we follow this policy of us becoming an aggressive supporter of local farming, for example, we have become part of the story and not just the teller of stories. (interview with author)

Consequently, Eden is perhaps most fruitfully conceptualized as being open minded, displaying, as Bruner (1990, p30) puts it, 'a willingness to construe knowledge and values from multiple perspectives without loss of commitment to one's own values'. This open-mindedness is closely allied to the idea that the project is an 'open work, created only in the play of its users, who are free to perform and communicate individual or collaborative experiences of objects and situations according to their own designs' (Carr, 2001, p180). Some visitors and organizations seemingly project their own desires and goals onto Eden, expecting it to be a role model of their own conception. For others, despite the sustainability message of connectedness and connectivity, Eden is many things. As one Friend of Eden remarked, 'you don't have to like plants to like Eden'. My interviews and discussions with visitors indicate that a few people do actually have transformative learning experiences as a result of their visit, although these may take place over time rather than being instant or immediate. For example, for Tina, who works in a primary school in the West Yorkshire city of Bradford, Eden is inspirational, connecting very much with her own lived experience, anxieties, hopes and emerging aspirations. Eden offers 'a whole learning thing', what Frey (1998) terms a 'total experience', because they don't tell you what to do but 'actually live what they say. The things like the recycling bins, separate bins for everything – nothing's wasted. It is a lifestyle and I think they live that lifestyle. That does come across. It is not like a giant greenhouse. It's not just like a thing to do with flowers and plants, it's actually a whole learning thing while you're there.' Tina continues:

For me, it all sort of fell into place – the real big picture stuff and how when you see something or have an idea you can make it happen, That was the inspirational part of it for me, which wasn't to do with environment or the plants, or the growing or what they were used for, but that has come since. It's become an exciting thing now. It was really about how this idea came about, the self-belief, the sheer determination about getting it up' and running.

I work in a primary school and we have a huge amount of land, and I do like parental and community involvement, but I also look at the business side as well and I've engaged over the last year, I've got in touch with the community environmental project, which includes groups of businesses promoting science, technology, engineering and maths. Some adults who are connected with the school because they've heard their children, nieces or nephews who go there [be so enthusiastic] have formed groups and we've secured some funding for each of these groups. And the very wild uncultivated land around the school we're now developing into four external classrooms, classroom areas – we might have a wetland area, we might have a nature trail area, a flower meadow area. Every child in school will visit all sections of the land and learn about them, apply them to their learning and lifestyles. And we're developing an external amphitheatre to do the work in as well. We've now got growing beds out in the grounds so we are growing our own fruit and vegetables, which our kitchens will use. And the children have set up a gardening club to run that. And because the area is quite large we can let other primary schools in the district visit at a greatly reduced cost, which can then mean we can afford to maintain and sustain it. They get the benefit as well because being in a city there is not a huge amount of green space. We've pinched ideas from Eden brochures or what other places have done and it's all coming along really, really nicely. And that can be developed from a starting point of zero. We know it can be achieved because we've seen it being achieved. It's going to be our mini Eden if you like. We've got the underlying sense of what it's about at heart, so children will see how things group, how they are important, what they can be used for, recycling – how that works, affects lives and families. That's something the children will grow up with. (interview with author)

More generally, engineers tend to marvel at the engineering and architecture; keen gardeners explore the plants, enjoying the experience of recognizing specimens they grow in their own gardens or keep as houseplants; artists and photographers explore colour, shape and image; the religious see Creation, frequently referring to the biomes as 'cathedral-like'; environmentalists admire the work but often say that Eden has not stimulated them to do anything new because they do it already; and activists are frequently critical – about the parking, the energy used to maintain constant temperatures and humidity in the biomes or the need to pump away water to prevent Boldelva from flooding. Most visitors, except perhaps practising artists, seem to be blind to the artwork, failing to perceive the underlying environmental message informing its design and placing.

Although there is not the space here to discuss all the interviews, letters, emails and discussions I have had in relation to the Eden Project, it is worth quoting two more by way of illustration. Sheila, a young mother, told me:

> I work in the social services department at my local county council. The council has decided to try to minimize its 'environmental footprint' through recycling, electric cars, renewable energy and other initiatives. I'm an 'environmental champion'. The Eden Project stands for me as a positive example of what people can achieve. It helps when I feel despondent about pollution and war; hopefully there will be a planet left for my grandchildren... (interview with author)

And Jim, a retired aviation engineer, remarked:

> As an engineer, my first interest in the biomes was their construction.
>
> What a superb method of solving a difficult problem. Having gone all the way around the tropical biome once, I now tend to stay at the lower levels, which is what I did when the family went around. I sat for about half an hour by the spice section. What held my attention was the interest and the involvement of the children. They were looking at everything. There may be hope for our planet yet. Obviously, a lot of that interest was generated by their parents, but also the enthusiasm and ready smiles of the attendant staff helped a great deal. Again it is instantly obvious that considerable thought has been given to the layout and presentation of the various species which are in the biomes. It has been put together by people who have a genuine interest and concern for the project.
>
> I find myself smiling a lot at Eden. It combines so much of what I value in the world – care for the environment, thought and ingenuity in the construction and layout of the whole site, and, particularly early in the morning before the crowds arrive, a feeling of peace and tranquillity. Long may it prosper. (interview with author)

Visitors are not treated as passive recipients, as inevitably they have their own personal agendas and are, and for the Eden team must be, free to choose when, where and what to learn. There is no context-setting AV presentation in the Visitor Centre, although the videos, *Eden: The Inside Story* and *The Gardening of Eden*, play in the shop and the Plant Takeaway installation may partially serve as an 'advanced organizer'. However, as yet Eden does not know precisely what visitors actually do take away, although Bagnall (2003, p96), in her study of Wigan Pier and the Museum of Science and Industry in Manchester, suggests visitors will 'selectively construct worlds based around their own experiences', reflecting 'the tension in contemporary Western society between reflexivity of behaviour and the degree to which such behaviour is socially embedded, located in social relations and routines'. For Falk and Dierking (2000, p2), 'learning is the reason people go to museums, and learning is the primary "good" that visitors to museums derive from their experience'. Visitors generally come both to learn and to be entertained. It is not an either–or (Falk, Moussouri and Coulson, 1998). The museum experience is about engaging people 'in educationally enjoyable experiences *from which they can take their own personal meaning*' and successful museums should go 'one step beyond experience and provide the ultimate offering, *transformation*' (Falk and Dierking, 2000, p76).

The new Core does offer more structured learning experiences, perhaps reorientating the project's overall approach to learning and sustainability. This education facility foregrounds sustainability and development issues far more overtly than in any other area of the site but does so without losing the sense of fun or interactive play that pervades spaces elsewhere. An undertow of political seriousness, however, is detectable in the exhibition designs and messages communicated through the displayed artefacts, games, activities, installations, images and signs. Traditional Ecological Knowledge is presented through various exhibits and displays as contrasting with the privileged, wasteful, materialistic and overdeveloped lifestyles of ourselves and others in the more economically developed world. Issues of environmental security, pollution, ownership, corporate power, transboundary pollution, biodiversity loss and over-fishing are characterizing contemporary existence. An exhibition on biomimicry uses video art, computer graphics, 3-D models and photographs to illustrate the importance of natural forms in sustainable design, using the architecture of the Core and biomes as examples. Visitors have the opportunity to express their own beliefs and feelings by creating messages on 'ideas cards', on noticeboards or by arranging magnetic letters on a metallic wall. Some of these messages might be silly but many, the vast majority, are totally in keeping with the new spirit of Eden – 'eat organic', 'use the car less', 'education @ its best', and so on.

Some of the signage used in the biomes also became slightly more politically assertive in 2005. Perhaps a first sign of the new seriousness was the staging of the African concert in the summer of 2005, which enabled Eden to re-orientate and rebrand itself slightly, and in so doing communicate more effectively and empathically with developing countries. The concert, available on DVD, shows that Eden has lost none of its marketing skill; but this commodity itself hosts an important message to non-white audiences as well as readers of *Songlines*, the world music magazine.

The experiences of indigenous peoples and those in developing countries are given prominence not as victims but as agents of their own sustainable futures. An exhibition of photographs, actions and events associated with the work of the Barefoot College in Tilona, in the Indian province of Rajasthan, highlights innovative methods of rainwater harvesting, use of solar energy, the empowerment of women, rural informal education, community health and traditional/cultural modes of communication such as the use of puppet theatre. One piece of signage reads, 'Literacy is what the children pick up in school. Education is what they receive from their environment, their community and their family'. Based on fundamental Ghandian principles of simplicity and austerity the Barefoot College was established over 30 years ago. Interaction with the rural community has taught members of the college to respect natural elements, so no rainfall is wasted and since 1986 solar power has been used as its sole source of energy. The college states that only technology which can be understood and repaired and which fulfils a basic need lies within the control of the community and should therefore be used. In the book accompanying the exhibition of the Barefoot Photographers of Tilona, the educational philosophy is neatly summarized thus (Barefoot College, 2000, p16):

> *Barefoot College always was a centre of learning and unlearning. It is a place where the teacher is also the learner and the learner the teacher – where everyone is expected to keep an open mind, try out new ideas, make mistakes and try again; where innovation, taking risks and improvisation are expected because they have not been destroyed by the formal education system.*

At the end of 2005, by offering up alternative points of views from which to choose, Eden's Core is doing far more than allowing people to make up their own minds.

THE EARTH CENTRE AND THE CENTRE FOR ALTERNATIVE TECHNOLOGY

Completely different but complementing the Eden Project is the Centre for Alternative Technology (CAT). In a relatively isolated part of rural west Wales, CAT has succeeded in generating a regional, national and international impact by offering practical, expert and pragmatic guidance on green energy, sustainable construction, transport and lifestyle. Established in 1974 by the entrepreneur Gerard Morgan-Grenville, it is run by a cooperative of around 40 members as an educational resource and a visitor attraction offering examples of sustainable technologies and sustainable ways of living. Set in a former slate quarry, it has also regenerated an area which would otherwise have remained a virtual wasteland. It now attracts in excess of 70,000 visitors a year with a turnover of around £2m. The slate quarry legacy lies all around, allowing industrial heritage to form an important context to the future orientation of CAT. The centre shows that to be sustainable is both practical and possible but requires a continual process of learning, reflection and creativity. CAT politically contextualizes its focus on alternative energy sources and technologies in all its marketing and publicity materials, presenting its message in a relatively direct and unmediated way. When I visited I was struck by the compact nature of the site compared with Eden and, apart from the cliff railway, the absence of spectacular iconic structures. It is functional and serious, though again not lacking a sense of play, resonance or wonder. It makes you think and concentrate and the learning experiences emanating from it are clearly focused. This is what needs to be done to make your home more energy efficient and these are ways to do it – with this message CAT is far less polysemic or polyvocal than Eden, and the approach works well, particularly as the climate of the times urgently demands serious action. Ann MacCarry, an education officer at CAT, told *The Daily Telegraph* (14 January 2006) that children are beginning to apply 'eco pester power' as they become familiar with the ecological footprints games, on-line quizzes and other related activities. More and more children, she said, want to know more about their family's impact on the environment. The CAT website (www.cat.org.uk) states:

> As we move into the 21st century it is becoming clear that following more than 100 years of intensive population growth and industrial development, human activity is beginning to unsettle many of the natural self-organizing systems on our planet. However, with a little forethought and a change of course in our lifestyles and practices, it is hoped that more sustainable development might be achieved. Embracing a sense of responsibility for the future of our global environment and society is looking to become a necessary requisite for sustained and healthy living long into the third millennium. Adopting more sustainable living practice whilst requiring some effort on an individual's part offers rich rewards both immediately and in the foreseeable future.
>
> CAT's emphasis to sustainable living focuses on practical alternatives in key fields such as construction, energy, food supply, water and sewage treatment. Whilst these are essentials, it is also important to remember that for healthy, balanced and truly sustainable living, environmental, community and economic elements of lifestyle must be reconciled and developed not one at the cost of another but in parallel where possible.

CAT therefore offers the visitor a practical, intimate, instructive, user-friendly approach to examining one's environmental impact and one's conscience; from energy saving and recycling methods throughout the home to sustainable gardening practices, growing and composting methods. CAT has a demonstration house for the visitor to walk around with video loops explaining clearly what can easily be done to make a domestic dwelling more environmentally sound

Figure 3.2 *Flyer for the Centre for Alternative Technology, Powys: Reaching large numbers of people through clearly focused and integrated activities*

and less resource-intensive. Around the site artwork and 3-D installations often constructed from found materials directly address environmental and energy themes. The emphasis is again on the clarity of the message rather than oblique artistic metaphor. The centre also offers formal accredited learning programmes, including a Master's course on sustainable architecture run in association with the University of East London, and a range of informal learning experiences, on-site and online opportunities to buy a variety of goods and services, including detailed technical guides on eco-building and renovation, small outdoor equipment and artefacts as well as everyday gifts bearing the CAT logo. It markets practical green solutions to establishing an organic or wildlife garden, rainwater harvesting, cleaning the patio or listening to the radio (wind-up/solar powered, of course). It is purposeful and tightly focused, clearly articulating a set of values and beliefs that are increasingly relevant as our oil-driven economy looks increasingly precarious and unsustainable. This is undoubtedly one of the reasons why the organization has steadily grown in scope and reputation despite its relatively isolated location for more than 30 years.

The Earth Centre, by contrast, was both more ambitious and radical than either the Eden Project or CAT, and this perhaps is one of the reasons for its short and troubled existence. Conceived in the late 1980s in the wake of the Brundtland Report, which called for major educational campaigns for sustainable development, former Greenpeace Managing Director Jonathan Smales recognized the need for a major sustainable education and sustainability resource project that would lead by example. Set in an industrially depressed area of South Yorkshire where coal had been worked for over one hundred years, Conisbrough and Denaby Main were economically and socially deprived communities and by the early 1990s surrounded by contaminated land and suffering an unemployment rate of around 30 per cent. The Earth Centre was designated a Millennium Landmark Project in 1996 but never drew all of the earmarked £50m because of its failure to attract the required match funding. The Earth Centre did, however, succeed in turning 400 acres of acid coal spoil into an ecology park by planting 120,000 trees and by importing soil created from various combinations of sewage sludge, green refuse, farm manure, waste from mushroom farming, as well as topsoil from local land being developed for building construction. The resulting ecology or country park became an open access amenity for all, using over half the total funds the centre received. This was something rarely mentioned, let alone praised, in the media coverage of its failure. Opening in April 1999 with some very favourable but relatively low-key publicity, the centre's buildings and outdoor exhibition areas occupied a site of around 25 acres. It attracted a number of high-profile, establishment supporters, including Sir Crispin Tickell and Derek Osborn. In 2002 its Welcome Hall was nominated for an architectural design award. Indeed the buildings themselves, although lacking the spectacular visual appeal of the Eden biomes, were built to the highest green specifications and were at the time extremely innovative and influential. Unfortunately the centre never achieved the visitor numbers it needed to break even financially, attracting about a third of the planned 320,000 in its first year. Job redundancies were announced within the first six months and, despite internal reorganizations and reconceptualizations, the centre closed in 2004.

Jonathan Smales was keen to present casual visitors and formal education groups with a challenge to established thinking, established ways of living and being, and established ways of learning. As he wrote in *The Guardian* (Smales, 1999), he had no intention of the Earth Centre being just another wheel on the burgeoning eco-tourist bandwagon:

> *For many, eco-tourism has come to mean any visit to a place of natural interest or beauty. For others, it implies a heightened sense of responsibility in the tourist, taking great care not to damage the very thing they have come to see. But it should also include consideration of how we travel to and around the precious destination, a reduction in the frequency of visits to special places in order to improve the quality of the visit and the decision, sometimes, not to visit; the need for greater collective action and investment to safeguard or enhance the special place; the importance of high standards in green building and other development not only in the refurbishment of existing premises and places but also for new developments; changes in agriculture and other enterprises to diversify the economic base and strengthen local cultures.*
>
> *Before making a trip, especially one involving a car, why not first consider taking full advantage of the world on our doorsteps? Look again closely at what is already there in front of our noses and just beyond our backyards and gardens. And if it's not up to much, improve it.*

What was perhaps most interesting about the centre was its ambition and radicalism, which, however, for its former education officer Glenn Strachan were just part of its problem. An emphasis on change, reflection and challenge pervaded the Earth Centre's educational philosophy and pricing strategy – if you arrived by car you were charged £4 more than if you cycled, walked or travelled to the centre by train. I even heard rumour that the centre staff once discussed not accepting credit cards because they were made of plastic. The aim throughout was again to connect with people's everyday life experience and offer ways in which they could consider the social, environmental and economic aspects of sustainable development. In some ways this was similar to the Eden Project, but, as Glenn told me, it was more 'overt'. The Earth Centre, he said:

> *was attempting to say to visitors, 'when you come onto this site leave established thinking behind, suspend belief to some extent and we'll take you through all the things that are recognizable in your everyday life, like transport, food, retail goods, gardens, but we'll show you a different way of doing all those things and then*

hopefully you can take some of those ideas away with you and then apply them'. For example, the cafeteria and the restaurant at the Earth Centre has sustainably sourced food – organic in some cases, local as well – and it made this very overt to the visitors who used the facilities. All the goods in the shops were sustainably sourced – fair trade, many products used from recycled materials. We stocked Patagonia ware, which had fleeces made from recycled plastic bottles, and it wasn't just that they were there but they tried to be an exhibition in themselves and explain to people where these goods had come from, so that when people went away maybe they would start thinking and question-ing things they see in normal shops. Maybe they would ask the question when they go into a cafeteria or restaurant – 'Where does this food come from? Is it local?' ... If you arrived by car you'd pay more although you were able to park your car for free on the site. This caused quite a stir and in a way it was meant to do that – create debate and challenge about these sorts of issues. Some visitors felt they were being unjustly discriminated against. It certainly had an impact, but not one that was necessarily supportive of the financial development of the Earth Centre.

We wanted to bring in a reflective process to the visitor experience so that they would consider some of the things they had done and what differences they could make if they imple-mented some of the ideas outside the Earth Centre in their learning and living. I think this was true in all the programmes we put together and was demonstrated best by the programme we had based around the Kurdish yurt, where visitors experi-enced what it was like to live a nomadic lifestyle where you are dependent for all your needs on locally produced things and waste was something that was rarely produced at all – absolutely best use of everything. And then to reflect on how they currently lived their lives, what their current houses were made of, where their food came from, where their clothes came from, what their clothes were made of, what their toys were made of and so on and to be able to see the difference. Not that we wanted them to be nomads, just that they appreciated the huge amount of resources that went into supporting their current lifestyle and ways in which those resources could be reduced. It's very much now talked of in terms of ecological footprinting, although we didn't use that term at the time. (interview with author)

The large Planet Earth Galleries, exhibition spaces designed by Feilden Clegg Bradley Architects, were built into a hillside with the façade constructed out of local magnesium limestone. Below the galleries was an area combining the idea of the Roman hypocaust with contemporary environmental modelling techniques, intended to act as an effective temperature regulator to ensure comfort in both summer and winter. The galleries incorporated two major exhibitions: the Planet Earth Experience and Action for the Future. The former was set in a large, dark space, with the basic message that, although the world is a beautiful place, our way of living is rapidly destroying the natural ecosystems upon which we depend. Visitors were invited to explore the changing relationships between people, nature and technology. The Planet Earth Experience was marketed as the world's first 'cyberhenge', with slabs of standing glass holding sculptures denoting various aspects of life on earth. Huge glowing globes symbolized ecological threats to the planet and lights, projections and prisms combined with a specially designed soundscape produced an unsettling and theatrical visitor experience. An installation of Solar Spectrum Art attempted to immerse the visitor in intense primary colours, symbolizing possibilities of a better, more sustainable future. That was the idea, but it was one that was lost on many visitors, including, I am afraid, me.

By contrast, the exhibition Action for the Future was a light, bright, optimistic space designed by the Dutch company OPERA. By presenting numerous ideas and visions for a more sustainable world, the intention was to prepare visitors for the remainder of the site by prompting them to reflect on what sustainable actions they could apply when they left. To facilitate this process, the concept of sustainability was divided into 16 themes, each with an animated installation or 'icon' representing it, which visitors would come across elsewhere on the site. 'Magic' windows invited visitors to see a 'fantastic future' at home, in the city, in the countryside, indeed all over the world, as visions of sustainable regeneration were demonstrated time and time again.

Nature Works, conceived and partly designed by local children, naturalists and community groups, explored the diverse freshwater and terrestrial habitats found in the Earth Centre's 400-acre Ecology Park. Direct hands-on and exploratory play and learning by children and adults was actively encouraged by both the design and centre guides. Specially constructed podiums exhibited different habitats, with visitors being able to 'pond-dip' from indoor tanks to collect algae, bugs and fish in jam jars. Children and adults alike participated and, being a city boy for most of my life, this was my first and to date only experience of pond dipping. Visitors were also able to see some of the creatures they collected magnified many times on large overhead screens. The building was a demonstration green construction – a simple timber and glass structure designed by Letts Wheeler Architects, a young practice formed in 1996 and interested in working with artists on environmental and sustainability issues. Located between the Cadeby stream and a wildlife pond, its steel frame had cladding made from indigenous softwood, and the roof was constructed from reconstituted waste timber.

Fine art, sculpture and design were therefore principle elements of the Earth Centre's educational experience, but visitor reactions to it were not always favourable. There was the issue of legibility, symbolism and meaning as well as taste, perhaps a reflection on the lack of good art education in Britain's schools. Interestingly the artwork at Eden seems to be very much part of the backdrop – almost invisible, meaningless or silent to many visitors but adding to the overall aesthetic pleasure the project offers. John Vidal, writing in the week prior to the centre's opening, mixed his enthusiastic report in The Guardian with a little scepticism:

> *The centrepiece of this optimistic laboratory of life is the Earth Galleries, a long, low, super-efficient building cut into the hill behind it. There's a wall of waste and the ceiling is full of knack-ered motor parts and scrap. The whole building has a raw, industrial feel. Into this space, George Tsypin, a Russian opera designer based in New York, has created a glass 'henge', with huge plates of glass set around a revolving stage.*
>
> *Goodness knows what people will see. Tsypin is not too sure himself. His installation is abstract and complex, throwing up infinitely changing images of the living world. Activated by sensors linked to computers, flashes of beauty, terror, calm, speed, harmony are thrown on to the glass walls; they and the music, the sounds of jets, traffic or of utter peace, the light inside, even the speed at which the exhibition unfolds, all change according to the number of people inside the hall, and how they move around.* (Vidal, 1999)

At the centre's relaunch in May 2001, a mere few hundred visitors and supporters arrived, which was an obvious disappointment to the organizers. My personal recollection is of the site seeming vast and empty, smoke drifting everywhere from a barbecue, and still some unfinished but quietly impressive buildings. This was not my first visit to the centre, but it was for some of those I spoke to. One woman who attended a lecture on permaculture gardening noted, 'It was all a bit too alternative for me, carrying your wee in yellow plastic buckets. It might be alright in the country but not something you can do in a town.' Although no major formal evaluation of visitor experience was ever undertaken, it was, as Glenn suggested, the radicalism and ambition that seemed to mark the Earth Centre apart from rather than interact with the everyday. Although it was about connecting, it failed to connect with people, with popular culture and with the popular imagination. It simply did not resonate with everyday life experiences or at least failed to do so for sufficient numbers of visitors. This led to the ratcheting up of financial pressure and to Jonathan Smales being replaced as Chief Executive by Suzy England, whose brief was to be much more visitor-savvy. Additional grant money and other sponsorship were found. A pirate ship, a crazy golf course and an indoor 'Amazon Adventure' play area were constructed. The radical and ambitious sustainability messages were muted, causing much annoyance to some dedicated staff members whose ecological consciences had led them to work for the centre in the first place and take pay cuts to keep it going. Unfortunately, the Earth Centre was still off the beaten tourist track and nothing could really be done about that. Millions of people simply did not go to Doncaster for their holidays or a relaxing weekend break, and the centre's messages were possibly too complicated as well as too radical to get across in the local and national media. Arguably it was a massive and combined conception, design, communication and marketing failure. Glenn again:

> *The Earth Centre was focused on sustainable development right from the very beginning and it was a huge challenge to base something on sustainable development, for sustainable development means little enough to people today in 2005. If you mention the Eden Project to people they think of plants and gardens, and yes there are sustainability messages within that, but the hook for people is the amazing plants in amazing settings, the biomes. The Centre for Alternative Technology focuses very much on energy and alternative technologies, but it is wind turbines, solar panels, and so again this is very tangible to people. This contributes to the overall concept of sustainable development but the hook is to go and see wind turbines and how solar panels work, alternative energy for transport, energy conservation in building. It is very much about technology – the hard physical things. The Earth Centre tried to pull together the social, economic and environmental aspects of sustainability. It's a very complicated picture and a very difficult picture to sell to large numbers of people.*
>
> *You could say the Eden Project focuses on plants and then gets across messages about sustainability when people are already there. This is possibly a better way of engaging the public, for that is where the public are at the moment. They are not, and certainly weren't back in the late nineties, bursting to go and see something about sustainable development, because for the vast majority of people it doesn't mean that much to them. The issue of climate change is permeating people's thinking now and they are making the connections. In the UK people have experienced a very reductionist form of education, where they compartmentalize things. And what we are trying to do when educating people about sustainability is to make them appreciate the connections, to give them a more holistic view, a more systems view of the world, and that is quite hard and is not going to attract people along. You have to get them in on one thing that really attracts them and then bring sustainability in, possibly in a more informal way. We should have focused on one thing – biodiversity or architecture or something. The Earth Centre was a little bit ahead of its time.* (interview with author)

Celebrating CAT's twenty-fifth anniversary, Gerard Morgan-Grenville told *The Guardian* (Schwarz, 2000) that the new Earth Centre was 'a theme park lacking a coherent message', while also suggesting that neither Greenpeace nor Friends of the Earth offer a learning centre where anyone can go. At the time of writing, the Earth Centre's Ecology Park public amenity remains open to

a) Flyer for the Earth Centre
b) Part of the interior
c) External view showing an
adjacent pond

Figure 3.3 *The Earth Centre, South Yorkshire: An idea
too complicated to sell to large numbers of people?*

the public but the buildings are closed and unused, with the most vivid record
of the Earth Centre's history being the website of a local primary school, which
proudly records its involvement with the centre.

LESSONS?

The three institutions discussed in this chapter have or had similarities in their
educational mission, range of formal and informal learning activities, use of
their buildings' architecture and design as an informal learning opportunity,
and links with schools, colleges and universities. The Earth Centre hosted a
few international conferences and I once addressed a group of school inspec-
tors on the Education for Sustainable Development Regional Strategy for
Yorkshire and the Humber produced by Yorkshire's ESD Forum. Fielden Clegg
Bradley won a RIBA award in 2002 for the Solar Canopy and Arrivals Building
and Bill Dunster's conference hall, made emphatically from recycled materials,
won significant praise and would later inform the design of his BedZed sustain-

able housing development in South London. Both Eden and CAT are also closely associated with further and higher education course development and social, educational and scientific research. Eden is increasingly working overseas, making significant contributions to sustainable design, horticulture, land reclamation, education, sensory learning, eco-tourism and much more. The Core was opened with a celebratory high-profile conference entitled 'The Rainforest Gathering', sponsored by both Eden and the Association for Tropical Biology and aimed at a specialist, student and general audience. Speakers from major universities and conservation organizations addressed issues ranging from biodiversity, forest regeneration, finance, conservation, climate change and the struggles of indigenous peoples to public media and communication, learning and education. The Earth Centre offered workshops on sustainability and citizenship and residential programmes, hosted conferences, and linked single-day school visits to various aspects of the National Curriculum. In its first six months it hosted many school visits and, through its 'academy', offered a six-week primer on sustainability delivered at the Miners' Welfare Institute for local people who were to be employed at the centre. This increased local skill and employability as well as income levels for many people. Glenn recalls:

> *The Earth Centre brought in speakers from a wide range of organizations, including the Findhorn community in Scotland, local universities and customer care experts, and when the centre faced financial difficulties, the team spirit of those who had been through that six-week experience was absolutely amazing because there was a real democratic ethos. When difficult times came they pulled together. They worked in a democratic way with the management to help find solutions. For those people it had a real impact, shifting their mindsets, at least for the vast majority of them, in terms of how they viewed the world around them.*
> (interview with author)

So what are the lessons? To innovate and to stimulate. To be ahead of the times but not apart from them. To model a future and lead by example. To speak the language of the everyday, but to reflect critically upon it, with it. To maintain a clear sense of purpose and to encourage learning that is fun, participatory and rewarding, but above all necessary. To ensure that learning and sustainability are integral to our life experiences. To interpret the world, but also to change it.

4

Building Sustainable Neighbourhoods and Communities

This chapter looks at the nature of community and design, construction and living in a more sustainable environment. Examples ranging from a new social housing project to an alternative community established in response to social deprivation are discussed as spaces in which to live and from which to learn. The chapter comprises sections on:

- Changing places;
- Parish maps and community gardens;
- Towards building sustainable communities;
- Designing sustainable communities;
- Learning ecologies; and
- Spaces to live, spaces from which to learn.

CHANGING PLACES

The Eden Project, the Earth Centre and the Centre for Alternative Technology all attempt (or attempted) to reach out into various local and distant communities. But the concept of community, like so many others, is open to interpretation and academic discussion – although most of the time we seem to know, feel or intuit what is meant when terms like democracy or community are used in everyday conversation; the meanings of words are derived from their use and application. (The same, however, cannot be said for sustainability or sustainable development.) In recent years, there has been a resurgence of public policy interest in 'community' because it seems this is something we have lost and is at the heart of many of our numerous social, political, cultural and environmental ills. The communitarian writer Amitai Etzioni (1995) has written of the 'spirit of community', the need for social cohesion, social inclusion and social capital – all terms open to interpretation, discussion, debate and disagreement. Nevertheless, taking an anthropological approach, I wish to view community more as a symbolic cultural construct than a structural one. In other words, although communities may be firmly rooted in a particular place, they do not have to be in order to be considered communities; what makes them so is that people believe them to be so – they share meanings, values, attitudes, practices, lifestyles and identities distinguishing them from others in a more or less general way. Immigrant populations retain contact with their cultures and countries of origin through satellite television, the internet, videos, imported 'ethnic' food and so on. Community, writes Cohen (1985, p13), 'hinges crucially on consciousness'. People may share certain ways of behaving, and while there are always differences in what these actions mean, crucially, what separates one community from another is that members share more with each other than they do with others. Thus people will use, share and own the same symbols but interpret them slightly differently. They may even adopt or rearticulate ones emanating from other cultures or from changes in the global economy, corporate marketing and the global media. So one activity, a festival or a celebration, may serve as a cultural space for different communities to come together, to share, learn, play or display. This is the case with the predominantly Afro-Caribbean annual Notting Hill Carnival in London and the traditional South Asian Mela transferred to Bradford and other UK cities. Derived from the Sanskrit for 'to meet', the Mela is an arts, craft, music, literary, community and cultural festival. With artists and activities from many different backgrounds, the Mela now has a number of different significations including (following civic disturbances in many northern British towns) community cohesion, ethnic harmony, intercultural learning and also, to adopt Illich's (1975) phrase, 'a tool for conviviality'. Cohen writes:

> *The quintessential referent of community is that its members make, or believe they make, a similar sense of things either generally or with respect to specific and significant interests, and, further, that they think that that sense may differ from one made elsewhere. The reality of community in people's experience thus inheres in their attachment or commitment to a common body of symbols.* (Cohen, 1985, p16)

It is also possible to talk of communities of practice, community development, community organization, community action, community education, community economic development, community justice, community regeneration, professional community, business community, virtual communities, ethnic communities, occupational communities, communities of place, communities of interest or community feeling as well as simply community. We learn in and from these and other communities; we become who we are in communities whether they are place-based or not.

A geographical location will generate a common body of symbols; it will nurture stories and histories that ground people in an understanding of who or what they are and where they come from. As a child, I remember seeing myself as a Londoner, as both sides of my family had done for generations, but we were from south of the river, not from the East End and certainly not from the north or west. In effect, it boiled down to a specific area bounded by its own cultural heritage and meanings – winkles and shrimps, street markets,

Charlie Chaplin, pubs, shops, people and, as a very young child, bomb sites which still existed nearly 20 years after the Luftwaffe had flown their last sortie. All these places had different meanings, which as I grew older changed. My area of London became increasingly more cosmopolitan, yuppie and 'ethnic'. Places change and our understanding of their, and our, identities change too. Our subjectivities, our lifestyles and our cultural practices are connected to the wider environment. Today the area I grew up in is reported to have vibrant English, Afro-Caribbean, Chinese, Columbian and other ethnic communities; the estate on which I lived for years, once scheduled for demolition because it lacked modern amenities, partially remains as a result of resident action, with the tiny apartments selling for over £200,000. The old terraces are now, according to the estate agents' marketing blurb, 'well-built, Victorian artisan dwellings set in the middle of a vibrant bohemian artistic community and within easy reach of the Globe Theatre, Tate Modern, the National Film Theatre', and so on. In April 2005 the local council agreed to protect the place by designating it a 'conservation area' – the best preserved 150-year-old mews workshops or yards in London in a gentrified and economically regenerated area of north Southwark. The big modern tower blocks built in the late 1960s and 1970s to house many of those moved from my old estate have themselves been pulled down because, like Thamesmead further east along the river, these buildings, albeit designed with the paternalist good assumption that the built environment determines human behaviour and the quality of life, largely ignored the capacity of people to shape their own built and cultural environments – a space ordered for the dwellers rather than a space ordered by the dwellers. Spontaneous social organization was replaced by social engineering and so reduced feelings of personal or emotional ownership given by unplanned use and informal adaptation – the creation of identities and relationships, the sharing of cultural values, the redefining of spaces with window boxes, television aerials, murals or graffiti art. The built environment, like other technologies, provides individuals and groups with certain 'affordances', but top–down direction often excludes 'the mutability of space which is a site for the construction and expression of identities' (Miles, 2000, p64). The consequence of this may be responses to disenfranchisement that are categorized as anti-social and uncivil. But it is important to be able to express oneself, and perhaps better for the graffiti artists to adorn dedicated walls in community leisure sites than someone's garden wall, a train or a bus stop. There is a difference between vandalism and artistic or political expression, but this too may be a matter of interpretation and its temporal location (Cresswell, 1998).

The world changes and, because my memory and understanding of that part of London was closed off when I went to university in west Wales in the mid 1970s, I was surprised to learn how parts of my early world had survived and prospered in my absence. Even my old primary school now exhibits its ecological credentials on its website, but the point of this personal digression is that, apart from changing, places offer different meanings and afford different possibilities at different times. It is through action, learning and

Figure 4.1 *Graffiti Wall, Tiverton, Devon: A fenced-off public space dedicated to creative expression, situated within a leisure centre*

engagement that we are able to fashion change, including more sustainable possibilities for our environment in relation, of course, to those globalizing forces that impinge so heavily upon us. We cannot truly learn about ourselves, or our environments, without being reflective, and we certainly cannot learn about or from our environments if we perceive them as simply being there – a static backcloth to the theatre of our lives. That we engage with our environments, and that the places we interact with are essentially dynamic, is still worth saying because we can and frequently do forget. Places are shaped by the constellation of social relationships existing on a local and global scale – just think about where the food stacked on supermarket shelves originates, about who made the trainers and where, and about what we do when we enter the store. The geographer Doreen Massey put it like this:

> *If one moves in from the satellite towards the globe, holding all those networks of social relations and movements and communications in one's head, then each 'place' can be seen as a particular, unique, point of their intersection. It is, indeed, a meeting place. Instead, then, of thinking of places as areas with boundaries around, they can be imagined as articulated moments in networks*

of social relations and understandings, but where a large propor-
tion of those relations, experiences and understandings are
constructed on a far larger scale than what we happen to define
for that moment as the place itself, whether that be a street, or a
region or even a continent. And this in turn allows a sense of
place which is extroverted, which includes a consciousness of its
links with the wider world, which integrates in a positive way the
global and the local. (Massey, 1994, pp154–5)

If people are to relate the general to the specific, the global to the local, then it will occur in their 'lived' everyday worlds and, as adult educators know so well, the best place to start a critical and reflexive learning journey is where people are, with what they experience and what they know (or think they know) (Knowles, 1983; Brookfield, 1986).

PARISH MAPS AND COMMUNITY GARDENS

Neighbourhood-based initiatives like parish mapping and the development and running of community gardens or city farms can serve a number of purposes with outcomes that interlock in a truly sustainable fashion. The charity Common Ground initiated the community capacity building process of parish mapping in the 1980s. In England a parish is the smallest and an ancient unit of local administration, with boundaries often corresponding to natural or geographic contours. Parish mapping involves members of a particular parish working together with artists to produce a map that articulates what the locality means to them and also possibly to visitors. The parish map is not a scaled or precise exercise in cartography (and is not exclusive to rural areas), but it is highly visual, narrative, emotive and personal. It is an expression of community values and community learning, of memory and local knowledge. Sue Clifford, a founding director of Common Ground, writes:

Knowing your place, taking some active part in its upkeep,
passing on wisdom, being open to ideas, people, development,
change but in sympathy with nature and culture which have
brought it this far will open the doors of dissent. But conversa-
tion, tolerance and the passing on of memories are civilizing
forces. Whatever the forms of knowledge we shall need for the
next millennium, humanity and imagination must take a high
priority in organizing them.

In making a parish map you can come together to hold the
frame where you want it to be, you can throw light on the things
which are important to you, and you may find courage to speak
with passion about why all this matters. (Clifford, no date)

The drawing together and representation of local knowledge is one element in the conservation of local ecologies and indeed of the three ecologies identified by Guattari (2000).

Many community gardens and city farms are located in areas of de-industrialization or inner-city deprivation, sometimes near areas with high degrees of toxic contamination, illegal dumping of waste and poor health. They too bring people together and develop a sense of place and belonging. Their value lies in their contribution to the social and ecological restoration of the locality, providing healthy green space but also offering far more – growing food locally reduces food miles, enabling people to work in the outdoors, contributing modestly to meeting an income gap, positively affecting health and well-being, nurturing a sense of community or belongingness, developing new skills and knowledge and restoring a sense of worth and identity. Growing food may not be the major reason for a community garden scheme's existence, but all will be influenced by the wants and needs of the locality (Holland, 2004). In the US, a number of community gardens address issues relating to drugs, gun culture, inner-city crime, alienation, skills development, low personal esteem, and feelings of low collective and individual efficacy. Catherine Sneed of the San Francisco Garden Project writes movingly of her work with former prisoners (Sneed, 1997). She notes the stupidity of keeping people in jail instead of preparing them for a job and the appalling social conditions of many black communities, which, among other things, lack hope as well as employment and general opportunity. Learning about nutrition and parenting is an important element of the Garden Project, encouraging people to leave both the crack and the junk food behind. Ferris, Norman and Sempik write of similar experiences:

> The effect of guns and drugs on poor neighbourhoods in American cities has been devastating. Although the bay area must be among the richest communities in the world, social polarization is also very high, with 'people of colour' suffering the greatest deprivation. Community gardens are now being used to develop alternatives for young people exposed to the drugs and crime economy... Strong Roots Gardens are gardens which offer job training and earning opportunities to African-Americans and other socially excluded young people. (Norman and Sempik, 2001, p564)

In Britain, the Women's Environment Network and the Black Environmental Network have also been engaged in supporting community gardens in Bradford, London, Birmingham, Glasgow, Sheffield, Bristol, Manchester, Newcastle and elsewhere. The Hulme Garden Centre flourishes in the once formerly depressed but now regenerated area of central Manchester (Whittingham, 2005). Established in 1999, the Concrete to Coriander and Bangladesh Women's Community Garden at Small Heath Park in Birmingham has thrived thanks to the efforts of CSV Environment and a financial grant

---

BOX 4.1 FROM CONCRETE TO CORIANDER AND BANGLADESH WOMEN'S COMMUNITY GARDEN, BIRMINGHAM

Over 25 women meet two or three times a week in Small Heath Park, east Birmingham, to plant vegetables for the family table. Some come with children or grandchildren, with daughters or other family members. The atmosphere is mostly relaxed and friendly, although as the membership increased, some small disputes erupted, for example on why some members have more planting space than others. At the general meetings we have open and frank discussions about current problems and try to sort them out because we value the idea of being together and love the activity of planting and growing as a group.

Participants vary in age from early twenties to seventies and many join through the invitation of existing members. We know each other well and know a lot about each other's families, like who is not well and who is getting better. The group is more than just a garden club; it is for many a social event to look forward to each week. We teach each other languages: I teach the ladies some words in English and in return I learn Bangladeshi words like '*Bala asonny?*' – 'How are you?' This is what I say on Monday morning when I arrive at the garden. I also know the days of the week: '*shonibar*', '*mongolbar*', '*budbar*', etc. Birmingham women and children came together to learn more about composting and to see the Small Heath site.

Source: Taste a Better Future Network Newsletter, Autumn 2002, no 5

---

from the National Lottery Charities Board. The project, featured briefly on BBC television's *Gardener's World* in 2005, has three major objectives:

1 To establish women's gardening groups and provide horticultural training to members of these groups;
2 To implement good allotment practices such as organic vegetable growing, recycling, water conservation and composting; and
3 To learn about and adopt a healthier lifestyle through gardening, improved diet and exercise.

There are countless gardening clubs and allotments in many parts of the world and, apart from providing many people with immense pleasure and satisfaction, they offer opportunities for friendship, sharing, competition and companionship. Working in a garden or allotment can generate detailed ecological and geographic knowledge, help an individual keep fit, and offer a physical, personal and sensual experience of place – of the land, soil, nature, personal control, achievement and degree of empowerment. It is always satisfying to create something that is both pleasing to the eye and pleasing to the taste buds. In my own village there is an extremely well attended gardening club which meets on the first Wednesday of every month. Club members, mainly though not exclusively elderly, organize visits to local gardens and projects (including Eden) and invite horticultural and, occasionally, environmental experts to talk about plants, propagation or related issues. The Garden Club also organizes the village flower and produce show, which runs on alternate years with a local gardens open event. Not every gardening club member adheres to organic principles, but many members do and, although the club is socially and culturally conservative, the entries of the local eco-community that lies just outside the village settlement area are always welcome. Although different and alternative, they too are part of the community of gardeners. In North Yorkshire, on the edge of Harrogate, a garden centre and nursery called Horticap employs people with learning difficulties. Far from being cheap labour, these workers enjoy a sense of purpose and worth by doing a useful job, being paid for it and interacting gently with the general public. Gardens are wonderful things – powerful, restorative, pleasing and potentially at the cutting edge of social learning and sustainability. My wife and I used to buy our Christmas trees from Horticap.

TOWARDS BUILDING SUSTAINABLE COMMUNITIES

Nozick (1999), exploring various dimensions of sustainable community development in western Canada, suggests five action areas for successfully building and developing sustainable communities:

1 Enhancing local wealth through economic self-reliance, community economic development, etc.;
2 Gaining community control of local resources, eg local self-governance, control over land use and development of local co-operatives;
3 Becoming ecologically sustainable, eg energy-efficient land use and urban food production;
4 Meeting needs of individuals, eg health, safety, security, identity, and sense of belonging and connectedness to place; and
5 Building a community culture that binds people together over time.

Those involved in sustainable community development will often say that existing structures, relations and processes of power, systems of administration, finance and governance, and vested interests must be contested as well as reformed for new sustainable habits, perspectives and values to be nurtured from the bottom up. Sustainable community regeneration and development processes inevitably involve multi-agency partnership working, conflict resolution, the development of new skills and aptitudes, and knowledge and understanding of values and visions of what the future could and should be. Invariably it will mean making connections of the global with the local, building new social and economic relationships, reflecting and learning from experience, making things happen, taking a lead, and living within the planet's ecological carrying capacity. However, community capacity building and the creation of more sustainable ways of being are also for most people rooted in the harsh material reality of making a living, surviving, perhaps, in a place-based environment. Interviewing residents in three working class estates in the UK, Burningham and Thrush (2001) concluded that people in disadvantaged groups feel strongly that they lack real personal influence over environmental problems. Focus groups were asked which environmental issues concerned them, but participants from these communities were often unfamiliar with the language of environmentalism, and when the discussion was steered towards wider environmental issues participants usually, and quite rapidly, returned to more pressing, day-to-day and immediate concerns. These people did not see the point in looking far beyond their own locality or to a time beyond the present, although there was an underlying concern for the young and future generations. Except for such issues as car or industrial pollution, which was part of their everyday life experience, the local–global connection was rarely made, though their existence and ultimate significance was appreciated. The authors quoted people from the North Wales community of Cefn Mawr:

> *'I don't think in the long term. Like I say I live for the day and see what tomorrow brings so I don't overly worry about these things.'*
>
> *'Well this is it, you have enough problems with your own to cope with so you don't worry about things that aren't actually affecting you at the moment...'*
>
> *'Well places like that [rainforests] are a long way from Cefn.'*
>
> *'Well they are, rainforests are a long way from Cefn, but this is how I look at it, they're not affecting me at the moment so don't tempt fate by thinking about it.'*
>
> *'But then, if you're like me, if I find something like that come on my telly I switch it off... because it scares me, I just don't want to know.'* (Burningham and Thrush, 2001)

The researchers offer a number of conclusions and practical recommendations for environmental activists, policymakers, and regeneration and sustainability professionals as well as residents living in these deprived areas. Of course, concern with local rather than broader global issues is not confined to people living in working-class urban environments or isolated rural farming communities, but the authors do suggest that it is through local issues that the broader ones can ultimately be addressed. They also recognize that residents are acutely sensitive to, and often offended by, the basically stigmatizing language of policymakers, white middle-class environmentalists, newspaper editors and academics who, from the outside, categorize such localities as deprived, poor, disadvantaged, polluted, and so on. This is more than a communication break-down, it is a sign that people in disadvantaged communities are objects of and for research, of policy intervention, of community capacity building. Whatever the case, people live in these communities – it is home, it is where their friends are and where social and work-related networks are rooted. More specifically, the authors note and reaffirm the importance of social relationships, social and collective learning, dialogue and discussion, sharing and participation. They write:

> *Our focus group discussions lend weight to the notion that environmental attitudes and concerns are not fixed but develop in the course of dialogue with others. In some groups, we were aware of some individuals shifting their position in the light of others' comments whilst others grew in confidence and expressed views on unfamiliar issues. Focus groups provide an excellent forum for collective learning about environmental issues.*
>
> *Involvement in group discussions may assist and empower those who take part. There were many examples of individuals passing on useful information to others: the location of recycling facilities; details of a mother and toddler group; or how to conserve water in the home. We also had occasional glimpses of the possibility of collective action through the expression of shared dissatisfaction. These observations suggest that discussion groups are an important way of involving people in local environmental projects or decision-making, at the same time helping to build social capital.* (Burningham and Thrush, 2001, p42)

Discussion groups are therefore one of the ways in which people can learn from each other and from their social and natural environments. It is one means by which people develop the intellectual tools to interrogate, reflect upon and evaluate experience and behaviour. And sometimes the places where people live, the exterior and interior spaces people inhabit, whether intimate or remote, threaten them with hazards of which they may be unaware but which can nonetheless hurt them physically and mentally. Air pollution, for example, conjures up images of smog-bound old London or contemporary Los Angeles, Mexico City or Shanghai, but frequently the air quality inside our homes and offices is poor and unhealthy – if only we knew it (Griggs, 2001; Saunders, 2002). And this applies to rich as well as poor areas. Griggs writes:

> *Today's homes and offices are environments invisibly polluted with thousands of synthetic chemicals – and the cleaner, more modern and efficient they are, the more polluted they are likely to be. Where do all these chemicals come from? Synthetic materials used in building and insulation, fibreboard, plywood, flooring, paints, resins, varnishes and finishes are all sources of noxious chemical emissions. Modern furnishings may make a further contribution – synthetic or semi-synthetic carpets and fabrics, plastics, fiberglass and the photocopier. All of these may give off emissions known as Volatile Organic Compounds (VOCs).* (Griggs, 2001, p105)

We can do something about this but first we need to know that the problem exists and then we have to set about dealing with it. But how? Television makeover or lifestyle entertainment shows rarely address these hazards, often focusing instead on how to sell and make money from your property. Consumer labelling may be inadequate at providing information in isolation; it is rarely sufficient to make a difference. Government public communication campaigns may help, though Bedford, Jones and Walker (2004, p24) noted with regard to the 'Are You Doing Your Bit?' campaign that advertising is not enough either – messages have to be discussed and reinforced by action and debate in other arenas. You can buy a guide to green living, but first you have to want to make that investment, see the need, and believe that something can be done and then do it.

One important way of influencing people's attitudes, values and behaviour is design, which, combined with public discussion and community involvement, may help people realize the positive benefit of ecologically sound concepts. Eco-design is relevant both to those living on ordinary housing estates and to those in upper-middle-class gated communities. It may help fashion an alternative, more sustainable, view of the world. Experience of space and place, of which sustainable design forms a part, therefore becomes, as indigenous peoples know so well, a key element within an overall ecology of learning about our selves and our understandings of how we connect with the wider social and natural worlds. This ecology of learning is experiential in the broadest sense, incorporating emotional, intuitive, rational, scientific and possibly mystical elements. We may attempt to consciously make sense of this experience by putting it all into words, concepts and theories – environmental justice, civic participation, social capital, sustainability, design, makeover – but often we simply feel things. We feel that composting or standing up to a developer or replacing dusty carpets with wooden flooring is the right thing to do. It is possible to feel safe and secure in a virtual community or feel injustice or environmental shame in the country or in the city. It is possible to feel that we are living healthy and contented lives, that the open or closed spaces, the coriander or concrete, are not alternate realities but integrated realities created by ourselves.

DESIGNING SUSTAINABLE COMMUNITIES

Architects and planners sometimes see design as a way of solving many personal, political, social, communal, environmental, criminal or cultural problems. And to some extent this is true. It is possible to design out crime or to design in affordances making for sustainable living. It is possible to design and plan a city or urban area according to ecological principles, taking due notice of the significance of local vegetation and soils, designing ecological methods for improving air and water quality and urban micro-climates, and recognizing the importance of wilderness to cities, higher urban population densities to human sociability and the intrinsic value of the ecological restoration of degraded or destroyed landscapes. Hough argues that designers must think clearly about how development contributes to environments, how biodiversity can be re-established and how natural resources can be drawn upon and sustained. Designers must recognize that a healthy human body is dependent on a healthy ecological life system. What's more, sustainability learning needs to begin at home, in the everyday:

> *Seeing nature whole, understanding interrelationships and connections between human and non-human life, therefore, begins with the places where most people live. The urban allot-ment garden, for instance, through the daily process of food growing, provides a realistic basis for understanding the cycle of the seasons, soil fertility, nutrition and health, the problem of pests and appropriate methods of control... One of the funda-mental tasks of reshaping the city is to focus on the human experience of one's home places, to recognize the existence and latent potential of natural, social and cultural environments to enrich urban places. This provides the best chance of spiritual growth and creative learning, since it lies at the heart of environ-mental education.* (Hough, 1995, pp25–6)

Following Hough, Hugh Barton (2000, pp89–90) argues that places, neigh-bourhoods, are best conceived as open eco-systems and that designers should base their work on six key principles if sustainable living environments are to be achieved and maintained and a community's ecological footprint reduced without compromising choice and opportunity. These are:

- **Increasing local autonomy** – wherever technically, socially or environmen-tally feasible people's needs, including work, services, energy, water and waste, should be met locally;
- **Increasing choice and diversity** – particularly as regards home, work, trans-port, open space, shopping, education and other services;
- **Responsiveness to place** – development should be responsive to the particu-lar geological, landscape, hydrological, biological and microclimatic conditions;
- **Connection and integration** – of residential settlements, neighbourhoods, towns and cities linked with the wider urban region(s);
- **Flexibility/adaptability** – including the design of multi-functional open and social space and buildings capable of changing use or adapting to new environmentally friendly technologies; and
- **User control** – governance and decision-making should be based on the principle of subsidiarity.

The idea that plants could be used to create a healthy eco-system within an indoor environment goes back to the work of NASA scientists in the 1970s. Plants, rubber or spider plants, for example, seem to be particularly beneficial, but they need to be properly placed to interact with any mechanical heating, air conditioning or circulation systems maintaining temperature, humidity and air quality levels (Wolverton, 1998; Griggs 2001). Technological inventions that observe and imitate nature can lead to the design and construction of healthy, aesthetically attractive, eco-efficient and sustainable living environments for humans and non-humans alike (Benyus, 2002; Roelofs, 1999; McDonough and Braungart, 2002). Energy-intensive landscapes such as lawned, manicured gardens can be redesigned to become plentiful and biodiverse ecosystems. We may learn to gather energy like a leaf or weave fibres like a spider, design ventilation systems based on the structure of a termite mound or base a roof design on the structure of a cauliflower like the Core at the Eden Project:

> *The natural world provides an immense database of designs that can inspire creative thoughts. For instance, butterfly scales produce their optical effects via effects such as diffraction, multi-layer interference, scattering and fluorescence, all of which are known to the scientific community. However, what is interesting is the way they combine these effects in seemingly random ways that would not necessarily occur to the designer. It is important to recognize the valuable contribution made by engineers of all kinds in helping the biologist and the biophysicist to unravel the design principles behind the natural world. It is also the synergy between these disciplines that will provide the means of increasing our understanding of what nature does and being aware of advantages as well as limitations towards delivering sustainable buildings. Rich rewards lie in a variety of established and emerging technologies, not only in taking the design rules and paradigms offered to us by nature's systems, but also trying to take advantage of some of its self-assembly processes, self-repair processes and optimum use of sensors and monitoring of our environment. Sustainable building components are waiting to be discovered and adapted from nature's designs. (Godfaurd et al, 2005, p 327)*

Cost-effective ecological homes need not use complicated technologies; the selection of low embodied energy and non-toxic materials, combined with energy- and water-efficient design, should easily help produce a healthy building that has a relatively low environmental impact. Using local materials and labour wherever possible could reduce construction costs, at the same time providing local employment and contributing to the development of a sustainable skills base. If buildings are orientated towards the sun, avoiding wind and frost pockets, together with appropriate planting, pond construction reflecting light, correct glazing ratios and the inclusion of thermal mass to reduce temperature fluctuation, then comfortable working and living environments can be created. The co-evolution of social and cultural expectations with new technologies is discussed by Shove (2003). She notes that people today feel comfortable with an indoor temperature of around 21–22°C and that, although there are variations to do with climate, habit and economics, what is interesting to remember is that in 1970 the average indoor temperature in UK homes was around 13°C. We tend to wear fewer clothes indoors and expect to do so; in hot weather many people like to have air conditioning in the home and in the car. We expect to feel comfortable, and feeling comfortable is culturally and temporally relative. We take more showers and baths, like freshly laundered clothes everyday and use a lot of water in the process. About 70 per cent of domestic water consumption in the UK is used for cleaning, putting a premium on energy consumption. It is well known that in conventional buildings over half the domestic energy use is for either heating or cooling. Consumption is rooted in everyday practice and more sustainable living needs to be rooted there too.

I spoke with one of the senior partners of a firm of Devon-based green architects, Gale and Snowden, who have won awards for their community buildings and housing developments. They design new schools, training centres and museum buildings as well as ecologically refurbishing existing buildings. They work with both the private and public sectors and keenly believe green building and design illustrate what is possible and desirable, can influence informal learning processes and can shape pro-environmental behaviour. The Oak Meadow social housing development in South Molton consists of 35 dwellings – 23 houses and 12 flats – and won the Green Apple and the Devon Environment Business Initiative Awards for Sustainability and Sustainable Construction in 2003 and 2004 respectively. The development has attracted significant local and national media attention and public policy interest. Built to very high green specifications, the design brief achieved a BREEAM (Building Research Establishment Environmental Assessment Method) rating of Very Good, providing a template and catalyst for future social housing projects. The eco-design maximizes passive solar gain, passive cooling, energy efficiency, use of daylight, low-use water appliances and rainwater collection. Hard interior surfaces throughout prevent the breeding of dustmites. The use of organic paints and waxes and sustainable materials with low embodied energy, timber window frames, radial wiring in bedrooms avoiding electromagnetic fields, and bicycle sheds and organic garden composters are also provided. David Gale spoke of the immense potential of ecological design and development, if executed sensitively:

> *I think you can do development and integrate it into ecology and make things better. You can go around the countryside and ask, 'Is this nice countryside or it the most polluting industry we have – monoculture fields everywhere using lots of fertilizers and pesticides?' You can have a development, which is better than having a field which is just being used for rapeseed or something and have more plant life, more animals, more carbon dioxide exhaustion and more people living in it as well if they are integrated*

properly. At the moment, 'development' has a certain connota-
tion. The opposite is designing with natural systems and
designing people into the ecology of the planet. We work with
ecologists and permaculturalists to enhance what naturally lives
and grows on the sites. People are biological beings like every-
thing else, so there is no reason why we can't work our inputs
and outputs to be cyclical and work better. (interview with
author)

Oak Meadow is an attractive and impressive development although there have
been a few problems, partly the result of the building contractors and sub-
contractors not fully understanding the requirements of the green design brief.
Their knowledge and skills at that time were possibly not always up to the job
– some skills updating was certainly needed – leading to problems with grey
water recycling, higher than anticipated water bills because the contractors
fitted power showers by mistake, the installation of inappropriate photo-
voltaics, which have made some of the built-in cool larders not as cool as they
might have been, and delays in the original construction due to the difficulty of
sourcing certain products. The Sustainable Living Co-ordinator of the Devon
and Cornwall Housing Association, responsible for the management of the
estate, told me that some of the units were not constructed fully in accordance
with their green design specifications because of cost factors. Britain, even in
eco-friendly Devon, is still behind many other countries like Germany, Sweden
and Denmark in sustainable construction. However, on the subject of Oak
Meadow and another project, the Woolsery Village Hall, David Gale assured
me that ecological design has the potential to change people's lives, to encourage learning by offering examples and demonstrations of not only what is
possible, but what is better:

There is a couple who live at the end [of the development] who
have said living here has actually changed, completely uplifted,
their lives. And that is why we are here. That's what we want to
do. It not just to make buildings ecological, it's for people as well
– healthy design for the planet and people... This community hall
– the community wanted a low-running-cost building and they
wanted it to be environmentally sensitive. The community has
put up a big plaque explaining how it all works – inside-out
buildings, blockwork on the inside and the insulation on the
outside so there is the thermal mass and resistance to the
footballs. They have done it themselves and they are quite proud
of it... What we tend to do with our community projects is use
local skill and labour as well as local materials [where possible],
then the people living there have more ownership of the building.
The local economy is reinforced by spending money for local
skills and so on. So for this community project, which was lottery
funded, we found out very early on from the community members

who and what people could do in terms of helping with the build-
ing fabric and so we used local joiners and cabinet-makers on the
reception desk, lockers and changing areas. Sounds small but all
these little things add up, particularly if you can use local timber.
You then have at least some of the lottery money staying in the
community rather than going off to an outside contractor. (interview with author)

Not everyone living in Oak Meadow wishes to demonstrate exemplary sustainable lifestyles, though many residents have changed their attitudes and values
at least in part through living there. The design of the dwellings offers the
appropriate affordances, but for this to develop further, other factors, including personal values, desires and a positive experience nurturing ongoing
commitment, are needed as reinforcements. You don't have to be green to live
in Oak Meadow but you might start to go green when living there. Alison, a
single mother with two young children, had previously lived in a flat above a
shop and had already been concerned to turn appliances off when not in use,
to pass things around and to recycle, but living in Oak Meadow has been
genuinely transformative:

For us it's fantastic. Brilliant partly because where we were before
was draughty, in a flat above a shop, no garden, things like that,
not just connected with it being eco-friendly but everything. The
bills are cheaper, the house is warm, the children are happy and
we are healthier. Me and Michael are both asthmatic and that has
been better. We have had the odd stint of it but nothing very
much, nothing like we had before. It's made a huge difference.

For me it's nice because I have two little boys – a four- and a
five-year-old – and its going to be a way of life for them. They
are going to grow up knowing we recycle. I mean they do it
already – this goes into the recycling, this in the compost bin. It's
a natural way of life for them. It's not like it's been forced on
them or anything. Just like second nature for them to do it, to
turn off the light. It's never going to be a question in their mind.
It's partly a budget thing and partly that's the way we are –
passing things on, not just taking things down to the recycling.
(interview with author)

Although some of the residents had known each other before moving in, the
housing association invited new residents to a meeting before they took posses-
sion to kick-start the getting-to-know-you process. The seating plan of the
meeting room replicated the spatial location of the new estate, so people sat
near their new neighbours. The fact that the development was special facilitated an emergent sense of community, reciprocal social relationships
exemplified and reproduced in many small ways – babysitting, putting out
each other's recycling bins, taking turns to take the children to school, children

playing together in a neighbour's garden and households sharing home-grown vegetables produced in their own small gardens. Before moving in each household was offered a tree by the association, and that too could be traded. Alison remembered how her neighbours were 'gutted' when they realized they had given her their cherry tree. Alison again:

> *I like growing my own vegetables. It was quite amazing really. We moved in December so we thought the first year we won't have much but we had cabbages for a good few months, we had two small crops of potatoes and there was a lot of sharing as well. Gill was often popping over with lettuces and carrots and things, which also do well for my rabbit and guinea pig. I do like the community and there is certainly a group of people on this estate that are well into 'yeah, pass this along, home-grown food'. I like having home grown food because it's cheaper and because its nice and because it makes you think 'we did that'.* (interview with author)

What living on the estate seems to have enabled is a normalization of eco-friendly behaviour both for those who were previously disposed to this way of thinking and living and for those who were not. Recycling water is normal. Although family members may take regular baths, the water is now shared. Although some people still put their power showers fully on, some reflection on what this means regarding what is both 'normal' for Oak Meadow and environmentally acceptable means many householders choose not to. Many people ensure their eco-efficient washing machines are only used when there is a full load. This is normal. The technology allows this choice to be made and reflective learning informs how and why this choice should be made. There may be more than the once traditional weekly wash, but it seems there are far fewer than the 274 per annum average for UK households (Shove, 2003). And once changes are made they can be repeated; they can constitute a different way of living without having to cross the line and be seen as alternative, odd, different, eco. Thus certain aspects of green consumer behaviour may be hardwired into the home; it is still possible to ally oneself with general standards of thermal comfort and cleanliness and be green. Alison sums it up:

> *Quite honestly, if I was loaded and I was going to build my own place, this is what I would love. It's my sort of thing. I think we do have a duty to protect the planet. It doesn't take an awful lot to do just that little bit extra. So for me, it's fantastic because I can do it and have it basically handed to me on a plate. If anything it makes me feel a bit special. I'm very lucky really that I've got one of these houses. Before I came here I did try to remember to turn lights off and put lids on saucepans and things like that but living here has just made it easier. It's just like an obvious thing to do.* (interview with author)

Figure 4.2 *Oak Meadow, South Molton, Devon: 'Quite honestly, if I was loaded and I was going to build my own place, this is what I would love'*

Some other residents, perhaps not quite so predisposed as Alison, have also been persuaded by their houses to think and act differently. Dorothy and Ken live in a house with three children and feel that everyone in the neighbourhood 'gels together'. There is a generalized trust symbolized by the comment of one resident that she would trust her house key with any one of her immediate neighbours. Living at Oak Meadow is both special (thanks to local media coverage) and normal. Dorothy put it to me clearly:

> *I think a lot of people thought that just because you had one of these houses you had to change everything about you. No. This is my home. I have to have it for me. I'm not going to do it just because someone says you have to. No carpets – that's fine. I love the floor, no problem. Love the floors.* (interview with author)

Living at Oak Meadow has subtly but positively affected everyday routines without any sense of intrusive or disturbing change, so that after a short while it is now other, less green, people who seem different, lazy or uncaring. Cultural norms and values have shifted and meanings have altered. A green community isn't a just green or alternative community but a decent one, a responsible, a pleasant and a desirable one. Other areas seem different too, and these feelings are shared and create a sense of pride and satisfaction, of belonging and togetherness, of being different but necessarily so. Dorothy again:

> *I think you do change. I have changed. I think more about what I'm doing, like chucking things away. Well, I have a big family and when you're preparing vegetables, you have a lot of potatoes, so I put the peelings out in the compost bin. I think you are just who you are. It just becomes normal, yeah. Lots of my friends say 'oh, I can't be bothered to tip that in the bucket' and I say 'but why? because really that's all it is'. A lot of people want to come in and see what they're like. From the outside a lot of my friends thought they looked like Trago Mills, like sheds. This is what they've said but when they come in it's like, 'oh my God, it's lovely'. It's just fun living here, natural fun.* (interview with author)

The UK Housing Corporation, which finances the construction of many new affordable homes, intends that all new build in its multi-million pound 2006–08 investment programme will meet the *EcoHomes* 'Very Good' standard. This will undoubtedly mean many more builders, construction firms, architectural practices, planners, building engineers and others needing to learn new skills and techniques and acquiring knowledge about a range of sustainable building materials. Demonstration projects like Oak Meadow, BedZed, various eco-homes (especially those featured on television), the work of Eden and, particularly, organizations like the Somerset College of Arts and Technology, a Centre for Vocational Excellence in Sustainable Construction, and its Genesis Project (see Chapter 7) will become extremely significant in shaping and delivering learning about sustainable technologies and building practices.

Many aspects of residents' everyday life that formerly went unrecognized in their practical consciousness have been brought to the fore, deliberated upon and developed on the estate. A community is forming that offers residents the opportunity to live at least certain parts of their lives more consistently with what Borgmann termed 'focal practices'. This may be strengthened with the formation of an Eco Team led by the Sustainable Living Coordinator and a very enthusiastic estate officer who, as she told me, works 'insidiously'. If people complain about their electricity bill she suggests a way of dealing with this is to lower their thermostat a degree or two, saving money, reducing energy consumption and doing a little bit more for the planet in the process. In early 2006 Global Action Plan's (GAP's) 'Action in the Home' initiative was started – residents monitor their waste, consumption and travel to be more aware of the ecological impact of their actions and work towards further greening their lifestyles. I attended Oak Meadow's first two Eco Team meetings held early on Friday evenings in January and February and witnessed a sincere engagement with the project from members of ten or eleven households. Many of these individuals were already aware of environmental issues, resulting largely from living on the estate, so I felt that if any Eco Team could be successful then most likely this one would be. In the community building, we saw extracts from a GAP DVD on waste and recycling, discussed our own behaviour – How much do we throw out? How much what do we recycle? – and listened to a brief talk from council officer Nick Scott on recycling. Nick, who has written easy-read guides on reducing, reusing and recycling waste, visits schools and community groups showing what can be done and how. We were shown a large plastic composting bin, a demonstration wormery with a Perspex front and a local authority DVD featuring Nick dressed as a scarecrow explaining the joys of household recycling. The learning was relaxed, discursive, situated, purposeful, social and fun. The aim was to make a difference and ultimately to demonstrate to others living in Oak Meadow that it is possible to be more green but still normal.

Architecture and technology enables certain things to happen, but ultimately you have got to do, and want to do, things yourself. It is certainly true that architects can design and have designed small communities and indeed whole cities or city regions and that not all have lived up to the philanthropic or utopian ideas (or fantasies) of their designers. Twentieth-century urban history is replete with stories of old slums being cleared away and shiny new ones being built in their place only to be themselves demolished a couple of decades later. It is also true that many buildings, new and old, are notoriously energy inefficient and totally unsustainable. The problem is compounded by the fact that today the majority of the world's population are urban, exurban or suburban dwellers. Nevertheless, this living environment is also a learning environment. Our lived experience shapes our everyday routines and practices. Our urban, suburban or rural lifestyles distinguish us from others, giving us a sense of who we are and even where we may belong. Our lived experience is the raw material of our own personal and social learning about (un)sustainability, and without a doubt access to nature, to open green space, is a fundamental human need without which the urban dweller is likely to experience a deterioration in health and well-being. Ecological design of schools and classrooms of the future can also improve student achievement and the quality of the school experience. Over twenty years ago the Waterloo Schools Counties Board in Ontario, Canada, set up the first environmentally controlled classroom built with natural materials, sealed concrete floors, wooden furniture, efficient air-filtration and purification, natural light, and windows that opened and used learning materials that were pure and natural. The effect on student achievement and behaviour was noticeable (Griggs, 2001, p110). The Scottish Executive has its own eco-school design programme motivated by the recognition that a healthy and ecologically sound learning environment facilitates learning and achievement. There are a number of eco-schools in Devon using the environment as an important resource for learning. What can happen in primary schools can happen in our own backyards and living rooms if we have the will and the capacity to make it so. Change happens. Let's make it happen.

LEARNING ECOLOGIES

The experience of green space, of nearby nature, is pleasing to the eye and other senses; it has a restorative function often helping to clear the head after a busy day or relieve feelings of stress and anxiety. The psychologists Kaplan and Kaplan identify the benefits aesthetic natural environments offer:

> *First, aesthetic natural environments give pleasure; they are satis-fying to experience. Second, such settings support human functioning. They provide a context in which people can manage information effectively; they permit people to move about and to explore with comfort and confidence. And, finally, such environments foster the recovery from mental fatigue. They permit tired individuals to regain effective functioning.* (Kaplan, 1995, p196)

Roof gardens are also becoming increasingly popular with planners, architects and urban inhabitants in North America, Japan and parts of Europe. Apart from the aesthetic pleasures they provide, roof gardens also absorb urban pollution, increase the energy efficiency of buildings by providing insulation, produce cooling in summer, absorb noise, create wildlife habitats and offer additional space for vegetable growing which could in turn reduce environmental damage by cutting down on the need for imported food and reduce rainwater run-off. Green roofs can absorb up to 80 per cent of the moisture and retain it. There are some interesting examples of roof gardens on both public and private buildings. The Ford Motor Company's Rouge Factory in Michigan boasts the largest roof garden, at 454,000 square feet and the CUE (Centre for Understanding and the Environment) building at the Horniman Museum in London has as its roof a living and evolving wildflower meadow. Also in London, companies that design and create roof gardens for private houses and flats are doing good business. For Worpole (2000) green spaces, particularly parks, offer privacy and escape from domestic demands and responsibilities, and although other, harder, (semi) public spaces can also generate feelings of belonging and even intimacy, there is no associated sense of guilt, as there may be on a therapeutic trip to a shopping mall, that one is not spending money on consumer goods when one should be. However, the meanings people attach to various places differ – a park or a public square may be a place for solitary reflection or for meeting people. An urban woodland may be desirable because it offers a connection to nature. Wilder urban places, for example former derelict sites or railway sidings, may encourage birds and animals to return, enhancing biodiversity and no longer being crudely perceived as waste ground. The protection of open spaces, the nurturing of a vibrant and convivial street culture, farmers' markets, safe places for walking and cycling and more environmentally friendly dwellings and refurbishments are public supports and places facilitating a more sustainable and healthier everyday life.

In the information age, argues Catherine Ward Thompson, urban open space, whether green or grey, is more important than ever:

> *Modern telecommunications and information technologies mean that our community is increasingly a 'virtual' one, based on friendships and shared interests regardless of the geography of individuals. But although we may have regular contact with friends who live thousands of miles away, we can also easily communicate with large numbers of local contacts. The internet has allowed groups to plan and organize events and open space use much more readily than ever before. Whether it is a rally against the World Trade Organization in Seattle, involving tens of thousands of people, or simply an informal game of Frisbee in the local park among friends, email and the mobile telephone allow such use of public open space to be organized very quickly, with very low overhead costs, and (as we have seen recently) very effectively. So, although the electronic revolution means we no longer need to go into the streets of our towns and cities to find out the news or to arrange to meet people and organize events, ... it does mean that we can now use those streets, squares and parks with much greater confidence that we will find what we want there, meet whom we want, be able to do what we choose. Given that we are social animals, and that we crave real contact with each other and with nature, perhaps public open space will be more, and not less, used in future than it has in recent decades.*
> (Thompson, 2002, p68)

The practices of community participation, democratic engagement, social communication and social relationships will undoubtedly be affected by the massive changes in information and communication technology (ICT) that are altering the nature of civic networks and social networking, pressure group campaigning, education, urban management, leisure, politics, the labour process and social inclusivity. The relationship between social capital and the internet is a complex one, as with sustainability more generally. For instance, although I have referred to community and social capital as being basically geographically located – rooted in actual space and place – considerable attention has also been focused on virtual communities and communities of interest that are not confined spatially or indeed temporally. Bordiga et al write:

> *What focus groups do suggest, however, is the intriguing possibility that extant community structure and levels of social capital may play an important mediating role in understanding the impact of internet access on social relationships and psychological wellbeing. Similarly, extant community structure and levels of social capital may also mediate the impact of internet access on the forms of individual and collective action in a community.*

> *Research on the personal and social motivations that dispose*
> *people to volunteer and sustain their volunteerism, for example,*
> *suggest that communities with strong social ties and connectivity*
> *may be more promotive of volunteerism and other forms of*
> *citizen participation than communities characterized by lower*
> *levels of social capital.* (Bordiga et al, 2002, p138)

The urbanist Kevin Lynch (1981) saw cities and urban areas not so much as an ecosystem but as an evolving 'learning ecology'. For Lynch, an ecological ecosystem is essentially made up of 'unthinking organisms' not conscious 'of their fatal involvement in the system and its consequences'. Ecosystems change and develop, reach maturity or a state of dynamic equilibrium, but they cannot be said to learn or initiate progressive developments. 'The inner experiences of the organisms – their purposes and images – are irrelevant; only their outward behaviour matters' (Lynch, 1981, p115). Within a human settlement people are conscious, capable of modifying their attitudes and behaviour, of envisioning a different future, of altering their way of doing things, of learning to see waste land as a reserve for wildlife. Human imagination, values, intentions, knowledge creation and information flows and the connection of inner experience with outer action all contribute to altering the conditions of possibility, of being flexible and adaptable, of organizing ideas and of successfully dealing with tensions, difficulties and conflict. For Lynch, a good human settlement is one that is characterized by a dynamic openness, accessibility, diversity, tolerance, adaptability and subsidiarity. Stability or recurrence is not something to be valued for itself or as a primary defining feature. If settlements are to become adaptable, tolerant and flexible, then the only way this can happen is if their inhabitants become adaptable, tolerant and flexible too. What people do in their neighbourhoods and communities, what constraints or freedoms they work with or within, will shape the nature of this learning ecology and people's learning within them. Although writing before the terms sustainability or sustainable development came into general use, Lynch's understanding of 'development' is worth reflecting on:

> *If development is a process of becoming more competent and*
> *more richly connected, then an increasing sense of connection to*
> *one's environment in space and time is one aspect of growth.*
> *Thus a good settlement is one which enhances the continuity of*
> *culture and the survival of its people, increases a sense of connec-*
> *tion in time and space, and permits or spurs individual growth:*
> *development, within continuity, via openness and connection.*
> (Lynch, 1981, pp116–17)

Failure to make these connections, to spur growth, leads to development that hardly warrants the name or at least to developments that are seemingly out of tune with time, space and other people. The recent 'development' in Ashley Vale, within the city of Bristol, is an example perhaps of a self-build project failing to realize its full potential of producing an ecologically sound and socially sustainable neighbourhood where local people retain full control of their aims and aspirations. Good self-build schemes should demonstrate the potential for people to work with each other to produce space and the basis for a society grounded in aesthetics and community rather than the usual apparatus of market exchange. Although there are good examples of this in both the affluent and non-affluent world, Ashley Vale offers a learning experience of another kind – an opportunity to learn how and why things can go wrong. This particular urban area is characterised by allotments, woods, wildlife and other green spaces, a city farm, some light industrial units, a culturally diverse population (some with 'alternative' lifestyles) and a range of urban amenities. In the late 1990s, to save this rural cityscape from a developer, a group of residents formed the Ashley Vale Action Group (AVAG), bought up some disused land with a view to selling plots for self-build and to a housing association to construct homes for the elderly. Many of the new self-built wooden houses now totally dwarf the older dwellings. The self-builders had a keener eye on the resale value of their new houses than values of aesthetic, ecological or social harmony, even though the self-builders did largely work with light and flexible timber frames to contain their environment impact. The planned homes for the elderly and new workspaces for local people have not, so far, appeared. Bristol City Council has argued that certain planning conditions have also not been met. So by 2005, some of the original residents were reported as feeling let down and angry with the whole project. Some members of the group possibly lacked the requisite project management knowledge and skills needed but did not know it at the time. Sarah Edghill, writing in *The Daily Telegraph* noted:

> All the criticism clearly stings. 'Initially, it made us angry... But most people are happy with what we've done and are right behind us. There are always individuals who complain, but they get heard only because they shout the loudest.
>
> 'We are building a community and we have tried damned hard. There are things I don't like about some of the new buildings, but we all do things differently. Overall, it's spectacular – certainly when compared with a Wimpey housing estate.'
>
> Meanwhile, building continues on the remaining houses, and AVAG hopes to convert the office block into workspace at some stage in the future. 'We were bound to make mistakes, we're only human,' says Ms Mackay [a founder member of AVAG], 'But it's been a learning experience for all of us. The whole point of being a community is that you learn to live together and put up with people's opinions and ways of doing things. We've gained so much from doing this that the little niggles aren't important.'
> (Edghill, 2005)

Successful community building is a highly connected learning process – a human settlement is, as Lynch said, a 'learning ecology'.

After coming in for some criticism over the Poundbury development in Dorset, which clearly articulated the Prince of Wales' views of good architecture and urban design, the Prince's Foundation for the Built Environment is involved in another project which is part of the UK Government's 'Sustainable Communities' vision. Based very much on ideas derived from American new urbanism, which is now unkindly associated with the towns of Seaside (used in the film *The Truman Show*) and the Disney Corporation's Celebration, both in Florida, the new 'sustainable community' of Upton in Northamptonshire has been designed and built according to codes drafted in consultation with local people. The aim is to make the new development people- and car-friendly, traditional in style but not a social or historical pastiche, with affordable housing visually indistinguishable from privately owned dwellings. UPVC windows and doors have been banned and TV aerials and dishes are discretely displayed only where appropriate. Although some architects and consultants have criticized the development – too much space for cars, rather cheap-looking interiors – local interest in Upton is increasing because the quality of both design and construction is better than many new housebuilding developments (Weaver, 2005), largely because genuine interest has been shown in the everyday lived environments people inhabit. However, although there may be elements of top–down benevolent paternalism, this has been offset by, and through, dialogue, consultation and communication, resulting in the usual tendency of designers to privilege planned space, being tempered by a necessity to reflect on the social lived space of the everyday, of people.

SPACES TO LIVE, SPACES FROM WHICH TO LEARN

As Lefebvre argues (1991b, p289), every social organization or society has a characteristic spatial practice, ie the close association between daily reality and urban reality, that offers an understanding of its values and domain assumptions – 'the space of a (social) order is hidden in the order of space'. When the rational and the abstract become real the possibility of violence becomes real too, since space is instrumental, 'the most general of tools'. It does violence to the everyday, as seen in Thamesmead, the Aylesbury and Heygate estates and possibly in Seaside, Celebration and Poundbury. This is because, for Lefebvre (1991b, pp38–9), societies produce space in two ways. First, conceptual 'representations of space' are designed or produced by scientists, planners, architects, urbanists, academics, and so on. Second, experiential space, 'representational spaces', the space of users, people, inhabitants – 'space as directly lived through its associated images and symbols ... the dominated space – and hence passively experienced space which the imagination seeks to change and appropriate' is formed. Representational spaces therefore overlay physical spaces and together shape and are shaped by economic and social forces, tensions and conflicts, or, for Lefebvre, capitalism and neo-capitalism. Nonetheless, there are implications attached to the dominance of representations of space over lived experiences of space, and these boil down to the marginalization of ordinary people, ordinary dwellers in the land, producing a subjectivity, a way of living and being, subject to a world conceived, designed, constructed and policed by others. Lefebvre writes:

> *The user's space is* lived – *not represented (or conceived). When compared with the abstract space of the experts (architects, urbanists, planners), the space of the everyday activities of users is a concrete one, which is to say, subjective. As a space of 'subjects' rather than of calculations, as a representational space, it has an origin, and that origin is childhood, with its hardships, its achievements and its lacks. Lived space bears the stamp of the conflict between an inevitable, if long and difficult, maturation process and a failure to mature that leaves particular original resources and reserves untouched. It is in this space that the 'private' realm asserts itself, albeit more or less vigorously, and always in a conflictual way, against the public one.* (Lefebvre, 1991, p362)

It is probably this conflict, together with the experience of alienation and/or physical deprivation, and which Lefebvre also writes of extensively, that has motivated the creation and occasional flourishing of utopian communities, eco-villages and communal living experiments (Pepper, 1991; Hardy, 2000). The best known of these in the UK is probably Findhorn in the north of Scotland, subject of a three-part Channel 4 television documentary in 2005 entitled *The Haven*. This programme attempted to examine the motivations and inspirations informing the community's establishment in the 1960s, the spirituality of its members and the democratic nature of its organization and governance. Inevitably there were scenes of community members hugging trees or holding hands and dancing in circles, but there were also scenes addressing issues relating to the aesthetic attractiveness and environmental necessity of green building and design and the contribution Findhorn has made to this practice (Talbot, 1995). Many members of alternative, intentional or utopian communities believe their way of life offers visions and practical examples of sustainable living, of sharing and supportiveness, of socially harmonious methods of organization and decision-making, possibilities of emotional and personal well-being, strong social relationships, a sense of belonging and a profound sense of place. Living in an intentional community is by all accounts not without its problems – and members tend to come and go – but these communities do offer values, practices and learning opportunities that may be necessary to, and constitutive of, a more socially and environmentally sustainable society generally. It is time for elements of the alternative to be mainstreamed.

I spoke with some members of the Beech Hill Community in Devon one cold but sunny Sunday morning, having originally intended to attend a whole volunteering weekend, which I was prevented from doing because of the story of modern life – pressures of work. Three volunteers joined the community that weekend to learn more, and perhaps to see if living in this intentional community was for them. The community members explained how decisions were arrived at through consensus at weekly meetings, how people shared domestic and building maintenance tasks, how an atmosphere of tolerance and reciprocity governed everyday actions and relationships at least while living in the community itself. The main building, a large farmhouse dating back to the seventeenth century, has communal kitchen and living room spaces. The members occupy their own rooms, which vary in size and are rented for a very small sum. The community was intentional in the literal sense of the word. Members lived there and lived their values because that was their intention, their goal. Theirs is a voluntary commitment, offering a stark contrast to the values and experiences of the world outside, so to join would, apart from needing the agreement of existing members, require a sharing of ecological and democratic values and a belief that such a mode of living was socially and personally fulfilling. As one potential new member said, joining would represent 'a leap of faith' because living within and as part of a communal unit would mean a step away from the individualist, consumerist and competitive lifestyle that most of us experience and reproduce in our own everyday actions. One community member remarked that to live in an intentional community 'you have got to like and want to get on with others, you have got to share and cooperate, but the benefits are real'. For whatever you put into the community, he went on, you get more out of the experience whether it be cooking a communal meal once every ten days and having nine other meals prepared for you or living in a splendid building that would have been impossible in any other context except one that involves having a substantial income. It was the feeling of being appreciated by others that community members said contrasted most strongly with the experience of social life, particularly work life outside, where whatever you do or however hard you work more is demanded of you with little or no recognition given in return. Work at Beech Hill is undertaken not for goods and consumer durables but to maintain a sense of community, a sense of purpose, to maintain individual and social well-being. It is perhaps the very fact that people do, can and have attempted to live in this way from the time of the Diggers (a seventeenth-century radical/anarchist group active during the English Civil War) and before that testifies to the enduring appeal of alternative values, lifestyles and possibilities. Members of Beech Hill and communities like it are at one extreme of the continuum, but like everyone else are nonetheless still tied to the mundane realities of having to earn a living to pay bills and adhere to planning regulations and constraints when building work needs to be done. These communities do, however, offer opportunities for others to learn how to be different, how to change and how to persevere.

Very different to Beech Hill is Dignity Village, situated on the outskirts of Portland, Oregon. This is an alternative community of another type. Formerly a mobile tent city, it was started in 2000 by some homeless people living in

---

Box 4.2 Beech Hill Community, Devon

Beech Hill Community is an international community of 19 individuals occupying a large rural manor house, outbuildings and about seven acres of land in mid Devon. Members do not have any particular religious, spiritual or political affiliation but try to live in a sustainable manner using wood-burning stoves to heat the property and are looking for ways to utilize alternative energy sources like biomass, wind and solar. Beech Hill Property Holdings Ltd (BHPH) owns the freehold of the property, grounds and most of the accommodation in the main house. Some self-contained units of accommodation have been sold leasehold to individuals and families and Beech Hill Community Co-op Ltd manages the property on behalf of BHPH.

Not everyone living at Beech Hill is a co-op member, although membership is preferred as members contribute work to the cooperative and make the decisions which affect the community's future. Co-op members congregate weekly in a general meeting, where decisions are arrived at by consensus. Sub-groups for gardening, building maintenance, administration and course centre are delegated authority to execute specific tasks. Each co-op member is expected to undertake work necessary to maintain the communal living environment and manage the property. All residents contribute to the household work that needs to be done as in any other home.

Some members work part-time outside the community in order to earn money to pay various bills. Being in a very rural setting, there is of necessity a car pool; most, though not all, meals are vegetarian; evening meals are usually communal. Most members get together each evening, for celebrations and on days when they all work together. In 2005 members' ages ranged from 12 to 61, with the children going to local schools.

The community has good contacts with neighbouring farmers and the local village, which enjoys the benefit of a local Composting Scheme based at Beech Hill, and members are part of our Local Exchange Trading System (LETS). The community hosts various courses and offers bed and breakfast to walkers using the Two Moors Way footpath as a way of generating additional income. It also holds occasional open days.

Source: Adapted from www.diggersanddreamers.org.uk/record_detail.php?eight=beechill

---

one of the most affluent and sustainable cities in America. When I visited in 2004 it looked like a shanty town or favela, with makeshift buildings, rudimentary facilities and unmet environmental health needs. More than anything this creation of a lived space, a spatial practice, is a response to and a social comment upon US material affluence, consumerism and inadequate social welfare provision. It is a self-managed community with a cooperative farm, independent of any official government support or aid. The men and women living in Dignity Village are creating their own cultural and physical space out of necessity and thereby regaining some control over their lives through sharing, cooperating and working together. They have been able to regain some self-respect and self-esteem by developing new practical skills and capabilities of democratic participation and decision-making. They also host craft courses in association with local schools. Villagers have created a safe, relatively secure, alcohol- and drug-free environment where members connect and support each other without experiencing the stigma they would do, and did, in the wider society. The village also prepares members to return to this wider society when they are ready. Motivated initially by need and supported by some members of a local university and other citizens of Portland, the village has attracted considerable academic and public attention. With plans for the community to go green and become a permanent model of a socially and ecologically sustainable community, Dignity presents itself as a learning opportunity for people on the outside. In its proposals for the future, villagers have stated:

> *Dignity is poised to become a unique prototype for synergistically addressing two critical social issues at once – homelessness and sustainable green development, issues that are normally addressed quite separately. Through a hands-on process of involvement, Dignity will enable Government agencies, social service providers, educational institutions and private citizens to exchange knowledge and resources directly in a context of learning and teaching that will produce social and environmental benefits for the whole society.*
>
> *From a 'green building' perspective, homeless people who have internalized a strong vision for creating a sustainable life/work environment are ideally situated to demonstrate to the larger, more conventionally-housed community how much can be accomplished using very little in terms of material wealth or resources. Somewhat ironically, this is true precisely because homeless people have already been conditioned – albeit through unfortunate necessity – to make the best use of the very limited resources at their disposal.* (www.outofthedoorways.org/proposal/ DignityProposal.html)

When I saw the proposals and architect's sketches laid out in 2004 on wet and muddy ground, the whole thing seemed highly aspirational, but then so is fashioning a more sustainable world. As Lefebvre would have remarked, signs of possibility are found in everyday places, and although Dignity is a space that is far from ordinary, everyday or routine, it is an existential response to dispossession, alienation and disenfranchisement. In Dignity, and elsewhere, everyday practical activities become the foundation for reflection, a critique and meditation on the unsustainability of everyday life in post-industrial, postmodern, globalized neo-capitalist society:

> *Above all we must demonstrate the breadth and magnificence of the possibilities which are opening out for man, and which are so*

really possible, so near, so rationally achievable (once the politi-cal obstacles are shattered) that this proximity of what is possible can only be taken for one of the meanings (painfully and fright-ening unconscious) of the famous 'modern disquiet', the anguish caused by 'existence' as it still is! (Lefebvre, 1991a, p229)

5

Social Learning and Community Action

This chapter explores a range of practices, activities and learning experiences involved in the building of sustainable communities. Topics discussed include environmental justice, social capital and 'backcasting', and specific examples of sustainable community development projects in the UK and Canada are examined. The chapter comprises sections on:

- Learning for environment justice;
- The Market and Coastal Towns Initiative;
- Community learning;
- Social learning in the Georgia Basin Futures Project;
- Bioregionalism; and
- Skills for Building Sustainable Communities.

LEARNING FOR ENVIRONMENTAL JUSTICE

Urban and rural deprivation have characterized and blighted many communities in the UK, US, France and other parts of Europe. The decline of heavy industries turning once lively industrial areas into rustbelts or heritage parks is quite common, and many of these areas have experienced multiple forms of deprivation. Frequently, ethnic minority groups, people on low incomes and single parents have suffered disproportionately from environmental degradation ranging from dog mess to organized fly-tipping and toxic pollution. Poorly maintained sink estates harbour ill health, drug problems, anti-social behaviour and high crime rates. These areas frequently lack playgrounds and open green spaces. Many are often located near polluting factories or waste or simply too close to noisy, unhealthy and dangerous roads. The elderly on these estates are likely to experience 'fuel poverty', which might lead to death from hypothermia in the winter because they cannot afford to heat their homes properly. The poor often eat less nutritious convenience foods, compounding health and behavioural problems. Research by Friends of the Earth (2001) revealed that 662 of the UK's largest factories were in areas where the average household income was less than £15,000, whereas only five were in areas of average household income of £30,000 or more. In 1996 the UK's biggest factories released more than 10,000 tonnes of cancer-causing chemicals. Many communities have therefore become engaged in economic, social, cultural and sustainable regeneration projects, some financed by regional and central government. For Eden, CAT and the Earth Centre, sustainable community development and regeneration is, or was, part of their wider brief. Friends of the Earth Scotland have made environmental justice a central concern in their national campaigning, successfully influencing the policies of the Scottish Executive in the process.

The 'Agents for Environmental Justice' project (Agents for Environmental Justice and Scandrett, 2003) employed popular education approaches and techniques to create community agents from activists worried about many issues affecting their communities – opencast mining, fish farms, quarrying, GM crops, poor housing, economic development and waste. The communities were supported by these agents, who as students in adult education were also learning to apply the insights gained from academic study in a curriculum jointly designed and negotiated by Friends of the Earth Scotland (FoES) and by educators at Queen Margaret University College in Edinburgh. The open studies programme at Queen Margaret offers modules in environmental justice, human rights, globalization, citizenship and many other related subjects, which could lead ultimately to a higher education certificate. Academic knowledge is taken out of the ivory tower and made relevant to the everyday life issues, struggles and needs of local people. As Scandrett, O'Leary and Martinez (2006, p22) write, 'The knowledge content of the learning is not simply disseminated, but rather produced from dialogues between the body of academic knowledge embodied in the University College, the campaigning of FoES, and the diverse skills and experience of people and their communities and organizations living with environmental injustice and engaged in struggles to overcome it.' In this way, realizing the aims of Gelpi (1979), lifelong learning becomes truly meaningful when contradictions and injustices are recognized as part of the adult curriculum and when, with the help of educators sensitive to these injustices and community needs, social action is taken to remedy them. Indeed, similar to the US experience, British law courts seem particularly inept at righting environmental wrongs, possibly because the people who suffer most from the environmentally irresponsible actions of big corporations and governments lack the skills, knowledge and support necessary to make their voices heard. The victims of the disaster at Union Carbide's chemical plant in the Indian town of Bhopal know this full well (Williams, 1998). Some communities in the developed world also suffer the consequences of environmental pollution and injustice, and not all community members are content to remain victims, as the Hollywood movie *Erin Brockovich* has so effectively dramatized. Indeed, one of the most famous examples of the struggle for environmental justice is that over toxic contamination in Love Canal, where a whole community, and one woman in particular, learnt how to organize and be heard (Livesey, 2003).

In the US, grass-roots environmental justice campaigners have noted that people of colour and the poor are more likely to suffer from environmental degradation than other groups. These activists, including some academics, have vigorously opposed unjust treatment by public bodies and large private corporations who seem to sacrifice human health for profit, expose people to harmful chemicals, exploit the vulnerability of disenfranchised communities, subsidize ecological destruction, create an industry around risk assessment and fail to adequately develop pollution prevention strategies. By contrast, the rich have always been able to afford cleaner and healthier environments. Bullard and Johnson (2000, p573) conclude that environmental and economic justice are closely entwined:

> *The poisoning of African Americans in Louisiana's 'cancer alley', Native Americans on reservations and Mexicans in the border towns have their roots in the same economic system, a system characterized by economic exploitation, racial oppression, and devaluation of human life and natural environment. Both race and class factors place low-income and people-of-colour communities at special risk. Although environmental and civil rights laws have been on the books for more than three decades, all communities have not received the same benefits from their application, implementation and enforcement.* (Bullard and Johnson 2000, p573)

This led Agyeman et al (2002, p78) to argue that:

> *[Sustainability] cannot be simply a 'green', or 'environmental' concern, important though environmental aspects of sustainability are. A truly sustainable society is one where wider questions of social needs and welfare and economic opportunity are integrally related to environmental limits imposed by supporting ecosystems.* (Agyeman et al, 2002, p78)

Bridger and Luloff (1999, p380) offer a useful review of the social and community dimension of sustainable development. For them, grounding the experience of sustainability in everyday lived realities renders the terms 'sustainable society' or 'sustainable world' meaningful to a wide constituency of people:

> *By shifting the focus on sustainability to the local level, changes are seen and felt in a much more immediate manner. Besides, discussions of a sustainable society or a sustainable world are meaningless to most people, since they require levels of abstraction that are not relevant in daily life. The locality, by contrast, is the level of social organization where the consequences of environmental degradation are most keenly felt and where successful intervention is most noticeable. And, of equal importance, there*

*tends to be greater confidence in government action at the local
level. The combination of these factors creates a climate much
more conducive to the kind of long-term political mobilization
implicit in the term sustainable development... Sustainable
community development may ultimately be the most effective
means of demonstrating the possibility that sustainability can be
achieved on a broader scale, precisely because it places the concept
of sustainability 'in a context within which it may be validated as
a process'. By moving to the local level, the odds of generating
concrete examples of sustainable development are increased.*

*As these successes become a tangible aspect of daily life, the
concept of sustainability will acquire the widespread legitimacy
and acceptance that has thus far proved elusive.* (Bridger and
Luloff, 1999, p380)

Social capital provides the means by which groups and individuals communicate, enter into dialogue, resolve conflicts, identify and solve problems, and realize collective and individual potential as agents of sustainable development. Just as we talk about ecological carrying capacity, perhaps there is a need, as Roseland (1998) suggests, to speak of the need to nurture and increase our 'social caring capacity'. Leonard and Onyx (2004, pp3–4) identify five basic elements of social capital:

1   **Interlocking networks of relationships** between individual and groups;
2   **Reciprocity** – the individual provides a service to others, or acts for the benefit of others at a personal cost, but in the general expectation that this act will be reciprocated sometime in the future;
3   **Trust** – a willingness to take risks in a social context based on a sense of confidence that others will act in mutually supportive ways;
4   **Social norms** that provide a form of informal social control that obviates the need for more formal institutionalized legal sanctions; and
5   **Collective efficacy** or **personal agency** within a social context – the development of social capital requires the active and willing engagement of citizens working together within a participative community.

The development of social capital, together with numerous public and private sector agencies, community groups, local government bodies, and elected officials, is frequently central to many urban and rural regeneration initiatives (Roberts and Sykes, 2000; Carley et al, 2000). Where these relationships of trust and reciprocity are found wanting, a great deal of work and leadership is required to nurture and facilitate any sense of social connectivity. This rarely happens by itself unless stimulated by an external threat, and even then, as many campaign groups will testify, success builds upon on an already existing social infrastructure, culture of participation and availability of skills and motivations. Robert Putnam and many other writers acknowledge the significance of formal and substantive equality (characterized as 'horizontal'

BOX 5.1 A SOCIAL CAPITAL FRAMEWORK

A social capital framework can be used to analyse the resources present in a community that are available for use in community development. It can identify strengths and weakness, or areas where intervention can improve the community's social capital resources. The framework we propose can also be used to evaluate the success of an intervention strategy. We suggest that a social capital framework to analyse community development, including adult education, should consider:

- The **balance between internal and external networks**. Bonding networks are a necessary but insufficient component of social capital. Networks extending outside the community are of two types: bridging networks (these could be with other communities or among professionals working in community development) and linking networks with people or institutions at other levels of power;
- The **presence and diversity of brokers** who are able to operationalize the bridging and linking networks;
- The **levels of self-confidence and self-esteem** of community members and **skills** in working together, including conflict resolution;
- **Norms** present in the community, especially norms of inclusion/exclusion and reciprocity; and
- The extent to which the community of analysis has **shared visions** for its future.

Source: Kilpatrick, Field and Falk (2003, p430)

---

relationships) as essential for effective organizational functioning and civic participation. There is some dispute, though, over whether the social ties between individuals need to be strong, and a distinction is often made between bonding and bridging social capital (Putnam, 2000; Woolcock and Narayan, 2000). Bonding social capital tends to be characterized by dense multifunctional ties and strong and generally localized trust, whereas bridging social capital is characterized by weak ties. Woolcock and Narayan argue that bonding social capital is an effective defence against poverty but less valuable for economic and social development – the difference between getting by and getting on. This is because connections between groups and organizations that need a higher level of overt reciprocity inevitably operate on lower levels of trust and may be largely instrumental. Portes (1998) notes that strong ties and social norms may enforce a conformity that militates against working with others, leading to a desire for a form of social exclusivity or even the reproduction of undesirable traits such as ethnic prejudice, political marginalization, suspicion and even unwarranted fear of others. The increased numbers of gated communities in the US, Europe, including the UK, South Africa and even China is arguably one manifestation of this (Romig, 2005).

Contemporary policy failures to engage people in political and civic affairs are seen by Putnam (2000) as caused by a decline in membership of voluntary associations that produce the social capital upon which participation and engagement relies. Relationships and networks of reciprocity, trustworthiness, obligation and perceived mutual benefit are key to the generation and maintenance of this social capital. Putnam's 1993 study of regional democracy in Italy suggests an important causal link between social capital and citizenship participation, political literacy and government efficiency and effectiveness. As James Coleman writes:

> *Social capital is an important resource for individuals and can greatly affect their ability to act and their perceived quality of life. They have the capability of bringing such capital into being. Yet because many of the benefits of actions that bring social capital into being are experienced by persons other than the person so acting, it is not in that person's interest to bring it into being. The result is that most forms of social capital are created or destroyed as a by-product of other activities.* (Coleman, 1990, p317)

THE MARKET AND COASTAL TOWNS INITIATIVE

The Market and Coastal Towns Initiative (MCTi) in the south-west of England is an example of an area-based community-led regeneration strategy building on and developing pre-existing social infrastructures and social capital networks. Significant development work is being undertaken, many skills and much knowledge developed, but the primary motivation is not to right an environmental or social wrong but to fashion a better environment in which to live and work. The project is partly funded indirectly by the state, through the South West Regional Development Agency (SWRDA). The aim is to build capacity among a cluster of private, voluntary and public sector organizations, groups and individuals who will identify goals, develop strategies, design action plans, identify indicators, secure funding, and monitor and evaluate progress for a variety of projects enabling various towns and their hinterlands to nurture their social, economic and environmental development over a 20- to 30-year period. This is quite a challenge and, at the time of writing, with the MCTi still in its infancy, success has been uneven. One group, which succeeded in bringing together representatives from a wide range of organizations, produced a detailed strategy by 2003 but failed to secure funding for any of its projects. This was because steering group members did not fully understand what projects would attract the necessary public or private funding and, partly, because members did not have the skills to negotiate, broker or 'lever' monies and support from key players. Failure, following on from more than a year of hard work, resulted in a gradual fragmentation of the community coalition and mutual social relationships of trust and reciprocity, with members looking once again to pursue their individual interests rather than jointly agreed aims. Growing suspicion of the Market and Coastal Towns Association (MCTA) set up by SWRDA to be responsible for supporting and guiding, but not funding, these community-led initiatives did not help either. At the final meeting the slow disintegration seemed complete: local stakeholders met with the MCTA and a professional facilitator, whose company had produced the how-to manual or MCTi sourcebook, but little progress was made. There were calls for directly funded project workers, whereas the MCTi process required the identification and training of 'community agents', local people appointed and paid a small sum to help their community implement the plan. These agents could have either administrative or developmental responsibilities, but, as the chair of this particular local group noted, these tasks would need time, skills, knowledge and probably contacts most local people did not have. The bridging capital and the learning opportunities, requisite skills and collateral knowledge, supportive leadership and social and community relationships that could have averted disappointment and disillusion were simply lacking. Indeed, the belief that this 'community-led' initiative would only secure funding if it conformed strictly to the economic criteria laid down by various funding agencies – criteria beyond the control of local people – was shared by many people whose experience of the process was quite extensive. One person told me 'the money is simply not there' for the things the community sees as important or necessary. The learning experience reinforced scepticism and feelings of powerlessness and civic apathy.

The Tiverton and Exe Valley group, working within the same MCTi parameters and geographically located adjacent to the one just described, started a little later and was able to learn from other group's mistakes. It could also draw on the time and expertise of a small number of very experienced, skilled and highly educated people from business, the voluntary and community sector, and higher education. A steering group was easily formed and initial 'seed' funding from the MCTA was secured to develop a range of activities, which encompassed a broadly based 'community event' held in a local hotel. Focus groups were organized to explore issues relating to the environment, agriculture and tourism, sport and recreation, transport and waste reduction, the community and voluntary sectors, health and housing, heritage and the arts, economy, commerce, information and communications technology, industry, energy, and education. The aims of the focus groups were to identify challenges and possible projects for future development, to evaluate the development potential of the particular core area, and to look for ways in which potential activities could link with those in other fields. These projects would then form part of the overall strategy and action plan, itself based on the accumulation and analysis of much data, information and local knowledge on the locality's economy, natural environment, degree of civic participation, skill levels, and so on. Fern Clarke, coordinator for the Tiverton and the Exe Valley MCTi, spoke to me of the massive amount of time, energy and commitment required just to keep the process moving forward. A geographer by training, a part-time higher education tutor by profession and a naturally gifted administrator who admits the need to continuously develop her ICT skills, Fern believes that the necessary learning comes from doing, that coordination is seeking connections and that leading is essentially identifying opportunities and finding common ground:

I try to attend as many of the focus group meetings as I can, not to massively input but simply to keep a watching eye on the way the discussions are going, and if projects emerge that look very promising but maybe could be inter-thematic, I can then pass information across to the appropriate focus groups and say 'this particular focus group is thinking of this particular idea and it will involve transport or it will involve agriculture or whatever and maybe you will want to be involved in that project in some particular way'. What we found last autumn was that the sport and recreation group came up with a very exciting project for a water activity centre on the Exe. That fits in quite well with Devon County Council, who are putting forward tourism as a very important economic aspect and identified a weakness in terms of watersports activities. So we are hoping that putting forward a project like that, it will get DCC backing. And that also involves, obviously, transport, as you have to get to this activity centre. If it is to be an income generator in mid Devon with knock-on tourism effects, one of the things the agriculture and tourism group came up with was the idea of reopening the Exe Valley railway route to cyclists and to walkers. And on that group we have [a person] whose son runs the Bickleigh narrow-gauge steam railway, which is very, very short at the moment but has the potential to be a big attraction. I'm almost acting as a broker and facilitator. If we can open the activity centre and the pathway and bring people up on the narrow-gauge railway, it will be great fun and will open itself up to a lot of tourists in mid and south Devon. We can then develop the activity centre with add-on projects like woodland walks, perhaps a playground area, a café, a centre where sports equipment can be stored, which could also benefit and be available to local people. I had no idea my role would develop like this but its great fun. (interview with author)

Leadership is not necessarily the preserve of one person but can be distributed throughout the community and based on the skills, experience, knowledge and enthusiasm of various members. This provides the social legitimacy and ratio-nale for taking on a leadership role, although often a specific individual, or a few motivated and committed individuals, are necessary to get things started. Leadership and organization are a necessary requirement for any successful community development or business venture. Fern, and a group of five or six others, all with extensive community or business experience, are central to the successful development of the Tiverton and Exe Valley MCTi. Their leader-ship, organization and learning of new skills and capacities have facilitated the emergence of a 'community of practice' through a sharing of information, experience and knowledge. Often this sharing, the development of relation-ships, and the recognition of tensions or differing interests occurred through

Figure 5.1 *The Market and Coastal Towns Initiative (MCTi), Tiverton, Devon: The 'community event', offering space and opportunity for dialogue, discussion and democratic participation*

the telling of stories about living in the locality, or on an estate, or of a personal or family experience. This verbal communication of everyday observations vividly articulated needs and frustrations – we all tell stories to explain things, to help understand ourselves, others and the environments we inhabit. On one visit to Oak Meadow a postman told me how he regularly sees people putting the wrong type of rubbish in the kerbside recycling bins. Dorothy told me the story of how her family had eaten the runner beans she had grown at the Christmas meal, expressing the sheer joy of growing your own vegetables. At the Tiverton community event and subsequent focus-group meetings, members told each other stories about farm incomes, local government bureaucracy, business ventures or dull meetings with parish councillors. People make sense of their experience through stories and, although it may seem odd that focus groups sometimes prefer story-telling to devising strategic aims, objectives, action points, business plans and project proposals, it is from these narratives that people form new social relationships. It is from stories, perhaps, that communities are formed and action evolves.

Of course some tales are better than others, more interesting or relevant, truer or more coherent, more consistent with the way people are or how the world seems to be. People have the rational capacity to evaluate stories, to make moral judgements and to use them to resolve issues, disputes and problems, but the conclusions reached are dependent on a number of factors: information sources, other people, technologies, cultural proclivities and predispositions, ignorance and wishful thinking. In the Introduction I started with my account of the flood in order to make sense of my experience as well as the experiences and actions of my neighbours. Journalists tell stories all the time in order to reach their readers. We sometimes paint pictures, draw parish maps or take photographs to make our stories meaningful to ourselves and others. Our yarns and anecdotes also tell a great deal about us to other people. John Forester (1999), a well-known American planner and teacher, has discussed the importance of stories in planning practice and notes that, although it is not always clear how we learn from stories in practice settings, or from friends, we can learn a great deal from them if we have a mind to. He identifies five points for consideration. First, we learn from friends because they tell us stories designed to matter to us through their empathy, thoughtfulness and familiarity with our lives, actions and experiences. Second, we learn from friends because we may be able to use their words as a way of making sense of our own interests, commitments or worries. They might help us 'see the light', or at least not miss the wood for the trees, and so help us realize what we are doing or being. Good friends can be critical because we trust their motives – they want to help. Third, we learn from friends particularly when they do not offer us glib simplistic solutions. With luck they may help us come to grips with difficult and complex situations by being pragmatic, practical and non-judgemental, except perhaps when we ask them to be otherwise. Fourth, we learn from friends because they help us think things over, reflect on our previous actions and maybe look to the future by reminding us what really matters. They might help us focus our actions and activities. Finally, we learn from friends and focus groups because we are often presented with a world of shared interest, concerns and passions. Friends are facilitators in one sense and leaders in another. They are trusted and normally respected individuals. Working in a community setting, one therefore hopes that one will be working with friends as well as colleagues and neighbours. Forester writes:

> *The type of friendship from which we should consider learning is therefore not the friendship of long affection and intimacy, but the friendship of mutual concern, of care and respect for the other's practice of citizenship, their full participation in the political world. This is the friendship of appreciation of the hopes and political possibilities of the other, the friendship recognizing, too, the vulnerabilities of these hopes and possibilities.* (Forester, 1999, p36)

The realization of important friendships, hopes and possibilities frequently occurs within ritualized social gatherings as well as community development initiatives where dialogue and deliberation feature prominently. Within these cultural spaces, people learn from what others say, from what others do or have done, and from the way they say and do things. Actions may not always be exemplary, but a great deal of learning can be derived from a partial success or even a complete failure. Often learning is incidental, picked up from details that may not seem terribly important. A group member may feel reluctant to speak because of the seemingly trivial nature of the issue or experience shared. These details, as Forester (1999, p133) notes, are 'often claims about value', about what needs protection, what is cared for or what we are afraid of. Brainstorming in groups, writing down concerns or issues on Post-it notes or flip charts, and undertaking SWOT (strengths–weaknesses– opportunities– threats) exercises bring focus to values and *re-mind* people of what they consider important. These participatory rituals of story-telling, listening, brainstorming, identification and 'feeding back' may function as transformative learning experiences in three ways: they may produce or reproduce a public sense of self or more clearly articulate a specific social identity; they may serve to concentrate group attention on processes of selection or of collective decision-making; and they may enable group members to organize or raise value claims, for example the need to preserve the countryside, to provide employment for young people, to encourage eco-friendly tourism, to wire up businesses or to involve the churches. Learning, therefore, can be cognitive, affective and collectively rooted in local knowledge and the everyday concerns of everyday living. These meetings can build capacity and widen horizons, can offer a participatory experience, a sense of empowerment and a taste of a sustainable democratic process, although obviously its long-term realization depends upon many other factors – relationships of power and political decision-making, economic and other vested interests, horse-trading, argument and perseverance, and plain bloody mindedness (Forester, 1999; Flyvbjerg, 1998). On the importance of process, Forester writes:

> *As ritualized groupings and conversations occur with conventions and rules of their own (even those of ordinary small talk in a coffee break), participants find themselves not only bound by these rules but enabled by them as well. Not only are certain forms of formal argument and posturing precluded at times, but other forms of listening and being heard become possible in these new arenas of meetings of parties and, in some cases, previous disputants. So too do seductive information technologies (interactive computing, multimedia systems and sophisticated mapping programs, for example) pose both threats and opportunities, for different forms of representation enable different forms of interaction and deliberation, different forms of emotional responsiveness, memory, insight, and perception.* (Forester, 1999, p149)

This is not to say that every type of community or neighbourhood meeting is equally valid or productive – some are hijacked by individuals who are able to 'shout the loudest' or by just 'sounding off'. What is important here is the need and capacity to listen and be wary of the unpredictability of the experience, or, as a successful business-woman kept reminding people, 'we have one mouth and two ears, which means you should do twice as much listening as talking'. Rarely do people know what a group is 'bound to come up with' in advance, whatever they might say. Goals and ideas are frequently identified and clarified through dialogue and discussion, and when this happens a palpable sense of achievement emerges. Each group will develop its own dynamic, and whether passionate or rational, focused or unfocused, the deliberative process brings people together in a common purpose. I spoke with one participant at the community event a couple of months after the discussions and asked her what she felt now. Laura, a keen environmentalist, took some time and replied thoughtfully:

> *People were enthusiastic about the event, but I think people were very easily sidetracked to follow their own hobbyhorses. So I tended to be rather fragmented unless there was somebody cracking the whip and bringing everybody back into line. I'm not sure how much was actually reached in the way of a result. A lot of things were talked about, but I think it will take a long time for someone to make any sort of decisions. All the people in the 'voluntary' group I was in had vast experience; they were older ladies and they had experience of working within that area. They were all looking at it from different perspectives, which was a good thing, I guess. They all seemed to want to bare their souls and get something off their chest personally, which I didn't feel was moving the issue forward generally. I suppose it all depends on whether there was a goal to be achieved fairly rapidly or whether it was just like-minded people getting together to talk things over. I felt it should have been more focused perhaps. A lot of them seemed to go off on complete tangents, on things which seemed to have affected them personally in their own work lives. Putting things on Post-its and sticking them on a wall was good because it focused people on putting forward succinctly ideas which were informed and sparked by the group and their talking together, mulling over ideas, and I know a lot of people did work very quickly to do that. Some ideas seemed very valid and stirred imagination, interest and excitement. It certainly motivated people. I found it interesting but I was a bit out of my depth. I didn't have the knowledge and experience to impart very much. I felt I was more of a listener than a speaker. The 'housing' group was more of a free for all – people had their own ideas but nobody seemed to be a particular expert in any field in the group I was with. So it was more general. I felt that group was in a way more interesting because they focused on the issues and went through an agenda. Some of them worked in housing, but they were so absolutely passionate about it that they were able to get through more things – an odd thing really.* (interview with author)

BOX 5.2 PROJECT IDEAS FROM COMMUNITY CONSULTATIONS AND FOCUS GROUP DISCUSSIONS OF THE TIVERTON AND EXE VALLEY MCTI, SEPTEMBER 2005

Housing and Design

- **Vision:** To encourage development of accessible, quality community facilities within housing developments that: raise local levels of skills, encourage and support parenting skills, encourage awareness of the shape of sustainable communities and personal responsibilities within those communities, and knit members of the communities together to give a community identity to the area;
- **Project:** Importance of local community buildings and their maintenance for maintaining healthy communities – project to design and build a new roof and first floor office facilities for Sunningmead Community Centre (original flat roof will need replacing within five years; office accommodation can be let, providing income to maintain centre);
- **Project:** Graffiti wall area – possibly by youth drop-in centre in market car park – to translate antisocial behaviour into skills;
- **Project:** Involve youth in considering the design and environmental impact of the built environment;
- Future use of sustainable building materials;
- Use all existing buildings before erecting new;
- Parenting classes – support for young parents;
- Village halls as focal points for community – crèche/activities/communication. Communities must have 'reason to be';
- Design the community not the house;
- Think in terms of balanced communities (number of jobs matched to labour supply, matched to housing, matched to community and service facilities);
- Try to design communities to minimize commuting;
- Important to have housing in the centre of the town so that the centre is a living community;
- Provide public open space – for people and wildlife within towns and villages;
- Retain and take care of public parks;
- Explore renewable energy – solar power on all new buildings;
- Build sustainably – buildings to last;
- More green space and community facilities within housing developments;
- Protect open space – use redundant buildings as basis for small redevelopment housing;
- Build smaller sustainable developments with open spaces that are protected;
- Use brownfield sites first;
- No more development without matching employment potential for increased number of residents;
- Limit multiple ownership of 'affordable' housing, ie ensure access to affordable housing ownership for the needy;

- Plan and provide a flood prevention scheme for Bickleigh;
- Convert barns in villages to housing;
- Halt the decline of green space in Tiverton;
- Improve the appearance of Tiverton;
- Improve the public toilets;
- Develop the old hospital in Tiverton;
- Provide a sustainable infrastructure to match sustainable employment; and
- Ensure that all housing developments provide quality sustainable housing.

COMMUNITY LEARNING

The EcoTeam experience, like the development of the focus-cum-action groups of the Tiverton MCTi, may also be seen as representing emergent 'communities of practice'. These communities may take a variety of forms but they all share a common basic structure. For Wenger, MacDermott and Snyder (2002, p29) these include:

- **Domain** – providing a common ground, purpose, value and sense of identity which both guides learning and gives meaning to actions;
- **Community** – creating the 'social fabric of learning', fostering social interactions, and relationships of trust, respect and reciprocity; and
- **Practice** – a set of frameworks, ideas, tools, information, styles, language, stories and documents that community members share.

Knowledge and resources develop, which allows the community to deal with its domain, guiding the questions, enabling (most) members to distinguish the trivial from the important, and helping with the organization of information, knowledge and understanding. As Wenger, MacDermott and Snyder note (2002, p32), 'the most successful communities of practice thrive where the goals and needs of an organization intersect with the passions and aspirations of participants'. And for participants to constitute a community, they may interact with one another in real or virtual time–space. Even a website can provide an identity and effectively project an image to others outside the group, even though, of course, a community is more than just a website. Communities need not be homogeneous, or even intimate, but they do need to hold certain things in common, including a capacity to undertake leadership roles when circumstances demand. If the community grows and develops, if the eco-team operates effectively and creatively, participants will stay together and others may join because membership offers some leadership, mutual benefit and gain. It creates goodwill and social capital, which is a predisposition for openness, cooperation and collaboration, communication, problem-solving, innovation, accountability, experimentation and social learning. Wenger et al state that successful practice building accompanies successful community building, in which members must also gain a sense of both collective and individual achievement.

Taking stock of present and past actions and achievements, of seemingly everyday – even trivial – conversations, is an important part of the social learning process among families, community groups and businesses. Discussions with a spouse about turning off the light, with the housing association's estate officer about reducing the household fuel bills, with a colleague about car sharing, or with a neighbour about purchasing locally produced food or putting the right type of waste in the appropriate coloured recycling bin could lead to developing predispositions and eventually habits of critical and evaluative reflection on conduct (Moon, 2004) that could become a basis for wider sustainable social practices:

> *Many of the most valuable community activities are the small, everyday interactions – informal discussions to solve a problem, or one-on-one exchanges of information about a tool, supplier, approach or database. The real values of these exchanges may not be evident immediately. When someone shares an insight, they often don't know how useful it was until the recipient reports how the idea was applied. The impact of applying an idea can take months to be realized. Thus, tracing the impact of a shared idea takes time and attention.* (Wenger, McDermott and Snyder, 2002, p60)

Reflecting is probably the hallmark of effective learning and is, for Jonathan Gosling, an international expert in leadership, an essential prerequisite for being a good leader and sustainability practitioner. He told me:

> *The beginning has to be reflectiveness. The basis for improving one's leadership ability, particularly with adults who have had a fair bit of experience, is reflecting on that experience, noticing what one does, noticing the impact one has, noticing the kinds of exercises of power you are prepared to go along with, or you find yourself contributing to. What really counts is noticing what really counts, the impact of what you do, how you take a stand if you need to. You don't really change the habits of a lifetime unless you develop the reflectiveness to look at that. That's the starting point.* (interview with author)

Gosling also noted that sustainable community development involves being able to learn from each other through stories, including those of how leaders in various fields have dealt with common problems. Life itself should be treated as a never-ending story. He said that apart from having the skills and capacity to collaborate with others, to be active and get things done, to have or develop 'worldly mindsets', and to be analytical, it is also important to see oneself as part of a bigger picture, as part of the continuing ebb and flow of social life and the many experiences it generates. We can perhaps learn much from perceiving the world historically or as an ongoing soap opera – a contemporary media-generated metaphor most of us can relate to and understand:

Telling stories is such an important way to do things. One of the things that has bedevilled community activism is trying to see community actions as projects and manage them as projects. OK, we are going to engage in this activity in the community, like resolving disputes, and we'll organize our dispute resolution service by bringing together this party with that party who are arguing together. We'll bring them together; they'll come to some agreement. We'll monitor it for a few months and then the case is closed and they're gone. That is really taken from a professional-ized case-orientated way of working. It looks very logical from the point of view of the people providing the mediation service, but from the point of view of the people who are in dispute this is just one episode in ongoing community affairs and activities. At some point you might be in outright dispute and you get media-tion, but then other things happen in life and life carries on. Case resolution is like a one-act play, but real life is much more like a soap opera. It goes on and on and on, never ending, with a bunch of interweaving different plot lines, and certain things come to the fore at some point, and then others. So one of the questions regarding community activism, community work and particularly conservation is: How can one sustain engagement with a number of different parties in a way which is much longer term than simply chunking it into specific services, operations and cases? I think that is a tough challenge, and one of the things that helps people to sustain that kind of engagement is having a sense of repose, a way of saying 'well, OK, that was a win, that was a bit of a loss, let's carry on'. Not being too moved, upset or excited, but being able to maintain a steady engagement, a steady pace of things over time. (Jonathan Gosling, interview with author)

SOCIAL LEARNING – THE GBFP

One approach to learning how to create a sustainable future in a defined geographical location has been outlined by John Robinson, who has devel-oped, and applied, the method of 'backcasting'. Based on an approach known as 'futures scenario building', which avoids the hazards of predicting the future in a world characterized by risk, uncertainty and complexity, this technique involves a form of dialogic and social learning. It has been used successfully in Canada, specifically within the bioregion surrounding Vancouver, and could be applied equally successfully elsewhere. Robinson writes:

The major distinguishing characteristic of backcasting is a concern with how desirable futures can be attained. It involves working backwards from a particular desired future end-point or set of goals to the present, in order to determine the physical feasibility of that future and the policy measures that would be required to reach that point. (Robinson, 2003, p842)

Largely normative in orientation, with possibilities of combining qualitative and narrative approaches with 'harder' quantitative methodologies, backcasting as practised by Robinson and his team from the University of British Columbia in the Georgia Basin Futures Project (GBFP) has also involved the participation of various non-academic stakeholders in an interactive research process. The aim is to ensure the social acceptability of the various trade-offs required in the design and potential realization of specific 'true to life' models of regional sustainability. It therefore involves the recognition and possible assimilation of the local knowledge, values and preferences of many people. The interactive research process is a clear example of social learning that is open and often unpredictable, aimed at cultural and moral developments and changes in social consciousness and institutional and socio-cultural relationships. Engaging with indicators allows people to participate in a social debate about desired futures whilst continually refining their understanding of what sustainability is all about. Robinson's perspective on sustainability envisions it as emerging from participatory and deliberative processes essentially about the type of future people want – desired futures based on a developing recognition of the inter-relationship between the ecological, social and economic. It is about people using their own experience to talk politics – understood in the broadest sense, not just voting for a political party at an election – and not, as Eliasoph (1998) documents, shying away from difficult or potentially controversial issues. It is through discussion and debate that differences can be settled, learning achieved and community resolve consolidated.

The goals of the GBFP include:

- To better understand the inter-related dynamics of the ecological, economic and social systems in the Georgia Basin, and to identify policy interventions which could enhance human well-being, while reducing the adverse environmental effects of human activities; and
- To evaluate the role of game-like simulation tools in enhancing public understanding of these dynamics and of the complex trade-offs involved in sustainability.

The backcasting technique is applicable to a wide variety of social contexts – communities, businesses, schools, colleges and universities – and for Dreborg (1996, p816), most appropriate when the subject to be studied is a major societal problem, in other words how society may become sustainable. Backcasting is not the same as forecasting, which uses analytic methods and techniques to predict the future. Forecasts are often needed in the development of plans, for evaluating the effects of different policies or developing models to indicate how one set of variables will interact with one or more sets of endogenous and exogenous variables. Most people are familiar with forecasting, as part of their everyday life experience, but not necessarily with backcasting.

They may avidly listen to the latest weather forecast and be annoyed when the future predicted is not one that matches reality; they may read the 'stars' – the astrological column in the local paper – to see what their future holds and may be equally disappointed. It is prior experiences like these that inform people's initial expectations of what is going to, or could, happen when engaging in visioning or backcasting activities, but it must be remembered that the under-pinning element of the GBFP is learning – learning to live, learning to be more sustainable and learning to recognize that the only place to start the journey is where you are at the moment. Robinson writes:

> *A crucial insight that has developed out of the GBFP is the recog-nition that the processes through which the scenarios are developed are as important as the scenario analysis tools themselves. This is true in two ways. First, it is important to expend significant thought and resources on designing and managing the processes through which users come to engage with the project. Different purposes, stakeholder interests, group sizes and modes of interaction will give rise to different forms of outcomes. The interests of community planners, for example, can be quite different from those of high school students or the local business community. Second, we have discovered that many of the most interesting forms of social engagement and learning seem to occur after GB-QUEST [computer modelling game] is shut down and the discussion turns to questions of implementa-tion and proposed action. In this sense the formal backcasting exercise can serve as the stimulus for processes of social interac-tion and learning that go well beyond the scenarios themselves.*
> (Robinson, 2003, p853)

The use of information and communications technology, particularly the GB-QUEST computer game, embeds and situates learning in a specific environment and specific processes of reflection, deliberation, participation and imagination. It relates lived experience, the articulation of individual and cultural identity, with a proactive and futures orientated perspective on planning, community participation and sustainable development. In this way people feel empowered, and actually are to some extent, because they are genuinely making a difference and, in partnership with other individuals and agencies, are responsible for realizing the outcomes they have themselves identified as desirable. They may select priorities for action such as reducing waste or defining values like putting people or the planet first and then see through the computer model how their suggested actions would be likely to affect their future. This approach is one possible means by which the policies, processes and products helping to realize sustainability may achieve 'buy-in' or stakeholder commitment. For example, working with a small island community off Vancouver, GBFP project workers adopted a Precede–Proceed (P/P) model to promote healthier living. Using community planning processes, residents had been searching for over ten years for a balance between the human well-being of their growing community and the environmental health of their island's ecosystem. According to the P/P model, a community's predisposition, enabling techniques and learning reinforcements are the essential elements for successful and widespread involvement. The model suggests that people will not alter their conduct and engage in more sustainable activities unless they are initially motivated or predisposed to do so. Second, once motivated, people must be enabled to take action, and when this has happened must be in some way rewarded for doing so. If a reward fails to materialize, it will be increasingly difficult to establish any form of meaningful and lasting commitment. QUEST therefore offered a range of predisposing elements, in the form of knowledge, attitudes, beliefs and values, that were used by project workers and community members to understand the issues, problems and actions their wants and needs entailed. In a workshop setting, with people using various worksheets, participants identified the skills, tools and resources needed to effect the desired changes in behaviour and to reinforce and reproduce this behaviour over time. Savelson writes:

> *Creation of healthy public policy, building supportive environments and supporting skills enhancement each offers a means to enable positive action on sustainability. Using the worksheets, information is gathered that determines what would facilitate and enable people to behave differently or change their environment. For example, green products are usually more expensive than other products and they are also not as prevalent in stores. To promote green products, an enabling strategy could focus on increasing their availability in stores and make them less costly... Reinforcing appropriate behaviors helps to establish structures that consistently act as levers, eg tax cuts for using green technologies, tax levies for driving cars or subsidized public transportation. The scale of these strategies can vary according to the need and capacity for the changes to be implemented.* (Savelson, 2005, p637)

Participant understanding of sustainability was reinforced and expanded upon by bringing about new insights, sometimes rooted in unforeseen consequences of their choices. QUEST enabled people to move from the general to the specific. It enabled people to relate their ideas about desired future outcomes to the realities of their everyday living environments, but it also showed that it would be difficult to apply these ideas in practice unless success was objectively possible and enablers were in place.

The GB-QUEST computer modelling system is complemented by the Georgia Basin Digital Library (GBDL), a three-year project designed to develop user-friendly tools, accessible via a web-based interface (GB-Explorer) supporting the integration of geo-scientific indicators with socio-economic factors. The GBDL provides access to information on such things as land use, transportation and natural resources as well as stories suggesting how the various elements inter-relate within a sustainable development context. Stories are able to present aspects of sustainable development that evade numeric measurement, such as personal inspiration or environmental aesthetics. Local stories fascinated and inspired users – enabling community memories to be passed on and information and knowledge to be gained – and were used by groups engaged in local advocacy campaigns, community planning or political protests. The aim was always to develop understanding and awareness of sustainability through facilitating the integration of users' local knowledge with more technical sources of information in the form of graphs, maps and other knowledge representations. This sometimes involved considerable skill and knowledge acquisition and the development of community capacity and individual capabilities. The underlying pedagogic purpose of these related GBFP projects has been to engender attitudinal and behavioural change through what is in effect the provision of a transformative learning environment. Similar to users of other computer or video games, where players/learners are led to develop beyond their existing skill level or 'regime of competence', QUEST offers possibilities for active and critical learning that is both challenging and doable. 'Ideally users will play QUEST iteratively in order to learn about the tradeoffs between the choices offered within the model. Through this kind of iterative play it is assumed that users will move beyond a priori values to make more sophisticated choices,' write Carmichael et al (2005).

Robinson and his colleagues have also undertaken research on the cognitive changes people experience when playing QUEST and are planning a range of other activities building on what has been achieved in the project so far. Social learning, participation, social interaction and the application of new media technologies all figure importantly. Carmichael et al write:

> *The ability to engage with sustainability ideas (represented as stories or indicators, for example) in the context of place offers a powerful framework to provide meaning, context and focus to the bigger picture of what sustainability can be. To this end, we are exploring the use of landscape visualization, in the form of detailed three-dimensional representations of terrain, to represent current and future scenarios. We are exploring the feasibility of overlaying a GB-QUEST future scenario on the landscape so that stakeholders can get a sense of what their desired future might actually look and feel like – even flying over it and approaching it from different angles. The landscape visualization techniques are being developed for an immersive (surrounded by three large screens, the users start to feel that they are 'in' the landscape) and a web-based environment. In relation to sustainable community-level planning, we are also investigating the issue of scale and temporality between QUEST future scenarios and a local scale planning and modelling tool, such as CommunityViz.* (Carmichael et al, 2005, p201)

Social learning is therefore central to the process of building sustainable communities, environmental dispute resolution and many environmental impact processes and environment management activities (Sidaway, 2005; Keen and Mahanty, 2005). These social learning processes involve groups, communities, individuals, public and private sector organizations, and university researchers, working, possibly together, to identify, analyse and seek resolutions to problems. The aim of such learning partnerships is to apply their knowledge reflectively and constructively and to build trust as a basis for new networks and relationships. It is an ongoing, iterative process, inevitably influencing the dynamic of social networks, relationships, organizational arrangements and social structures. Groups may work individually or collaboratively to develop an agenda of new skills and capabilities, including techniques of cooperative inquiry, storytelling and human-centred participatory research, an approach which has been enacted successfully in both affluent and non-affluent worlds (Chambers, 1997; 2002). Glover (2003) writes of the personal, community and cultural stories a local group told of how they reclaimed as a community garden a small space within their decaying urban environment. This enabled them to experience the reality of making a difference through collective action and helped re-establish a sense of meaning and community identity. They became empowered by being able to offer and make good an alternative reality, an alternative story to the dominant narrative of social deprivation, crime, prostitution and environmental degradation. Community group members were therefore then able to talk of 'collective triumph' through community organization, showing the world they were something other than what was usually thought of them by outsiders. Thus the story of the Queen Anne Memorial Garden is one of overcoming – a story with a positive ending symbolizing the achievement of exerting control over an area of everyday existence and enhancing hopes of an improved and improving future.

BIOREGIONALISM

Many area- or community-based sustainable development or regeneration projects are bounded geographically, not so much by official government or local government boundaries (although this is sometimes the case), but by ecological, perhaps bioregional, parameters. Bioregionalism is a cultural idea closely associated with the cultural historian and writer Kirkpatrick Sale, whose *Dwellers in the Land* (1991) opened up a new debate and perspective on living in harmony with natural systems. The idea draws on both the natural and human sciences, particularly anthropology and history. Bioregionalism is therefore not about the environment as such; rather it is about 'specific life-places' people experience in their everyday lives. For Sale, the bioregionalist vision's one key idea is 'scale' – human scale settlements bounded by natural rather than human dictates and distinguishable from other areas by flora, fauna, water, climate, soils, landforms, and the human settlements and cultures these have given rise to. 'The borders between such areas are usually not rigid

– nature works with more flexibility and fluidity than that – but the general contours of the regions themselves are not hard to identify and indeed will probably be felt' (Sale, 1991, p54). When I first moved to the West Country and did some work in Cornwall, I remember people speaking of the region and the need for regional development and regional autonomy and realized only after a while that the region under discussion was Cornwall, which has its own local ecologies and ecosystems, local administration and business activities. It did not mean the South West. Cornwall does interact economically with the rest of England, and indeed Europe, but also articulates a bioregional identity that cuts off at the Tamar. Parts of Wales and Scotland also offer examples of bioregional consciousness.

Alexander (1996) notes that there are four ways in which bioregions may be delineated, but that for practical purposes it is probably best to view them as being largely products of culture and consciousness with geography setting limits or providing resources. He argues that 'accepting the fact that "natural" regions have begun to give way in people's lives and consciousness to functional ones (ie cultural regions), we should resolve to take advantage of whatever potential these hold for developing an attitude of ecological and social responsibility' (Alexander, 1996, pp172–3). Aberley (1993) suggests practical ways in which local communities may empower themselves through mapping their own bioregions and in so doing gain a greater understanding and sense of belonging to the localities in which they dwell. Sometimes accused of environmental determinism, Sale frequently alludes to the integration of tribal peoples in their natural environments as an example from which others may learn. Economic self-sufficiency, decentralization, community, participatory decision-making and gradualism are other key principles, but fundamentally it is about locating 'culture in nature through the praxis of living in place' (Carr, 2004, p77). Communities will be dependent on ecosystems, not the whole biosphere.

Bioregional thinking has been taken up by many groups and individuals, including eco-poets like Gary Snyder; restoration ecologists who wish to revive native plants and animals; urban ecologists who wish to 'nest' their redesigned towns and cities along ecological lines; community development workers who nurture community gardens and city farms; regeneration professionals who seek to redevelop urban and peri-urban localities and regions; and permaculturalists and organic farmers who wish to maintain local soils, water courses and native species. Bioregionalism has developed from a philosophy to a sociopolitical movement. However, critics point to a number of potential flaws in bioregional thinking. It seems, at least according to Barry (1999), that if you happen to live in a resource-poor bioregion then your standard and possibly quality of life may be poor also. The autarky or self-sufficiency imperative probably prevents or limits the possibility of redistributing or trading resources between bioregions. Then again, the various activities and tools used by bioregionalists in their efforts to build or rebuild sustainable communities or to renew or restore an intimate and necessary commitment between the social world and the natural have been taken up by many individuals, groups and

---

BOX 5.3 BIOREGIONALISM

Peter Berg (2002) defines bioregionalism as:

The unique overall pattern of natural characteristics that are found in a specific place. The main features are generally obvious throughout a continuous geographic terrain and include a particular climate and local aspects of seasons, landforms, watersheds, soils, and native plants and animals. People are also counted as an integral aspect of a place's life, as can be seen in the ecologically adaptive cultures of early inhabitants, and in the activities of present day reinhabitants who attempt to harmonize in a sustainable way with the place where they live.

There are three main goals to the bioregionalist project:

1   To restore and maintain local natural systems;
2   To practise sustainable ways to satisfy basic human needs such as food, water, energy, housing and materials; and
3   To support the work of reinhabitation.

---

organizations involved in ecological restoration. Higgs (2003) prefers to use the term 'focal restoration', understood as a practice that integrally restores what matters ecologically, socially and culturally. Influenced strongly by the culture and philosophy of indigenous peoples, the Canadian bioregionalist Mike Carr has extended the concept of social capital to encompass a spiritual embrace of the natural world so that relationships of respect and reciprocity accommodate the whole 'community of beings' and the earth on which we depend. He writes about 'ecosocial capital' and 'ecological kinship'. There is a certain alternative flavour to much bioregionalist thought and action which possibly seems at odds with most people's experiences and expectations of the everyday, particularly with the chanting, rituals and storytelling circles, but a great deal of bioregional practice is firmly rooted in everyday experiences, habits and predispositions. We get to know our locality not by reading an Ordinance Survey map but by walking the streets or country lanes, by creating or communicating to others a mental map of what is important, where and why. We engage with nature by walking in an urban park or camping out in a National Park, visiting a garden or tending our own. Bioregionalism is about feeling and being at home in the place we live in, and this necessarily means understanding that how urban and rural settlements have been designed and developed, how energy is sourced and used, how and where people work, travel, play and organize and govern themselves is extremely important. In this way being at home entails ecological, civic and domestic responsibilities. It also involves community building, culture-changing activities, embodied (lifelong) learning in place and through the practice of everyday life.

Higgs's critique of ecological and eco-cultural restoration as an element of bioregionalist thought and action leads him to a consideration of the place and influence of technology in and on everyday lives and contemporary culture. Following Borgmann (1984), Higgs (2003, p185) suggests that it is the 'communion between self, thing and environment (and perhaps also spirit) that generates profound meaning in our lives'. A 'thing' is inseparable from its context, involving both bodily and social engagement, whereas a 'device' is simply itself – a commodity to be consumed. There are particular practices, focal practices, that generate this meaning – going slow perhaps, enjoying celebratory meals, reading a bedtime story to one's children, or being in tune with an experience of the natural world that hasn't been served up as a Disneyfied, commodified package. You don't have to go to Disneyland to experience the commodification of nature, leisure or fulfilment. You can buy it in the mall or maybe just find it in a leisure resort or nature theme park. The new technologies which Higgs and Borgmann refer to as 'devices' ultimately do not deliver happiness or satisfaction, rather they distract us from what really matters, from things that have focusing qualities and that enable us to realize ourselves as human beings rather than as adjuncts of consumerism. For Borgmann, our fascination with mass-produced artefacts (devices again) – new cars, games consoles, DVDs, digital cameras – prevents, or even destroys, our capacity for focal practice, because increasingly we experience the world through our engagement with these objects, commodities or services, which are disconnected and disposable. Places become sites and homes machines for living in. The means become not simply constitutive of the ends but rather the ends themselves. The response then is to promote a practice that restores natural and human ecologies, social and bodily engagement with place, and in so doing generates and regenerates meaning. This focal restoration is not a return to a myth of a golden past, but the reality is that little things may actually count for quite a lot. To illustrate his position, Borgmann offers a seemingly antiquated illustration but one which today is perhaps not so quaint. I first came across Borgmann and Higgs when my wife and I were looking to replace the oil-fired central heating in our house with a couple of wood burning stoves. The increasing price of oil and its impact on the environment, the possibility of purchasing the wood from local sustainable sources, and the desire to have a more 'natural' domestic environment figured in our discussions. I also realized there was something in what Borgmann was saying, even though for me new digital media technologies offer potentially greater benefits and afford greater possibilities for future sustainable living than is sometimes recognized (see Chapter 7). In any case, Borgmann writes:

> *The experience of a thing is always and also a bodily and social engagement with the thing's world. In calling forth a manifold engagement, a thing necessarily provides more than one commodity. Thus a stove used to furnish more than mere warmth. It was a focus, a hearth, a place that gathered the work and leisure of a family and gave the house a centre. Its coldness marked the morning, and the spreading of its warmth the beginning of the day. It assigned to the different family members tasks that defined*

> *their place in the household... It provided for the entire family a*
> *regular and bodily engagement with the rhythm of the seasons*
> *that was woven together of the threat of cold and the solace of*
> *warmth, the smell of woodsmoke, the exertion of sawing and of*
> *carrying, the teaching of skills, and the fidelity to daily tasks. [...]*
> *Skill is intensive and refined world engagement. Skill, in turn, is*
> *bound up with social engagement. It moulds the person and gives*
> *the person character. Limitations of skill confine any one person's*
> *primary engagement with the world to a small area.* (Borgmann,
> 1984, pp41–42)

Focal things and focal practices require skill, patience and continual engage-ment. They are 'centring' things. They need to be both nurtured and practised. In restoring degraded land or building a new community, people necessarily collaborate, cooperate, share and learn socially and individually. They learn facts and skills. They learn to listen to others, to understand their own and other's emotions. They learn to be. So, for Higgs, adding the social to the ecological adds value to restoration practices because such activities promote:

> *community engagement, experimentation, local autonomy,*
> *regional variation and a level of creativity in working along with*
> *natural patterns and processes. It is the combination of value to*
> *nature and value to community that gives it the capacity to*
> *enhance a participatory politics.* (Higgs, 2003, p255)

The greater the level of participation, the more valuable the restoration project, because at the very least this acts as a counterweight to what Higgs sees as the growing danger to the integrity of the environmental movement, where cash donations are increasingly becoming substitutes for direct engagement and where there is a growing inference that basically social, political or environ-mental problems are susceptible to economic or financial solutions. There is also the conviction that a sustainable future will involve something other than globalized processes of mass consumption and mass production.

The charity Groundwork attempts to engage people in a range of social, economic and environmentally sustainable practices. It is in effect a federation of trusts operating in England, Wales and Northern Ireland and aiming to fashion a society composed of healthy, safe and environmentally responsible communities. The trusts work in partnership with a range of public, private and public sector agencies to improve disadvantaged or in other ways deprived areas by providing programmes that develop people's skills, encourage community participation and aid local businesses to prosper in an environ-mentally sustainable manner. Changing Places was a £60m government-funded Millennium Commission project aimed at revitalizing former industrial, environmentally degraded or under-utilized land in many areas of the UK. Many activities included the development of community parks, canal restora-tions, and the establishment of heritage cultural centres and walkways. For

---

Box 5.4 Saltmill Park

Saltmill is a reclaimed landfill site on the edge of Saltash town, Cornwall. Through the original Changing Places programme the site was transformed into a major community park. Groundwork has retained an involvement in the park since its completion and became aware that there were still further improvements that could be made. The young people in the area were asking for a more challenging skatepark, local residents wanted a play area for younger children, and as the park matured it became apparent that further landscaping was needed and that the local management group needed further support.

The drive to improve Saltmill came from local residents, under the banner of the Tamara Residents Association and KAUZE, a young people's group. These identified a number of elements as important – a play area for under-eights, further planting and, particularly, improvements to the skatepark.

Groundwork spent a day at the park in a marquee working with skaters and BMX riders to determine criteria for the improved skatepark. Young people were able to share their experience of other parks, whether they were successful or not, to inform the brief for the skatepark designer. The designer was also a local skater who had been involved in the building of an indoor facility in Saltash.

Whilst the skatepark was already popular, with users travelling from all over south-east Cornwall and Plymouth, it now offers a much better range of skating experience. Beginners have a good starting facility while added elements like increased depth to the ramps and improved transitions from one piece to another make it challenging for more advanced skaters.

Source: www.changingplaces.org.uk/index.asp?page=90

Groundwork it is important to incorporate the spirit, pride and history of the place in the regeneration practice. Collaboration with artists and the creation of arts projects, installations and sculptures figure significantly. Groundwork actively consults and encourages local community participation, seeking to ensure that the improvements undertaken are actually wanted, valued and owned by local people. 'Working with nature' frequently leads to less costly solutions and enhances biodiversity, while providing a base for future sustainability. Much was learnt from Changing Places and, in partnership with the University of Manchester, an ecological regeneration toolkit, Ecoregen, has been developed with financial aid from the EU's LIFE programme. The purpose of the toolkit is to continue the community-led aim of helping local people ecologically restore and regenerate derelict land in their vicinity. As Groundwork's website (www.groundwork.org.uk) states, 'Ecoregen describes how, by working together to improve land, people can gain new skills, make new friends, and develop a renewed sense of pride in where they live. By integrating local community needs with the natural ecology of derelict sites, Ecoregen aims to help people create truly sustainable landscapes.'

Many of Groundwork's projects have the express aim of linking people with nature by working with nature. The charity offers ideas about how to:

- Share and deepen an **ecological understanding** of a derelict site through learning together;
- Understand the **values and significance** of derelict sites, their wildlife, habitats and landscapes;
- Recognize and celebrate **cultural landscapes** on both older and newer derelict sites;
- Link people and nature through **art in the landscape**; and
- Encourage **local distinctiveness** and a sense of place.

I spoke with Rupert Goddard, the projects manager for Groundwork (in the southwest of England), who emphasized that people learn to care for and about their environment by being part of it and by having some control and responsibility for it. It is a product of genuine empowerment and real or effective democracy and it is people like Rupert whose dedicated and methodical work enable this to emerge and develop:

> *What I try to focus on personally is to use the environment to engage and motivate local people to improve the quality of their lives. What I've found is that if you can get people to make their environment nicer they tend to take more care of it. As soon as you get a group of residents to tidy up a planted area in the middle of the street, prune it down, make it look like someone is actually taking care of it, people seem to respect it. You don't get so much litter. People think, 'this land is being managed; I won't trash it'. It's very much the way forward, local people taking control over their green spaces and maintaining these spaces safely.* (interview with author)

Recycling and environmentalism are not simply middle class concerns. Rupert again:

> *I have just finished a project funded by the Neighbourhood Renewal Fund [NRF] to introduce doorstep recycling to the high-rise and multi-occupancy flats in the five NRF areas of Plymouth. These are deprived wards where the local authority waste department felt that the people in these flats didn't want to do recycling. We did a pilot project and showed that, actually, they do want to recycle, they just haven't got the service. It is very difficult to recycle from the doorstep of multi-occupancy flats because you've got so many doors to go to. So I've knocked on every door – over two or three hundred doors – tried to speak to every resident to explain what can go into their recycling bag, what mustn't go into it, and when the bag gets full they take it downstairs and tip the contents into a communal recycling bin. Residents think it is brilliant.* (interview with author)

Groundwork, like many voluntary organizations, is interested in working with businesses to secure additional funds for community projects and to encourage businesses to deepen their commitment to corporate social and environmental responsibility. To this end, in 2004 Groundwork negotiated a partnership project with United Utilities called United Futures, aiming to support up to 30 projects over three years. In the newsletter, *Groundwork 36*, the charity published an interview with John Roberts, chief executive of United Utilities, in which he discussed how corporate social responsibility (CSR) had changed from simply giving money to entering into genuine partnerships with local communities and organizations like Groundwork. Unfortunately, CSR has still to be valued seriously by other business and many shareholders.

SKILLS FOR BUILDING SUSTAINABLE COMMUNITIES

Partnership and cross-team working are key elements in sustainable community development, and the skills needed to flourish in such a difficult and testing environment involve learning how to lead and facilitate, how to be patient, how to listen, how to communicate empathetically and clearly, and how to get on with others. In 2004 the *Egan Review: Skills for Sustainable Communities* (ODPM, 2004) was published in the UK, identifying and discussing the wide range of skills deemed necessary to effectively build and maintain sustainable communities. Some of these skills can and are learnt in formal education, from online courses, or from the television, but many others, probably most, are best learnt in and through practice – situated, social, collaborative and cooperative learning operating within the three ecologies and firmly grounded on knowledge and understanding of key issues and perspectives. More instrumentally, the *Egan Review* presents seven components of a sustainable community and the knowledge, actions and generic skills believed necessary to deliver them:

1   **Social and cultural** – vibrant, harmonious and inclusive communities;
2   **Governance** – effective and inclusive participation, representation and leadership;
3   **Environmental** – providing places for people to live in an environmentally friendly way;
4   **Housing and the built environment** – a quality built and natural environment;
5   **Transport and connectivity** – good transport services and communication linking people to jobs, schools, health and other services;
6   **Economy** – a flourishing and diverse local economy; and
7   **Services** – a full range of appropriate, accessible, public, private, community and voluntary services. (ODPM, 2004, pp15–17)

This managerialist approach is aimed at efficiency as well as effectiveness. Businesses are the proverbial 'hard nuts to crack'; they tend to come in when a

Table 5.1 *Generic Skills, Behaviour and Knowledge Considered Essential for Delivering Sustainable Communities*

Skills	Ways of thinking	Ways of acting	Knowledge of
Inclusive visioning	Creative	Entrepreneurial	The seven sustainable communities components and how they interact
Project management	Strategic	Can-do mentality	Sustainable development, including best environmental practice
Leadership	Open to change	Cooperative	Housing and built environment
Breakthrough thinking/brokerage	Aware of limitations	Able to seek help	Transport and connectivity
Team/partnership working	Challenging assumptions	Humble	Wider national and local economy
Making it happen given constraints	Flexible	Committed to making it happen	Governance, citizenship and processes associated with local democracy
Process management/ change management	Clear	Respectful (of diversity and equal opportunity)	Spatial planning and master planning
Financial management and appraisal/ stakeholder management	Decisive; respectful and aware (of the contribution of other professionals); having a shared sense of purpose	Able to take action and to to work with local residents and residents/community groups	Urban design and urban coding; attracting financial capital
Analysis, decision-making, evaluation, learning from mistakes	Creative, open, empathic and reflective		Development processes
Communication	Clear, purposive and persuasive	Listening intelligently to the community; promoting development solutions	People, structures, processes and cultures
Conflict resolution	Empathic, critical, open and responsive	Listening to others; establishing dialogue; acting as facilitator and creatively when necessary; establishing trusting relationships	Issues, motivations, social and power relationships
Customer awareness	Curious and inquiring; reflective and evaluative	Sensitive; polite; dialogical; establishing clear relationships of communication and understanding	Feedback mechanisms

Source: adapted from ODPM (2004)

business opportunity beckons but otherwise may stay outside the process. Time is money, after all, so one aspect of learning and skills development consists in recognizing and understanding the connections between the economy, the community and the environment, which may seem a little abstract and theoretical but could easily translate into a concrete business activity, a clean river, a social amenity and a higher social and economic profile for the locality. It would also be the right thing to do. As Fern Clarke, of the Tiverton MCTi, said, 'The community and the environment focus groups come up with the projects and the business people then jump in.'

Thus one piece of knowledge and understanding that has been learnt is that if a proposal is presented to an individual business person with a clear objective, with clearly identified actions and with evident benefits, then it is certainly possible to motivate, stimulate and persuade wider stakeholder involvement. The actual demonstration or modelling of success, however, is also important. Simple information-giving or exhortation is not enough. Many reports, how-to manuals and sourcebooks are filled with good practice case studies, but the lessons from them need to be tied to a developing network of interested parties, activities and realistic outcomes. The nurturing of networks and the social, human and intellectual capital that may develop from them can then be celebrated at special events like awards ceremonies or communicated through continuing professional development (CPD) activities. Community- or locally-based businesses could learn how to gain and maintain a competitive advantage or increase market share by becoming more environmentally aware – more sustainable. So there is scope for deliberation and discussion and the identification and even realization of focal practices, although it is important to be wary of putting sustainability, let alone creativity, into a box. I remember talking to a couple of community workers and showing them a copy of Egan's generic skills: one turned to the other saying, 'Well, does this make sense to you?' 'Mmmm, well, yes... but...'

What really came through in my discussions with people 'building sustainable communities' is the importance of getting on with others, of distributing and sharing responsibility through as wide as possible a network of people and organizations, and of being as practical as possible. It is about establishing and maintaining connections which may in the first instance be with the people you know but which will also include those they in turn know, cumulatively producing a complex network of individuals, knowledge, skills and capacities from which to draw. The learning may be very basic, but nonetheless important – what is rudimentary to one person or organization may be a huge achievement or counter-intuitive for another. Fern, who has experience of teaching, of spatial planning and of working with people in the community, found her learning both basic and demanding: 'I had to learn really, really basic things about budgeting, how to put in simple claims and how to use Excel. I could be doing with going on a course about Excel.' She also told me about others who, despite having extensive experience in business, did not know how to apply their know-how to a new and relatively unfamiliar environment. Talking about one focus-group leader, she told me the story of a meeting called with no invitations to attend being sent to members and about how people would need cue cards to remind or tell them to do certain things at various stages of meetings or other activities. 'I discovered you can't assume anything', she said, but that once engaged the learning continues to grow in sophistication, detail and range. 'I've learnt so much about my town since I started,' a focus-group member told me. What is most important, then, in the development of sustainable communities is that people learn together, learn to share, learn to listen, learn to leave their hobby-horse at home, and learn how to make normal and commonplace activities and ideas that for some may at first seem unnecessary, irrelevant or just fanciful ultimately focal.

6

The Media, Sustainability and Learning

This chapter explores the role of the media – its power, potential and possibilities. The media is discussed in an attempt to outline an area that sustainability practitioners have yet to engage with fully. The chapter comprises sections on:

- Thinking about the media;
- Education for sustainable development – press and broadcasting;.
- Popular television and learning;
- Learning from public service broadcasting; and
- Advertising, marketing and culture jamming.

THINKING ABOUT THE MEDIA

It is hardly news that we live in a media-saturated, image-soaked and highly technological environment. This technology and media messaging arguably cultivates peculiar ways of thinking and acting, although it would be absurd to suggest that they *determine* the very nature of our existence, our thinking processes and our behaviours. We are not automatons. However, Gerbner et al do have a point when they write:

> *People are born into a symbolic environment with television as its mainstream; viewing shapes is a stable part of lifestyles and outlooks. Many of those with certain social and psychological characteristics, dispositions, and worldviews, as well as those who have fewer alternatives, use television as their major vehicle of cultural participation. To the extent that television dominates their sources of entertainment and information, continued exposure to its messages is likely to reiterate, confirm and nourish – that is, cultivate – its own values and perspectives.* (Gerbner et al, 2002, p49)

Moores (2000) shows how radio, television and new media technologies have rapidly become integrated into the day-to-day fabric of everyday living and how our understanding of our everyday lives is becoming increasingly 'mediated' (Thompson, 1996; de Zengotita, 2005). Despite all the new media developments, television remains a very important part of our symbolic environment – a source of information, comment and visual interpretation about a world beyond our own immediate experience. New media technologies generally are fundamentally changing and expanding in scope, reach and significance, reconstructing experiences of time, space and place in an increasingly globalizing network of electronic connections. The anthropologist Arjun Appadurai (1996, p33) has written influentially about the global cultural economy and the inter-relationship of five global cultural flows – 'ethnoscapes', 'mediascapes', 'technoscapes', 'financescapes' and 'ideoscapes'. He uses the suffix '-scape' to highlight the fluidity and irregularity of these landscapes and to 'indicate that these are not objectively given relations that look the same from every angle of vision, rather they are deeply perspectival constructs' shaped by language, politics, space and place. Appadurai continues:

> 'Mediascapes' refer both to the distribution of the electronic capabilities to produce and disseminate information (newspapers, magazines, television stations and film-production studios, which are now available to a growing number of private and public interests throughout the world) and to the images of the world created by these media. These images involve many complicated inflections, depending on their mode (documentary or entertainment), their hardware (electronic or pre-electronic), their audiences (local, national, transnational) and the interests of those who own and control them. What is most important about these mediascapes is that they provide (especially in their television, film, and cassette forms) large and complex repertoires of images, narratives, and ethnoscapes, to viewers throughout the world, in which the world of commodities and the world of news and politics are profoundly mixed. What this means is that many audiences around the world experience the media themselves as a complicated and interconnected repertoire of print, celluloid, electronic screens, and billboards. (Appadurai, 1996, p35)

From these mediascapes, people construct scripts of others' imagined lives, which may, and often do, become broken down into groups of visual and verbal metaphors which people live by (Lakoff and Johnson, 1980). This is not necessarily stereotyping but rather a shorthand way of encapsulating feelings and intuitions, producing pictures from limited and limiting materials. All the world's a holiday destination... What holiday bargains can be had? Can I fly to Rome for £15? Related to mediascapes are ideoscapes – chains of ideas, terms, images and values like freedom, democracy, growth, consumerism and, perhaps one might now add, sustainability. If the cultivation theory of television effects is in some way true, then it is likely, as O'Guinn and Shrum (1997) argue, that television plays a prominent role in reinforcing and reproducing materialism and consumerism. Extensive use of television, with its portrayal of affluent households in dramas and sitcoms, invites us to believe that we know how other people live beyond our immediate circle of friends and acquaintances. Those who watch a great deal of television are particularly likely to assume that the world is generally an affluent place, which may in turn inform social discussion and the nurturing of consumer wants and expectations. As the authors state, 'Although television may open windows on different social worlds, some of those worlds may look much better than one's own' (O'Guinn and Shrum, 1997, p291). Being brought up in a small flat in central London, I always wondered why everybody else seemed to live in detached houses with gardens. The BBC's 1970s suburban sitcom *The Good Life* was not my world, nor that of any of my neighbours; nevertheless, over 20 years ago John Caughey's (1984) ethnographic study of people's imaginary social worlds showed how descriptions of people's ideal homes often resembled the content of prominent television commercials and programmes.

Advertising, television, the internet, cinemas, mobiles, DV cameras, MP3 recorders and PDAs are part of the fast-changing techno-cultural fabric of modern living, with the waves of digital inventions dividing or conquering as they go. There has never been a shortage of media critics, from the early days of print in the 16th century, through photography and cinema in the 19th, television in the 20th, to the veritable explosion of new media information and communication technologies in the 21st. For some (Borgmann, 1984; Strong and Higgs, 2000), television is a prime example of a technological device that is both compelling and promising in the way it enriches our lives – by offering us new and different windows on worlds beyond our experience – yet also seems to disengage us, or at least make us feel disengaged, from what is important. It is quick, easy, convenient, private and readily available at the press of a button. Why go out bowling when I can watch something on the telly? Why go to the cinema when I can stay at home and watch a DVD without someone's head getting in the way of the picture? People in Europe and the US watch a great deal of television, often 20 or more hours a week, but being called a couch potato is not something to be proud of, even if we insist we are selective in our viewing habits. Maybe it is simply the unreflective, uncritical and passive viewing that is so shaming? Or maybe it is just a hang-up from the past? However, it need not be so – we need not be couch potatoes or use television and related media unreflectively, passively. It need not deskill, defocus or disempower us, although nerding out in front of the telly after a hard day seems to me to be as good a way to relax as any. As Ingold (2000) and Gibson (1979) argue, technology offers affordances that both enable and constrain, and much audience research shows that viewers, listeners and readers are not passively but actively constructing meaning from the various texts they engage with. Their social, cultural, gender, ethnic and other experiential environments are key to this meaning-making, and, although this largely constructivist view is not uniformly adhered to by academics, critics or even media practitioners, a great deal of media ethnography and qualitative research supports this position (Moores, 1993, 2000; Bird,

2003; Liebes and Katz, 1993; Buckingham and Scanlon, 2003; Miller et al, 1998).

Other writers have traditionally seen the media, old and new, as essentially a mode of social control, with mass audiences being massively doped and duped. Guy Debord (1995) argued that consumer capitalism is now essentially a 'society of the spectacle', with lived experience being increasingly substituted by media and advertising images, and active participation in civic affairs being replaced by a passive gaze. The media constructs 'pseudo-needs', using celebrities to project ideal fantasy lifestyles that invade everyday life so that the spectacle becomes the real world and opposition and dissent is absorbed, reorganized and transformed into more or less harmless commodities through a process he calls 'recuperation'. Thus through signs, icons and brands, the spectacular operates its global economic and symbolic hegemony – 'the spectacle has its roots in the fertile field of the economy, and it is the produce of that field which must in the end come to dominate the spectacular market' (Debord, 1995, p58). It makes sense. Nike, for instance, sell trainers by promoting the possibility of human transcendence through sport. The brand is both culturally sophisticated and extremely simple, capable of influencing people's practical consciousness by fashioning a personal and social identity through consumption, mobilizing sales worth billions of dollars (Goldman and Papson, 1998). However, the numerous activist campaigns linking the corporation with the exploitation of female and child labour in developing countries led Nike to green its image somewhat. Debord and his fellow 'situationists' also recognized the need for, and possibilities of, overturning, subverting and rearticulating the spectacle through practical action, play and critique. Debord does not endorse the political pessimism of the Mass Society and Frankfurt School theorists or subscribe to the One-Simensional Man thesis of Herbert Marcuse (1972).

Nevertheless there still seems to be a critical tendency to view the press, broadcasting media and now the internet as a major cause of many social and political ills, ranging from childhood obesity to international terrorism. But just as new media technologies enable drug dealers and terrorists to organize effectively, so the new technologies also offer scope for new communities of interest to develop, for anti-globalization movements to spread their message, for a participatory cyberdemocracy to emerge, for online independent media centres to form and for individuals to have their say, or their blog, publicly and sometimes quite effectively (Rheingold, 2002; Downing, 2001; Couldry and Curran, 2003). The media ecologist Marshall McLuhan coined the phrases 'the medium is the message' and 'global village', highlighting the immense influence media technologies have in shrinking our world and in shaping our perceptions of it, our place in it and even our subjectivity. 'Since all media are fragments of ourselves extended into the public domain,' writes McLuhan (1994, pp266–7), 'the action upon us of any one medium tends to bring the other senses into play in a new relation. As we read, we provide a soundtrack for the printed word; as we listen to the radio, we provide a visual accompaniment.' McLuhan also famously distinguished between 'hot' and 'cold' media.

A hot medium, like cinema, extends one single sense in 'high definition' – a 'state of being well filled with data' (1994, p22) – whereas a cold medium, like television, offers 'low definition', with much to be filled in by the user. Although this lyrical distinction is highly debatable, particularly in our multi-media, media-convergent age, the association of either high or low levels of participation being afforded by certain technologies is worth bearing in mind, not least because it is through doing, participating and learning from experience, through reflection, that key personal, social and cultural transformations are afforded. It is also the development of new or alternative practices that may empower people, enabling a sense of individual and collective efficacy to emerge. Or, to put it another way, getting people to believe they can make a difference by making a difference. McLuhan suggests that media technologies are also levellers and, potentially, intellectual and cultural liberators. He writes, albeit impressionistically:

> *Perhaps it is not very contradictory that when a medium becomes a means of depth experience, the old categories of 'classical' and 'popular' or of 'highbrow' no longer obtain. Watching a blue-baby heart operation on TV is an experience that will fit none of the categories. When LPs and hi-fi and stereo arrived, a depth approach to musical experience also came in. Everybody lost his inhibitions about 'highbrow' and the serious people lost their qualms about popular music and culture. Anything that is approached in depth acquires as much interest as the greatest matters. Because 'depth' means 'in inter-relation', not in isolation. Depth means insight, not point of view; and insight is a kind of mental involvement in a process that makes the content of the item seen quite secondary.* (McLuhan, 1994, p282)

For the media critic Neil Postman, the visual media, particularly television, are creating new forms of truth-telling 'favouring certain definitions of intelligence and wisdom' which dominate the contemporary symbolic environment, 'polluting' public discourse in the process. Referring to television news, Postman (1987, p104) writes, 'Credibility replaces reality as the decisive test of truth-telling; political leaders need not trouble themselves very much with reality provided that their performances consistently generate a sense of verisimilitude.' Television is also creating nations of amnesiacs with little sense or memory of the past, and, despite all the historical dramas and documentaries, nostalgia tends to win the day, rendering us all 'unfit to remember' since:

> *If remembering is to be something more than nostalgia, it requires a contextual basis – a theory, a vision, a metaphor – something within which facts can be organized and patterns discerned. The politics of image and instantaneous news provides no such context, are, in fact, hampered by attempts to provide any. A mirror records only what you are wearing today. It is silent about*

yesterday. With television, we vault ourselves into a continuous, incoherent present. (Postman, 1987, pp140–1)

Robert Putnam, in his book *Bowling Alone* (2000), argues strongly that although the link between social or leisure clubs and civic participation is strong, the decline in civic participation and social trust is caused by people watching too much television. Uslaner, however, disputes this, suggesting that local social and economic factors, rather than TV, are more likely to be the causes and noting that people who watch four or more hours of television a day are 11 per cent less likely to say their neighbourhood is violent than those who watch no television. Uslaner (1998, p463) was unable to detect any systematic media effects on either social trust or participation, although 'there is plenty of evidence that optimism leads to trust, which in turn plays an important role in fostering civic engagement'. Television is not necessarily all bad, but its effects and educative functions are something that should be actively discussed.

Postman is also highly critical of the educative function of television, or rather the claim that television can actually have such a function. Here he is not so much writing about the content of individual programmes but about the nature of the medium itself, since, like the American philosopher of education John Dewey, he is really interested in 'collateral learning', in the formation of enduring attitudes, the 'how' rather than the 'what' of learning. In this, he says, television pedagogy is predominantly about entertainment and amusement. It is visual, theatrical and essentially narrative, rather than being conceptually rigorous, sequential, challenging, linguistic or complex and requiring prior knowledge and exposition. Postman does recognize that television can stimulate learning in schools, colleges and universities and can effectively engage the emotions and communicate important messages, but, like McLuhan, he feels the real message is in the medium itself. For Postman, education is, and should remain, predominantly print-based and formal. But times and concepts of learning change and far greater value is now being placed today on informal and non-formal lifelong learning than previously. Postman persists, though, arguing that television and newer media technologies privilege certain types of learning, literacy, understanding and predispositions. As he wrote in *Technopoly* (1993), every technology is a product of a particular social, economic and political context, and associated with this is an 'agenda', a set of values and meanings that are not necessarily life-enhancing. A blog is not an essay, and most people will blog or email and only write essays when they are forced to – when 'in education'. Informal and non-formal learning is part of everyday life, and if television is also part of everyday life then the type of learning that TV affords is worth considerable attention by educators and sustainability practitioners. As Umberto Eco (1979, p15) wrote decades ago, 'If you want to use television for teaching somebody something, you have first to teach somebody how to use television.' And a teacher in this context could be either someone who works at a school or university or a member of a community or campaign group, government agency, media company, charity and so on. The television itself could be the teacher, because it does have the capacity say something to others, does have the capacity to show a world beyond the pub, club and living room. It is an affordance, if only we make it so. Using the term education in a fully encompassing manner, synonymous in many ways with the term 'learning', Eco (1979, p24) argues that 'a critically orientated education has to recognize the fact that television exists and is the principal source of education for adults and young people'. Those like Jerry Mander (2002) who are severely critical of television, who suggest it should be switched off permanently, are missing the point and an opportunity. Television, radio and related media have a great deal to offer learning and sustainability. 'Don't switch off television,' writes Eco (1979, p24), 'switch on your critical freedom.' This means watching selectively, critically and actively. It means being media literate.

Television, radio, the internet, advertising and computer games generate collateral learning and the 'scape' by which we continuously renew our understanding of the world about us and through which we filter and interpret new experiences. We must also be sufficiently aware of the processes by which we make meaning and how 'the culture industries' contribute to this meaning-making process. Consequently, the drive to develop media literacy among children and adults has been taken up by many organizations, educational theorists, pressure groups and critics, and it is undoubtedly the case that literacy is different in the new media age to how it was when print-based media dominated the scene (Kress, 2003). Eco's call for critical freedom can thus be read as a call for media literacy. As television, video games, the internet and mobile phone technology are defining features of our highly mediated consumer society (Budd, Craig and Steinman, 1999) and a means by which it is reproduced and reinforced, it is probably impossible for media literacy to be divorced from other 'literacies' – political, social, consumer or environmental. Commercials on television and advertising images in magazines encourage viewers to buy more, use more, become something special, transcend oneself and reach for something fresh, clean and fragrant. With the increasing prevalence of new screen media, writes Kress (2003, p48), the logic of the image is coming to dominate 'the ordering, shape, appearance and uses of writing. Writing will be subordinated to the logic of the screen, to the spatial logic of the image. Writing will inevitably become more image-like, and will be shaped by that logic... Pages are coming to resemble screens, both in terms of the much greater prevalence of images on the page as well as the appearance of the order of the screen in the layout of pages.' We consume images everywhere, virtually all the time. We produce them too, again virtually everywhere, as the award-winning documentary *Capturing the Friedmans* demonstrated so eerily. This is now standard in cultural and media analysis (Ewen, 1999; Gitlin, 2002; Schroeder, 2002; de Zengotita, 2005) but it is important to recognize that increasingly individuals are becoming their own media producers and are, like professional picture agencies, creating their own, copyright-free, stock images of the world. Fiske (1987) and Hartley (1999) argue that the individual user/consumer is also a producer and that a form of media DIY citizenship is emerging, undermining the social control arguments of so many media opponents. Our own digital snaps and digital videos represent not only our visual landscape but also an important aspect of our set of skills, frameworks of knowledge and understanding. Interestingly, many home snaps and movies conform to dominant commercial conceptualizations and cultural expectations. Amateur camera clubs have rules to enable judges to decide what makes a good image. A beautiful photograph of the natural world may look similar to an image in *National Geographic* or other visual rhetorics designed to be consumer-friendly or commercially engaging (Frosh, 2003). As anthropologists tell us, and as marketing executives know, we communicate through the ownership and display of consumer goods – cars, clothes, mobile phones, images – and in presenting ourselves to others we are presenting an image of ourselves, our lifestyles, values and mores. Media literacy, then, as the UK communications regulator states, is of paramount importance if we are to make this image-making work for, rather than against, the need to fashion a more sustainable world.

Increasingly there is a growing tendency to see the world through a lens, viewfinder or screen. We frame things and remember them by taking a picture or a home movie. Some time ago John Urry (1990) spoke of 'the tourist gaze' and more recently the educationalist Lowell Monke wrote of the consequences of this mediated environment on children's learning:

> *Having watched the Discovery Channel and worked with computer simulations that severely compress both time and space, children are typically disappointed when they first approach a pond or stream: the fish aren't jumping, the frogs aren't croaking, the deer aren't drinking, the otters aren't playing, and the raccoons (not to mention bears) aren't fishing. Their electronic experiences have led them to expect to see these things happening – all at once and with no effort on their part. This distortion can also result from a diet of television and movies, but the computer's powerful interactive capabilities greatly accelerate it. And the phenomenon affects more than just experiences with the natural world. It leaves students apathetic and impatient in any number of settings – from class discussions to science experiments. The result is that the child becomes less animated and less capable of appreciating what it means to be alive, what it means to belong in the world as a biological, social being.*
> (Monke, 2005)

Is this true? I wonder. As Gunter and McAleer (1997) and Buckingham (2000) demonstrate, children and young people are far more sophisticated viewers than many adults give them credit for. They can also tell the difference between Kermit and a real frog. They use television more than television uses them. Thus sustainability practitioners need to seek ways in which television and new media technologies can be used by children and adults to learn, to discuss,

BOX 6.1 WHAT IS MEDIA LITERACY?

There is no single, agreed definition of media literacy. There are parallels with traditional literacy – the ability to read and write text. Media literacy is the ability to 'read' and 'write' audiovisual information rather than text. At its simplest level media literacy is the ability to use a range of media and be able to understand the information received.

At a more advanced level it moves from merely recognizing and comprehending information to higher-order critical-thinking skills such as questioning, analysing and evaluating that information. This aspect of media literacy is sometimes referred to as 'critical viewing' or 'critical analysis'. Someone who is media literate may also be able to produce communications in electronic form, such as write emails, create web pages or video materials.

So media literacy is a range of skills including the ability to access, analyse, evaluate and produce communications in a variety of forms. Or put simply, the ability to operate the technology to find what you are looking for, to understand that material, to have an opinion about it and where necessary to respond to it. With these skills people will be able to exercise greater choice and be able better to protect themselves and their families from harmful or offensive materials.

A media-literate person should be able to, for instance, use an electronic programme guide to find the programme they want to watch. They may agree or not with the views of the programme-maker, or just enjoy the programme. They may also recognize that the programme-maker is trying to influence them in some way. They may interact with the programme using interactive features or by telephone. And they may respond to the programme by writing to or emailing the broadcaster with their point of view. People may also be able to use communications technology to create their own video and audio content.

Media-literate people should be able to use the internet to find information and accept that sometimes what they find may represent a particular view rather than a statement of objective fact. They will be able to control what they and their children see to avoid being offended. They may also be confident enough to be able to order and pay for goods and services online and to create their own website and contribute to a chatroom discussion. People's level of media literacy may change through time as they become more competent and confident in the use of communications technologies and as they 'consume' more content. People's ability to analyse critically the content they consume will depend on a number of factors. There are important roles for educators, broadcasters, internet service providers and others to understand and meet the needs of a wide and diverse range of groups.

Source: Ofcom (2004a)

to debate, to engage, to commit, to make a difference. Television is an affordance and, for me, Monke's view, and others like it, is an exaggeration, perhaps a warning – nothing more.

EDUCATION FOR SUSTAINABLE DEVELOPMENT – PRESS AND BROADCASTING

The implementation guidance for the UN's Decade for Education for Sustainable Development (ESD) 2005–2014 clearly articulates an inclusive education that occurs 'within a perspective of lifelong learning, engaging all possible learning spaces, formal, non-formal and informal, from early childhood to adult life' (UNESCO, 2005, p6). It conceptualizes ESD as being:

> *fundamentally about values, with respect at the centre: respect for others, including those of present and future generations, for difference and diversity, for the environment, for the resources of the planet we inhabit. Education enables us to understand ourselves and others and our links with the wider natural and social environment, and this understanding serves as a durable basis for building respect. Along with a sense of justice, responsibility, exploration and dialogue, ESD aims to move us to adopting behaviours and practices that enable all to live a full life without being deprived of basics.* (UNESCO, 2005, p5)

It also recognizes the importance of media organizations as key stakeholders in this process:

> *Journalists and media organizations have an important role to play in reporting on issues and in helping raise public awareness of the various dimensions and requirements of sustainable development. Their involvement can contribute to reinforcing access to information, communication and knowledge, as well as access to the know-how and capacities necessary for effective use of ICT in the framework of development programmes. This can include, for instance, the production of radio and television programmes with local content and on themes such as gender equality and universal basic education.* (UNESCO, 2005, p25)

In the UK, recent debates about the future of public service broadcasting (PSB) and the renewal of the BBC's charter have taken place at a time of serious political and environmental anxiety. Global terrorism, the war in Iraq, domestic security, globalization, climate change, genetic modification, continued environmental degradation, biodiversity loss, world poverty, famine and human rights abuses are major contemporary issues. There has been significant discussion about media reporting, embedded journalists and sensationalism but very little about the media's role in sustainable development. The communications regulator, the Office of Communications (Ofcom, 2004a; 2004b) and the BBC's own understanding of its role suggest that PSB, with its mission to inform, educate and entertain, to make people think, to broaden horizons, to address minority interests and so on, could be an important element in communicating sustainability. This was confirmed in the UK Government White Paper on the corporation's future, which confirmed six new 'public purposes' for the BBC – sustaining citizenship and civil society; promoting education and learning; stimulating creativity and cultural excellence (including film); reflecting the UK's nations, regions and communities; bringing the world to the UK and the UK to the world; and building digital Britain. The white paper also confirmed a set of five 'characteristics' that will distinguish the BBC's content for the next ten years (and possibly beyond) – high quality, challenging, original, innovative and engaging (DCMS, 2006). The UK's Sustainable Development Commission lobbied strenuously, albeit unsuccessfully, for the term sustainable development to be explicitly mentioned in the earlier consultative green paper (DCMS, 2005) when the UK Government was revising its own strategies on sustainable development, (*Securing the Future*, DEFRA, 2005) and various policy documents on education (DfES, 2004). Although sustainable development is still not mentioned by name, if PSB is perceived as one of the guarantors of 'the public sphere', it could conceivably facilitate a 'dialogue of values' (Ratner, 2004), enabling conversations about sustainable development to remain free, educative, constructive, participatory, inclusive and democratic. PSB would then become an integral part of the formal and informal learning process and, in the UK, where PSB does has a long history and is still extremely important, the BBC has a clear function in the overall broadcasting ecology to encourage or stimulate other media organizations and professionals to think, behave and communicate sustainability messages more often, more readily and more effectively.

So far the media's record, including that of public service broadcasters, is mixed. In the UK, according to a report by Futerra (2006) entitled 'Climate Fear V Climate Change', most British newspaper readers come across very few stories about climate change. Over three quarters (76 per cent) of UK national newspaper readers purchase tabloids or middle market newspapers – *The Sun, Daily Mirror, Daily Express, Daily Mail*, etc. – which publish only 16 per cent of the stories about climate change, with the remaining 84 per cent of climate-change stories being published in the 'quality' papers such as *The Independent, Independent on Sunday, The Financial Times, The Observer* and *The Guardian*. Most of the stories Futerra surveyed (59 per cent) focused on the negative effects that climate change brings, with no mention of potential or even current solutions, possibly reinforcing a sense of doom, gloom, hopelessness and powerlessness within readers. Admittedly, the concepts of sustainability and sustainable development are not easy to encompass in short media soundbites or graphic visuals. The traditional approach to news values militates against long-running stories that have no clear resolution or capacity to maintain audience attention (Smith, 2000), although undoubtedly the media has contributed to a public understanding and concern over development issues and environmental risks (Allan, Adam and Carter, 2000). Hargreaves, Lewis and Speers (2003) note that news media coverage of climate change allows audiences to frame and make sense of the issues in general terms, enabling most people to associate a range of human actions with negative environmental impacts. A broad public consensus on climate change is reflected in, and by, media coverage. BBC Radio has for many years broadcast highly informative series on environmental and sustainability issues – *Costing the Earth, Nature, Changing Places* – with some in-depth analysis and reporting within news and current affairs programming (*Today, In Business, File on Four*) and increasingly frequent discussions in magazine and talk show programmes like *Woman's Hour, You and Yours* and *Start the Week*. Some provocative factual TV programming – the BBC's *The Curse of Oil*, one-off *Horizon* documentaries on global warming and related issues, BBC Four's Storyville screenings like the harrowing *Darwin's Nightmare*, special seasons such as the BBC's 'Africa Lives' in the summer of 2005, Channel 4's short but incisive series of investigative reports on the developing world, *Unreported World*, ITV's award-winning documentary *Stealing a Nation* by John Pilger, the BBC's 2002 GM political thriller *Fields of Gold*, Saira Shah's 2001 Channel 4 documentary on women's oppression in Afghanistan *Beneath the Veil* – all arguably contribute to the development of a pro-environmental, pro-sustainability awareness. Interestingly, a number of students on Exeter's new MSc Sustainable Development programme named television as a source of their initial environmental awakening and inspiration. As Shanahan (1993) writes, the values underpinning environmental programming rarely offer radical alternatives to what, in other contexts, may be referred to as 'ecological modernization' (Mol and Spaargaren, 2000), although the urgency of the issue seems to be more clearly enunciated today than in the very recent past:

> *Indeed we might wonder whether the media can produce a situation where people believe they are saving the environment if they adopt media-endorsed strategies: recycling and purchasing 'environmentally friendly' products are examples of things that can be done without challenging the dominant paradigm. More and more companies are claiming to be friendly to the environment, and the symbolic environment has been flooded with blue and green images whose general message is that the environmentally friendly future is a corporate one. Oftentimes these messages seek to interpret environmentalism within the context of the current paradigm, preserving the general notion that consumption is a valid social goal.* (Shanahan, 1993, pp195–6)

Notwithstanding the controversies over BSE, GM and the crises of trust and confidence in official government and corporate communications (Beder, 2002), many journalists tend to defer to established institutional authorities uncritically. There are exceptions, however, when NGOs and campaign groups are able to identify failings in either official scientific evidence or, more significantly, in moral attitude. Greenpeace's campaigns surrounding the dumping of the Brent Spar and Shell's activities in Nigeria have become well-documented case studies (Smith, 2000), but Greenpeace video footage may only find its way on to PSB news channels when secured via a more 'reputable' journalistic source like Reuters. Natural history 'edutainment' programmes perhaps have a case to answer too. George Monbiot has criticized the anaesthetized presentation of nature in prestige BBC television series such as David Attenborough's *Life of Mammals*:

> *He shows us long, loving sequences of animals whose populations are collapsing, without a word about what is happening to them. Indeed, by seeking out those places, tiny as they may be, where the habitat is intact and the population is dense, the camera deliberately creates an impression of security and abundance. Attenborough cannot tell us that this is false, for if he did so his fantasy planet would collide with the one we inhabit, and his prelapsarian spell would be broken.* (Monbiot, 2002)

Attenborough's later highly acclaimed and widely sold series *The Blue Planet* managed to show the wonders of marine life and the technological sophistication of marine photography without any major discomforting discussion of the world's declining fishstocks. His three-part series in 2000, *The State of the Planet*, did address the serious issues of biodiversity loss, species extinction and environmental degradation, but as Cottle (2004) shows in his study of the production ecology of natural history programming, this focus on the environment is uncommon. Subscription satellite and cable channels like Discovery and National Geographic Television reach huge audiences, with the Discovery channels topping 650 million subscribers worldwide and National Geographic being broadcast in 133 countries, with 27 million subscribers in Europe. Many natural history programmes emphasize entertainment rather than science. The highly praised *Planet Earth*, a joint BBC/Discovery production first broadcast in 2006, depicts pristine natural wildernesses and in episode three can refer to Lake Baikal without even hinting at its environmental degradation. Not a human in sight. Lower down the 'quality' continuum, Steve Irwin has become a global celebrity because he wrestles with crocs, and film stars and academics – Charlotte Uhlenbroek, for example – are sometimes hired as presenters because of their attractive appearance. The fact is that environmental threat, ecological damage and the articulation of a strong conservation message can make programmes pretty downbeat (and expensive), limiting global marketing appeal. They are seen as potentially unsaleable. Such programmes may be acceptable for one-off documentaries and the occasional independent production, but not for mainstream commercial programming. As Cottle (2004, p97) writes, 'This chronic lack of engagement with and representation of the rise of ecological politics can only be seen as politically inexcusable.' At best, then, it can be argued that natural history programmes in the classic Attenborough mode encourage audiences to love and marvel at nature rather than engage with the concepts and politics of sustainable development. Lutz and Collins (1993), in their extensive study of *National Geographic*, persuasively argue that this popular glossy magazine and now its TV programming and film production (think of *March of the Penguins*) promotes a form of conservative environmental humanism while articulating what stands for universal values, even if this does relegate indigenous peoples to objects of concern, compassion and maybe to a lesser stage of socio-economic development. Penguins have 'children', not chicks.

Porter and Sims (quoted in Peck et al, 2004, p20) contend that the PSB media's requirement to adhere to due impartiality 'means the freedom to be impartial about matters of politics or culture within a socially agreed framework'. They go on to note that 'a broadcaster is not expected to be impartial about theft or murder, for instance. Being neutral on sustainable development is not exercising due impartiality, it only legitimizes an indefensible view way outside the international consensus'. Among other things, they recommend that media and entertainment companies should:

- *Cover environmental issues across a range of programming, from news and current affairs to entertainment and campaigns;*
- *Find ways of representing complex environmental problems in an accessible, relevant and interesting manner;*
- *Cover global as well as national and local environmental agendas;*
- *Give a balanced view of scientific research; and*
- *Examine the economic and political aspects of environmental problems.* (Peck, 2004, p20)

All of this is squarely in line with the legislative requirements of the UK's 2003 Communication Act, which outlines PSB requirements as including 'fair and well-informed debate, comprehensive and authoritative coverage of news and current affairs and a suitable quantity and range of programmes dealing with each of the following: science, religion and other beliefs, social issues, matters of international significance or interest and matters of specialist interest'. Additionally, Dover and Barnett show that, despite some notable exceptions, public service broadcasters in the UK have generally marginalized the developing world and global environmental issues. The amount of factual international programming on the four largest terrestrial channels was 40 per cent lower in 2003 than in 1989–90:

> *Increasingly prominent within factual international programming are genres that reveal little about the realities of life for non-British people living outside this country: travel programmes; series following British adventurers; documentaries about 'Brits abroad' and reality game-shows in 'exotic' locations. These programmes foreground British subjects, albeit in foreign locations. Factual programming about developing countries fell even more markedly.*

> *In 2000–01 factual international programming and develop-*
> *ing country factual programming had risen compared to the*
> *historic lows of 1998–99.*
>
> *These rises were due to an expansion of holiday travel*
> *programmes and the 'internationalization' of entertainment*
> *programme formats that had previously been filmed domestically*
> *(ie docu-soaps and reality game-shows such as* Survivor). (Dover
> and Barnett, 2004, p3)

Dover and Barnett conclude that the media does little to enable people to learn
about or engage with sustainability and development issues:

> *It is disappointing that our public service television framework is*
> *delivering a lower volume of programming about developing*
> *countries – even including entertainment formats – than ever*
> *before.* (Dover and Barnett, 2004, p32)

A report published by the PR consultancy CARMA International (2006),
'Western media coverage of humanitarian disasters', examined newspaper
reporting of earthquakes in Bam (Iran) and Kashmir (Pakistan), Hurricane
Katrina in the US and Hurricane Stanley in Central America, the Boxing Day
Tsunami and the humanitarian crisis in Darfur in nine countries including the
US, Australia and seven European countries. The conclusions make uncom-
fortable but perhaps unsurprising reading. Western economic and political
interests tended to be the focus of editorial attention. The predicament of US
residents in New Orleans was more newsworthy than that of the Central
Americans. The interest in the Tsunami was at least partially motivated by this
area being a popular tourist destination for Western tourists whereas Darfur,
Bam and Kashmir are certainly not. The case of Hurricane Stan indicates how
Westerners are offered primarily a self-interested perspective of the world
beyond its shores:

> *There simply was not enough of a political or economic interest,*
> *not only to* sustain *reporting of the ongoing humanitarian*
> *response but to* generate *such reporting in the first instance. The*
> *evidence of Stanley appears to be that if there is no economic or*
> *political mileage to be obtained from a crisis, media take the view*
> *that it is best not to actually turn off their readers by continuing*
> *to put the emergency in their faces.* (CARMA, 2006, p17)

If globalization has led to the erosion of natural environments and indigenous
cultures, then there is a danger that it may also lead to an erosion in the public
possibilities of informally learning from and understanding them. There are
certainly tensions and contradictions, strengths, weaknesses, opportunities and
threats. It's up to sustainability communicators and other practitioners to
reflect on these.

POPULAR TELEVISION AND LEARNING

Various programmes and information spots on, for example, smoking, obesity, better nutrition or taking exercise are quite commonplace in the UK media environment. *Gardeners World*, a popular prime-time TV programme, makes frequent mention of organic practices and broadcast a special in 2004 for World Environment Day. The comedian Bill Oddie's live series of programmes exploring wildlife habits and habitats on a Devon farm, *Springwatch*, had ratings that rivalled the reality show *Big Brother*, with a maximum 3.51m viewers compared with *Big Brother*'s 3.48m in the week ending 12 June 2005 (BARB, 2005). The BBC's 2004 health edutainment series *Fat Nation* and Channel 4's critically acclaimed *Jamie's School Dinners* are superb examples of encouraging social learning, online debate and socio-political action combined effectively with quality entertainment in the public interest. Indeed, the development of digital interactivity and web-based resources enables viewers to pursue learning in their own time at their own pace and has been a major PSB innovation in recent years. Every month approximately 4.6 million people visit one of the online sites that make up the BBC's factual services, and this is in addition to those accessing Channel 4's 'Think TV' online provision and more formal educational services. By the middle of October 2005 the BBC's Science and Nature online message board boasted 12,142 postings and by the end of May 2005 *Springwatch* events, including its associated viewers' survey, had produced 150,000 records. The 'end of term' report compiled by Nick Collinson (2005) stated, '*Springwatch* has proved a powerful vehicle for mobilizing people to take action for the natural world'. Among the findings:

- Bumblebees and butterflies were seen on average about three weeks earlier than 30 years ago;
- Hawthorn flowered about two and a half weeks earlier than 30 years ago;
- Swifts arrived about a week earlier this year than in recent warm years; and
- One species of bumblebee, *bombus terrestris*, is raising an extra generation because of milder winters.

The educationalist Albert Bandura, whose social learning theory has influenced the production of many edutainment series, is a firm supporter of the educational potential of television and radio, but notes that context or social mediation is extremely important. Part of this socially mediated context is now frequently virtual. Bandura writes:

> *In fostering large-scale changes, communication systems operate through two pathways. In the direct pathway, communication media promote changes by informing, enabling, motivating and guiding audience individuals. In the socially-mediated pathway,*

Figure 6.1 *BBC* Springwatch *advertisement: Popular television successfully encouraging informal learning and viewer involvement*

> *media influences are used to link participants to social networks and community settings. These places provide continued personalized guidance, as well as natural incentives and social supports for desired changes. The major share of behavioural and valuational changes are promoted within these social milieus. People are socially situated in interpersonal networks... At a more informal level, media influences lead viewers to discuss and negotiate matters of import with others in their lives. In the informal mode of social mediation, the media set in motion transactional experiences that further shape the course of change. Socially mediated influences can have stronger impacts than direct media influence.*
> (Bandura, 2004, pp76–77)

Popular TV formats like makeover shows are excellent vehicles for conveying all manner of sustainability messages. *Grand Designs*, broadcast on the UK's Channel 4 and More4, examines a wide range of practical, personal and financial issues associated with the sometimes fraught experience of self-build. Each programme focuses on a 'real-life couple' attempting to realize their dream of building their very own ideal home. By 2006 there have been three of these quite popular television series, along with a well-subscribed magazine and the inevitable website offering summaries of each home featured together with advice and guidance on property, construction, architecture, and green building materials and techniques and invitations to viewers to apply to appear on the series. Not all these dream homes can be considered eco-sustainable but some have been – a straw bale house in London, eco- homes in Carmarthen and Suffolk. Why not have a dream and then learn to live it? The presenter

Kevin McCloud is also the enthusiastic patron of the Genesis Project on sustainable construction at the Somerset College of Arts and Technology (see Chapter 7). What is perhaps interesting, and this is borne out to some extent by my discussions with communication and sustainability professionals, is that while its format, focusing on the stories of realizing people's dreams, resonates strongly with viewers, this dreaming is fostered by engagement with the practicalities and the pragmatics of construction – the use of appropriate materials, client relationships with architects and builders, the knowledge and skills of the builders (sometimes woefully inadequate where new eco-materials are concerned), the seasons, weather and, of course, good and bad financial budgeting. Many programmes effortlessly and accessibly chart participants' learning process and the learning curves. They do not baulk at showing that learning is not always easy or straightforward and that, particularly where the aim is the creation of a sustainable dwelling, problem identification as well as problem-solving are as much central features of the learning experience as they are of life. BBC2's 2006 series *It's Not Easy Being Green* offered possibilities of reaching a wider audience by following a family moving from one part of the country to Cornwall and seeing how they got on living a greener, but normal, lifestyle. Could the teenage daughter cope without all the modern conveniences? It is from the selection and consumption of goods and services and the normalization of everyday routines, habits, hopes and expectations that we construct our universe, stabilize it and make sense of it. Sustainability communicators could do well to look for more ways to rearticulate popular entertainment formats like the makeover show.

Pam Horton, one of the education officers at the Eden Project in Cornwall, told me how television and popular culture is used to stimulate school children's interest in plants. Workshops may be designed with a particular TV programme in mind and occasionally the presenter appears in person to cement the link. Television is being mediated by an organized event specially designed to address elements within Key Stage 3 of the National Curriculum. It is also fun, immersive and sensory. Pam explained:

> *Every workshop is designed with a hook. Even before the kids actually come here they are invited to take part in a challenge or a quest here, an invitation from a scientist to get them to want to come here and do it. When they are here the whole thing starts. And sometimes it's a role play. One of our very popular workshops, called 'Don't Forget Your Leech Socks', which has been evaluated quite extensively, is all about surviving in the rainforest and what things you will need for food, water and shelter. So the kids were invited to come and help with a documentary we are making – it's a bit of a Ray Mears-style workshop where they visit the Tropics [biome] for an hour and pick up all this information. How would they survive and what equipment would they need?*

> *The idea for Ray Mears sort of developed as the workshop progressed. As we started teaching it we thought "this guy does this on TV" so we talked about him a bit more and included him. He actually visited and took part. He actually ran a workshop with me with a group of kids. This was amazing. We learnt a lot from him. Kids can relate to him because they've seen him on TV, so we talk about him a bit more and they've seen these rubbish survival programmes, I'm a Celebrity Get Me Out of Here. They always talk about that and then we changed it to more his type of work, which is more "bushcraft" and plant adaptation and how they would use them to survive. They love it because as soon as they step into the Tropics they start looking at the plants. It's getting their creative imagination whirring. The stuff that comes out of that workshop is quite amazing.* (interview with author)

LEARNING FROM PUBLIC SERVICE BROADCASTING

'The BBC's Learning Impact' (BBC, 2004) identifies important programmes, partnerships and audience research that show learning in all its forms is an important part of the corporation's activities – Open University and *Bitesize* programmes (formal learning), social action campaigns on domestic violence like *Hitting Home* (informal targeted leaning) and numerous documentaries and entertainment programmes (informal learning from general programming). This goes, in varying degrees, for other PSB stations too. Children (Fisch, 2004) and adults (Stokes and Pankowski, 1988) do learn from the media and change their behaviour accordingly (Saunders et al, 2003). Television, as Hartley (1999) argues, does have pedagogic possibilities. And this learning may be either intentional or incidental, with studies showing that in some respects young people value and learn more about sensitive matters from what they see on the television than they do from formal schooling (Bragg and Buckingham, 2003). Many ethnographies show audiences productively, and complexly, using the media to learn to make sense of their everyday life experiences and social and personal identities while developing both real and virtual communities of interest and mutual support (Shattuc, 1997; Baym, 2000; Bird, 2003). Popular serial drama has been a prime medium for social messaging and informal lifelong learning in the UK from the early 1950s. The classic BBC radio soap *The Archers* addressed issues of agricultural innovation, and the first episode of BBC television's *The Grove Family* discussed community safety. In 2005 Channel 4's teenage soap *Hollyoaks* tackled issues relating to sexual health and testicular cancer and other British soaps such as *Brookside* and *EastEnders* have addressed a range of social problems including HIV/AIDS, sexual abuse, breast cancer and domestic violence. In the 1980s and 1990s the US comedian Bill Cosby devised a sitcom to promote a more positive image of African Americans to and for African Americans. In 2004 former *EastEnders* producer Matthew Robinson used his expertise to help design and produce a new soap for Cambodian Television, *Taste of Life*, to fight AIDS. *Soul City* in South Africa has being doing something similar for many years and radio soaps are used in many African countries, including Rwanda and Nigeria, to reach and educate people in rural areas about health, social and gender equality. Although some critics suggest that Western money and Western media know-how serve to communicate Western values to audiences in developing countries, many aid agencies and national governments have long advocated the educational value of broadcasting (Singhal et al, 2004).

Despite this obviously important work, PSB is threatened worldwide. In the US the Public Broadcasting Service (PBS) has been attacked by the Republican administration for its lack of balance in news and current affairs reporting, and in June 2005 it was announced that Federal funds to the Corporation for Public Broadcasting would be cut by 25 per cent (Farhi, 2005). Despite protests, political pressure on the PBS remains intense, even though it is becoming increasingly market-orientated and brand-focused:

> *The new entrepreneurial approach has progressed so far at PBS that it is becoming increasingly difficult to detect the public service model of broadcasting at work. Indeed, the rise of the new PBS raises important questions about the meaning of such concepts as public service and the public interest.* (Hoynes, 2003, p128)

Interestingly, given current debates in the US about rehabilitating DDT in order to (ostensibly) combat malaria in Africa, the 1993 PBS documentary in the American Experience series on Rachel Carson's *Silent Spring*, which highlighted the attacks on her work by a number of large corporations, is not, unlike many other programmes, available for public purchase as a DVD. The PSB ethos in the US has always been far weaker than in the UK, but even here seriously challenging PSB programming is frequently relegated to minority channels such as digital BBCFour and/or broadcast late at night (Ofcom 2004b; 2004c; 2005). Although audiences for such programmes have always been relatively small, the re-articulation of PSB, combined with the expansion of the multi-channel environment, means that it is likely that mass audiences for challenging and critical environmental programming may decline further. At the RSA and Arts Council sponsored conference Arts and Ecology in Bristol in 2005, BBC producer Jeremy Bristow, maker of *Kings of the Jungle*, *The Price of Prawns* and other environmental documentaries, rehearsed the problem succinctly for TV audiences and programme-makers alike. Although there could conceivably be more opportunities to make and watch challenging and critical programmes, the increasingly fragmented nature of the new media audience would mean fewer people would see them. Referring to his own experience with BBC4, Bristow suggested that even with repeats a programme like *Ape Hunters*, which investigated the bushmeat trade, would probably not be commissioned for either BBC1 or BBC2, where more benign natural history programming dominates. I asked him whether the multi-channel environment offered more or fewer advantages to programme-makers like him. He replied:

Can I say both? More opportunity and more fragmented. The environment programmes I used to do for BBC1 and BBC2 now go out on BBC4, capturing an audience of from 3, 4 and 5 million to 50,000, OK they are repeated a bit, but there's that order of reduction. To take up Martin's point, about The Blue Planet *[being 'dishonest because it portrayed the marine environment as being pristine and in no way damaged for the most part'], you are right up to a point. I mean they did produce a programme called* Trouble *that went out on BBC2 at the same time. It was one programme with some of the producers from* The Blue Planet. *Was it good enough? Not in my view; they didn't really make reference to it. It was off on its own and very few people watched it. It got a reasonable audience but we could go into that issue more. There's more 'ghetto-ization'. My fear is that, OK, I can make films that challenge the environment to an environmentally interested community and these are the films I make and can get to them. Can I make films where, hopefully, viewers who never thought about environmental issues before happen to switch on, get engaged and get motivated? The chances for that are getting less because of this fragmentation with all these channels. All that exists to some extent is that David Attenborough and* The Blue Planet *guide help create a sense of love of nature at least, even if, to some extent, they are helping portray a picture that doesn't reflect on the state of the oceans which we all know are in a desperate situation But maybe we are aware enough most of us to know that the oceans are in deep trouble and maybe we are still happy to go and enjoy a film which shows how wonderful these oceans can be. I'm not saying that's the official response on behalf of the BBC but that's probably one defence it's got.* (interview with author)

For Bristow, and for public service broadcasters and sustainability practitioners alike, what becomes important is not so much ratings but impact – discussions in the press, public debates, social learning through everyday conversations stimulated by the media, and, like *Springwatch*, public action. In other words making people think and do something. The lessons from PBS and BBCFour are that PSB broadcasters could increasingly target the more educated, 'thinking' and politically aware social demographics; and that where commercial satellite companies do offer programming that critically addresses environmental and sustainability issues, these will be largely confined to special-interest subscription channels where sustainability and the environment could develop a specific niche in a new media ecology. But PSB has had, and still has, a role in enabling ideas and experiences to be broadly shared, disseminated and discussed. It is not perfect and never has been but it does potentially offer an invaluable cultural and democratizing resource. People learn from each other, and if there is the opportunity to learn from different worlds and from different cultures, to learn about difficult and challenging environmental issues, then there must be something more than narrowcasting to market segments and special interest groups. Sustainable development is not a special interest; it is a process motivated by ecological problems that we unavoidably have in common, and it is in the public interest. PSB offers a broad platform for minority voices to be heard, potentially by large audiences, and should perhaps be perceived not only as part of our cultural inheritance but also as an element of the cultural commons we all need to protect and conserve rather than enclose. PSB could allow programmes made by indigenous people, rather than programmes made on them, to be seen more widely. For instance, the Canadian First Nation documentary filmmaker Barb Cranmer has made films on indigenous culture, knowledge and history financed by the National Film Board of Canada, the Canadian Television Fund, the Knowledge Network, the Aboriginal People's Television Network and other sources. *Laxwesa Wa* (1995) examines traditional fishing practices in British Columbia and documents native people's efforts to build a sustainable fishery for the future. Hardly commercial prime time, the work of Barb Cranmer represents the potential of 'minority' film and television to become an important vehicle in developing a public understanding of sustainable development, of alternative ways of working and being. The Inuit film *Atanarjuat* and films from Iran such as *The Circle* or *Ten*, recently screened on PSB channels in the UK, offer an alternative aesthetic and cultural world-view to that produced by globalizing Western film and television productions (Gauthier, 2004). Nonetheless, Hollywood films such as *Erin Brockovich* and *The Day After Tomorrow* have also engaged directly with environmental justice and climate change by telling gripping personalized and heroic stories of struggle and redemption. Although Postman may suggest that storytelling is not universally appropriate as an educational tool, it is certainly the case that storytelling is a universal phenomenon through which people learn ideas, values and ways of living and being. It was an important part of the culture of primitive peoples and remains so today, whether you are living in the outback of Australia or a skyscraper in Manhattan, whether you like to see yourself as a sophisticated urbanite, a Polish peasant, a Kalahari bushman or a middle-class greenie living in rural England. Stories are the stuff of television, of print journalism, of everyday discourse and are communicated through word, image, music and gesture. Stories may help people envision a different future, understand change or difference and observe, imagine or learn from role models. David Attenborough's documentaries tell stories about the lives of animals and plants and about the Earth and have undoubtedly opened up new worlds for many, many viewers. There is a danger that without a vibrant PSB, a public sphere – of multiple voices, multiple authorships, political confrontations and exchanges, digital interactivity, intercultural television with programmes belonging to more than one culture, opportunities for learning, debate and participation in 'the dialogue of values' that constitute sustainable development – may fail to develop as fully as it should.

ADVERTISING, MARKETING AND CULTURE JAMMING

Personalized stories, celebrity endorsements, marketing, advertising communication and other forms of social modelling are also part of our media and other cultural environments. Some of this is quite ephemeral. Some of it is literally an extra – actors sometimes step out of role on DVD extras, as Dennis Quaid does to present the 'Science of Tomorrow' documentary accompanying the feature *The Day After Tomorrow*. Robbie Williams presents a short film on child exploitation for UNICEF, initially shown in cinemas and later found as an 'extra' on *Intolerable Cruelty* – an unrelated screwball comedy starring George Clooney and Catherine Zeta Jones. Richard Gere has for many years publicly promoted the work of Survival International, which is aimed at protecting the rights of indigenous peoples. In newspaper advertisements the IVF specialist Lord Robert Winston endorses St Ivel's 'Advance' milk, which supposedly enables you 'to give your kids more Omega 3 without them noticing'. And BP uses 'ordinary people' in its television commercials in the US and UK as part of its wide-ranging marketing communication strategy to rebrand itself by moving 'beyond petroleum' to help wean Western consumer society off its dependence on fossil fuels and develop cleaner energy sources such as solar and natural gas. The corporation website (www.bp.com) states that 'we took a video camera, walked out onto the streets of several major metropolitan areas, stopped more than 400 strangers, and asked them their thoughts' on global climate change. The transcript shows how BP is associating itself with a general popular concern about environmental issues and is itself becoming a role model of responsible corporate citizenship (see Box 6.2).

The pressure group Corpwatch (www.corpwatch.org), commenting on BP's campaign, noted acidly:

> BP's re-branding as the 'Beyond Petroleum' company is perhaps the ultimate co-optation of environmentalists' language and message. Even apart from the twisting of language, BP's suggestion that producing more natural gas is somehow akin to global leadership is preposterous. Make that Beyond Preposterous.
>
> BP's claim to be 'the largest producer of solar energy in the world' is a little more serious. But being #1 for BP is so easy. It was achieved by spending US$45 million to buy the Solarex solar-energy corporation. That's a tiny fraction of the US$26.5 billion it spent to buy ARCO in order to increase BP's production capacity for oil. BP will spend US$5 billion over five years for oil exploration in Alaska alone. And, according to one group of BP shareholders, BP spent more on their new eco-friendly logo last year than on renewable energy.

Box 6.2 BP UK Advertisement: Do You Worry About Global Climate Change?

Question: Do you worry about global climate change?

Cabbie (London): I guess as I get older, yes, I am starting to worry about the environment now, the global warming...

Young Indian woman (London): I worry because I don't know much about it, but I know it's detrimental to our health.

Middle-aged business man (Chicago): We're destroying the capability of the planet to heal itself.

Young Asian woman (London): It's something we need to deal with and we need to deal with it today.

Text: We [BP] were the first major energy company to publicly acknowledge the need to take steps against climate change.

Our energy efficiency projects have reduced emissions by over 4 million tonnes since 2001, equivalent to the annual emissions of a city the size of Bristol.

Over the next 4 years we are planning to implement new projects to reduce emissions by another 4 million tonnes.

Source: www.bp.com/liveassets/bp_internet/globalbp/STAGING/global_assets/downloads/A/ABP_uk_campaign_worry_about_global_climate_change.pdf

---

> *When a company spends more on advertising its environmental friendliness than on environmental actions, that's greenwash.*
> (Bruno, 2000)

Television can also mediate consumer messages by acting as a consumer watchdog and by broadcasting programmes that explore unhealthy diets, laziness, obesity and even television addiction. Many use experts and celebrities to communicate the messages that are often part of much wider, and sometimes government initiated, public information/health and education campaigns. Channel 4's *Jamie's School Dinners*, focusing on celebrity chef Jamie Oliver's attempt to change first the school dinner system of one London borough and then the nation's, offers insights into the food system, human health, mass production and packaging, market economics, (un)sustainability, and macro- and micro-power relationships. The web-supported series *Honey, We're Killing the Kids and Honey*, broadcast in 2005, is another interesting example. There can be no better affective visual metaphor for the consequences of unsustainability than unhealthy children morphing digitally into desperately unhealthy adults. The parents are confronted with this digital transformation and assured by the presenter that the images are based on the most up-to-date scientific research and technical capability. Over three weeks, the unhealthy family is then given a series of tasks which involve such activities as cutting out the junk food, eating more fruit and vegetables, sitting round a table at meal times, taking more exercise, cutting down on their television watching and computer game playing, going to bed at structured (earlier) times, the whole family going on 'fun days' and, for the parents, perhaps stopping smoking. Six months later the TV cameras return to see how the family has got on. In *We're Killing the Kids – Revisited*, most families have improved their attitudes, values and behaviour. As a reward they are presented with revised digital morphs this time of their children growing into healthier, happier adults. Close-ups on the parent faces show expressions of joy where previously the audience witnessed tears of grief as they were told dramatically, 'you're killing your kids'. The emotional impact of this experience and of watching the programme can be quite considerable and have a discernable impact on behaviour. A follow-up exhibition was held at London's Science Museum, reinforcing the importance of the issues and allowing visitors to further engage with the issues highlighted in the television programme. (On a related issue, Phil, the organic farmer from Devon, told me that when a celebrity chef or food writer features a recipe using organic food his sales at the farmers' markets go up substantially.)

Programmes like these are part of, and sometimes initiate, much wider public campaigns involving the construction of new websites, interactive games and travelling exhibitions aimed at motivating viewers to participate and learn actively and purposefully. In 2003 and 2004 Gerard Hastings for the UK Government's Food Standard's Agency and Sonia Livingstone for Ofcom reported on childhood obesity and the detrimental effects on children's health partly caused by the persistent television advertising of junk foods to children. Livingstone concluded that research going back 40 years only detected 'modest direct effects of TV advertising on children's food preferences' but agreed with Gerbner that, given the cultural ubiquity of the media in our everyday lives, 'if accumulated total exposure is what counts, then almost everyone should be affected... It is clear, then, that the cards are stacked against finding evidence of effects'. Livingstone concludes:

> *Indirect effects are generally acknowledged to be important but are less often researched. There are however some indicative studies. For example it has been shown that television may normalize the image of an 'unhealthy' diet and consequently have an influence on 'unhealthy' food choices. Television viewing can also influence meal habits, which in turn may affect diet. Advertising on TV can lead to children pestering their parents for products, which may, if they are successful, lead to increased consumption of 'unhealthy' foods. Conversely, advertising, if mediated by parental comments, may have less effect. Similarly the consistent correlation between television viewing and 'unhealthy' food choices and/or childhood obesity has been hypothesized as being mediated by displacement of physical exercise and increased snacking. TV programmes and advertising*

> *have also been implicated in encouraging unrealistic expectations*
> *of ideal body size, especially for teenage girls, resulting in discon-*
> *tent with body image and attempts to diet.* (Livingstone, 2004,
> pp111–112)

Many parents look to advertised brands to provide quality products and feed their children accordingly. Vending machines and sponsorship in schools provide a platform for advertisers, and school meals sell themselves to pupils by modelling themselves on commercial principles. When children and their parents point to the importance of in-store promotions, they may have been primed to notice these by having previously seen a television advert. Television advertising sits within a whole web of interconnected influences. It feeds into other forms of promotion and affects children not only directly, but indirectly, through their friends and parents, who also watch television and see adverts and then go on to have their own separate impact on children's food choice.

> *Branding, packaging, 'fun foods' and interpersonal communica-*
> *tion through texting are all part of the indirect promotional*
> *effects, the mediascape, that percolate everyday life. As children*
> *develop, they grow in 'advertising literacy' – the ability to*
> *analyse, evaluate and critique advertising – but do not necessarily*
> *acquire a greater ability to resist advertising messages, largely*
> *because advertisers understand the most effective and subtle ways*
> *of reaching their identified markets.* (Livingstone, 2004, p131)

By the end of 2005, thanks to programmes like *Honey...*, *Fat Nation* and associated public communication campaigns, *The Grocer* reported that consumers were buying fewer calorific chocolate bars like Mars and Snickers, fewer sugary sweets and fatty crisps, fewer fizzy drinks popular with children, fewer frozen pizzas and ready to drink cocktails and more mineral waters and fruit juices, more rice and fresh and dry pasta, more crackers and cereal bars, more low cholesterol spreads and more premium dark and organic chocolate like Lindt and Green and Black's (recently taken over by the confectionary giant Cadbury's).

Although still important, conventional direct television advertising is becoming increasingly problematic in today's highly fragmented multi-channel, multi-media environment. Public information campaigns may look rather tired by association, even if they are sometimes dressed up with fun events, celebrity endorsements and television extravaganzas. Many marketing companies have developed a range of techniques, which come under the general term 'stealth marketing', to deal with this. This sometimes abstruse and surreptitious approach to presenting a new service or product involves word-of-mouth communication to selected consumers who may themselves be trendsetters or opinion leaders, so that eventually the product filters down to ordinary consumers. Although beset by ethical dilemmas, stealth marketing is more prevalent than many people believe and is 'here to stay' (Kaikati and Kaikati,

2004), not least because it seems to be very effective in seamlessly merging with everyday activities – going to school, having a drink in a bar, watching the football, a movie or TV chat show, chatting with a friend, playing a computer game, writing a blog. Kaikati and Kaikati identify a number of stealth marketing techniques including viral marketing – using a digital platform to spread a message ('word of mouse'); brand pushers – hired novice actors and actresses pushing a product in a real-life situation, for example by prominently using a brand new consumer item such as the latest cell phone/DV camera at a tourist venue; celebrity marketing – whereby a celebrity casually refers to a brand or product on a TV chat show; bait and tease marketing – such as Mercedes' mock film trailer shown in cinemas in the UK in 2002; and product placement in pop music, hip hop and video games:

> *In September 2002, Electronic Arts signed contracts to receive more than US$2 million for including McDonald's and Intel in its games. Gamers can participate in The Sims Online, an internet version of the popular PC game, in which the objective is to control virtual characters as they go about their lives. Players can play on PCs blazed with Intel's logo and are able to buy a McDonald's kiosk and sell its fast-food fare.* (Kaikati and Kaikati, 2004, p14)

The US advertising company Massive Inc. has worked with computer game developers to insert pre-defined 'ad areas' in its games. Clients include the US Navy, Coca Cola and Warner Bros. With the market for in-game advertising projected to rise from US$120m in 2004 to US$800m in 2009, this is big business, particularly as video, internet and computer games are becoming increasingly popular with younger people. However, as Calyton Dach (2006) reported in *Adbusters*, players of the law enforcement game SWAT4 posted instructions on the web for permanently blocking the ads. 'Expect players of other games to follow suit,' warned Dach, perhaps remembering from de Certeau how some individuals may develop certain tactics to contest and confront power relationships. The Demos/Green Alliance report 'Carrots, Sticks and Sermons' (Collins et al, 2003) also recognizes the importance of everyday life and the complexity of public behaviour. Using ideas already taken up by marketing companies engaged in viral marketing, the authors suggest that because environmental and sustainability matters are themselves complex and long term, it is difficult for many people to see any immediate benefit either to themselves or others if they change their behaviour, particularly as such changes might result in some personal or financial cost. (Changing to a greener electricity supply, for example, could quite easily mean a higher price per unit of electricity, as I recently discovered.) Gordon (2002) notes that purchasing decisions are frequently opportunistic, based on emotional impulses, cultural cues and wider trends. When public education or marketing campaigns are integrated effectively into social networks, patterns of everyday activity, cultural predispositions and proclivities, latent ideas, and assumptions of public behaviour may alter. Once new ideas, values or practices become more visible, or credible, more people will take them up. As Malcolm Gladwell (2000) writes there comes a time when there is 'a tipping point', and, as Seth Godin (2002) states in *Unleashing the Idea Virus*, it is the 'sneezers' (brand pushers or opinion leaders) that spread the word, idea or action. The Canadian government has recognized this with its 'Tools of Change' campaign (www.toolsofchange.com). Collins et al write:

> *Within all networks, the inter-relationships between members are at least as important as the actual members themselves. Network theory always asks about the links; what matters in a network is each person's degree of connectivity, rather than, for example, their status. Rather than asking people how they feel, or what they do, network theorists are interested in how they interact.*
>
> *It follows from the importance attached to inter-relationships that networks are seen to add up to more than the sum of their parts. 'Emergence' is a term that has been used to describe networks where low-level rules can translate cumulatively to higher level sophistication, without any apparent leadership, direction or coordination.* (Collins et al, 2003, p18)

It is almost certainly the heart rather than the head, the emotions that brand marketing, popular cinema, photography and television most often address. Sustainability practitioners need to recognize this and become eclectic in their approach, applying and adapting theories where the context and times demands. Systems theory, with one thing leading to or feeding back on another, is at the heart of this approach, and at the core of changing ideas and behaviour, the significance of social learning theory should be remembered. Many people take more notice of role models, peers or TV celebrities, and learn more from observing others and from receiving positive feedback than from simply reading public information leaflets or eco-labels on consumer packaging or going to a class.

Many campaign groups, large and small, are now using the media extremely effectively. By working with tabloid and broadsheet newspapers, the regional and faith press, trade and consumer titles, the 'Make Poverty History' campaign in 2005, which also included a huge demonstration in Edinburgh and the Live 8 event, succeeded in communicating to a huge audience, reaching 72 per cent of adults in the UK (34 million people). This significantly contributed to a high level of public awareness (87 per cent). The use of celebrities, advertising and Ofcom banning the finger clicking ad from television because it contravened the 2003 Communication Act forbidding political advertising generated additional coverage. The stylish black and white advertisement, with a voiceover by Liam Neeson, featured a range of celebrities including Bono, Claudia Schiffer, Brad Pitt, Emma Thompson and Bob Geldof, who, appearing one after the other, clicked their fingers at three second intervals to symbolize the fact that a child dies from a preventable disease

---

Box 6.3 Communication is Key for Success

The advertising sector plays a role in influencing consumption patterns by representing a link between producers and consumers. It is widely known to have creative talents and expertise. Such creativity is needed to translate the concept of sustainable consumption/lifestyle into different images to promote a product or service.

Response of business and advertising

Producers, who have to meet consumer needs effectively and in a sustainable manner, first explore what consumers want. Many surveys indicate that consumers are increasingly interested in 'the world beyond' the product they buy. They may not all take action, but the underlying trend is clear. And this holds true worldwide. Examples of UNEP trend studies are 'The Global Consumer Class' and 'Is the Future Yours?' (see UNEP's website: www.uneptie.org/sustain).

Source: McCann-Erickson/UNEP (2002)

---

somewhere in the world every three seconds. As the campaign took off, it became part of the news agenda and was able to exploit the 24-hour rolling news services with extensive coverage on news channels and online. Around 50 per cent of press articles analysed by Metrica mentioned at least one of Make Poverty History's three demands – trade justice, debt cancellation and more and better overseas aid. Richard Bagnall, Managing Director of Metrica, was quoted in an MPH press release as saying, 'The Make Poverty History campaign analysis demonstrated that 27 per cent of coverage achieved excellent message delivery. This was also reflected in market research which showed increasing levels of public awareness in relation to these strongly delivered messages.' The campaign also generated over three days of broadcast coverage, peaking around the G8 summit in July, when campaign spokespeople, many of them celebrities, featured in over 700 broadcast interviews, almost 300 on the first two days of July alone.

MPH showed what could be achieved on a large scale with traditional electronic media if the story resonates with journalistic and other priorities. In *Smart Mobs* Howard Rheingold (2002) argues that while new media communication and computing technologies amplify human talents for cooperation and can do an excellent job, the impacts of 'smart mob' technology may be both beneficial and/or destructive – used by some to support democracy and civil society protests and by others to coordinate terrorist attacks. Mobile communication devices and omnipresent computing – iPods, mobile phones, PDAs, etc. – make all this possible. Street demonstrators in the 1999 anti-WTO protests in Seattle used dynamically updated websites, cell-phones and 'swarming' tactics. In early 2001 citizens organizing public demonstrations by communicating with text messages overthrew the government of President

Joseph Estrada of the Philippines after a long period of discontent. As Rheingold says, smart mob technology is all around us – radio chips designed to replace barcodes; cybercafés; neighbourhood ICT centres; eBay; extremely inexpensive microprocessors embedded in everything from box tops to shoes (and beginning to permeate furniture, buildings and local communities) – and it is the function of research by biologists, sociologists, and economists into the nature of cooperation to seek to understand what is going on and could possibly go on in the future. Media corporations and government agencies are seeking to impose control, regulation and censorship, sometimes in the name of the war on terror; for Rheingold, if successful, this will damage if not destroy the democratic, creative and liberating potential of new technology and human capabilities. He warns:

> It is up to us to decide what 'human' means, exactly how it is different from 'machine', and what tasks ought and ought not to be trusted to either species of symbol-processing system. But some decisions must be made soon, while the technology is still young. And the deciding must be shared by as many citizens as possible, not just the experts. In that sense, the most important factor in whether we will all see the dawn of a humane, sustainable world in the twenty-first century will be how we deal with these machines a few of us thought up and a lot of us will be using. (Rheingold, 2000)

Of course, not everyone agrees that the new technologies offer the positives Rheingold envisions. We have already seen what Lowell Monke thinks, but computers and the internet are here to stay and are being used increasingly in all aspects of our everyday lives. The phenomena of citizen journalists, online newsrooms and independent media centres are something new and potentially liberating, and, although many 'indymedia' sites and blogs are sometimes ill-informed rants, not all are by any means. The increased potential for participation, direct action, free expression and critique is a welcome alternative to the dominance of corporate and state media, of Fox News and the failure of editorial policy to cover issues that do not meet the existing narrow criteria of newsworthiness or due impartiality. Citizen media projects may not always be successful. Some may be quite messy. But even if the distinction between producer and audience is blurred, perhaps this too is a useful antidote to the blurring of editorial and advertising/funding criteria in many commercial operations. A citizen journalist does not need a great deal of technical skill to post a comment (although to set up a site yourself does require significant knowledge and understanding of ICT). Serious thought went into the design and launch of Wikipedia, which in 2004 published its 500,000th article. Grass-roots activity, where anyone can post or amend an article, has flourished, grown and diversified, showing the immense capabilities the web has if used thoughtfully and responsibly. And most Wiki contributors are clearly using it in this way. For Dan Gillmor (2006, p150), a leading advocate of grass-roots journalism, the

Wikis represent 'an ideal journalistic tool under the right circumstances'. And, just as the multi-volume Encyclopaedia Britannica once adorned the living space of many households, participatory virtual reporting and knowledge sites are becoming a major feature of many people's virtual worlds today.

The technology also allows subversion or rearticulation of another kind. Since 1989 the group behind *Adbusters* magazine have been effectively turning the corporate PR messages against their originators in hilarious and sometimes quite pointed ways. 'Culture jamming' is a tactic available to anyone with a message, confidence and imagination, but is possibly most effective when occurring as part of a broader social movement campaign, for example human rights or global ecology. It is simultaneously empowering and an education in the theory and practice of communication, public relations and political power. It is a form of learning by doing, of social action, of subverting what Lasn (2000, p123) calls our dominant cultural memes, in other words those units 'of information (a catchphrase, a concept, a tune, a notion of fashion, philosophy or politics) that leaps from brain to brain to brain'. Memes pass through a culture like genes pass through generations and potent ones can change behaviour, perspectives on the world and even transform cultures. Lasn is a 'meme warrior' engaged in a 'meme war', and his principal enemy is corporate-sponsored consumerism. For Lasn, the anti-smoking ad and public communication campaigns exemplify how successful a meme war can be: 'I remember Yul Brynner, whose last creative act in the world, after a slow disintegration from lung cancer, was to come on TV just months from death, look the world in the eye and say, "Whatever you do, don't smoke"' (Lasn, 2000, p125). Another example is the famous 'subvertisement' which shows two cowboys riding together at sunset as if in a Marlboro ad but the caption reads, 'I miss my lung, Bob'. Through various acts of overturning and subversion the aim is to 'uncool' consumer culture – high (exploitative) fashion, car culture, corporate-dominated media products, junk food, the PR business – with strategies involving finding leverage points, using the law and reframing debates as well as a range of tactics such as initiating cyberpetitions, liberating billboards, confronting corporate PR professionals, producing your own media messages and mediaspots, and joining in with buy-nothing day or TV-turn-off weeks. See how the big corporations take to a loss of sales or advertising revenue. This cultural guerrilla warfare has had mixed success, though, since, as Rumbo (2002) and Heath and Potter (2005) argue, although adbusting is potentially a way of raising awareness and motivating change, corporate marketers have also adapted resistance efforts to their own purposes by developing eco niche products and markets for themselves. So, if a multi-national starts its own fair-trade brand is that a victory or a defeat for the culture jammers? If the culture jammers start marketing their own organic or fair-trade goods, is that simply reproducing the ethic of consumerism or part of a process by which new sustainable consumption patterns and new sustainable lifestyles can be fashioned? In some ways, culture jamming is in the avant-garde of consumerism and pro-sustainability communications in that it clarifies distorted or misleading messages and/or cultivates understanding of, and commitment to, sustainable goods, services, practices and maybe brands (Carducci, 2006). At the very least, it is part of the active learning process of developing a practical media literacy.

So what is my message? There are tensions and contradictions in the fact that the media can almost equally be seen as an opportunity or a threat, but there's a great deal at stake and everything to play for. The media is there, new and old – use it.

7

Reschooling Society

This chapter explores processes that are resocializing and reschooling society in a more sustainable direction. There is clear potential here and fine examples of groups, businesses and institutions making a difference, as well as a few uncertainties. The chapter comprises sections on:

- ICT and teleworking;
- ICT in community development;
- Computer games and learning;
- Learning to be sustainable: business and education; and
- Sustainability and the culture of everyday life.

ICT AND TELEWORKING

How many more times do we need to be told that we are living in a media-saturated and increasingly connected world, that new media technologies are changing the way we live our lives? As we have seen, there are plenty of media and technology critics – of television, of iPods, of the internet and personal computers – just as there were of the printed book and cinema in previous centuries (Ellul, 1964; Postman, 1993). If information and communications technology (ICT) is able to help dematerialize the economy, then it will also need to help resocialize and demobilize society; if it is to foster sustainability, it will do so because it also offers immense possibilities for global connectivity through which the values informing sustainable development may flow – respect for natural systems, tolerance and environmental justice, and the rights of non-human creatures and of future human generations. It is possible that the internet will enable people to see the consequences of their actions more clearly by being able to access and make sense of information from a huge variety of sources. For the present, 'cyberspace' is a global commons not yet completely colonized by corporate or governmental interests, although there is certainly a danger that this may occur in the not-too-distant future. Driskell and Lyon (2002) see the internet enhancing traditional communities in a local place or shared space. Virtual communities are not going to take over. We are not all about to become asocial automatons, plugged into the nearest piece of hardware, but on- and off-line relationships can, and do, easily complement one another. Email and other net services can fill in the gaps between face-to-face meetings and get-togethers for families, social groups, businesses, universities and diaspora communities. It may be better to view the net, like the telephone, as a means of communication that is quickly becoming an integral part of our everyday lives. Internet shopping is on the increase, with market analysts Verdict estimating that in the UK in 2005, £8.2bn worth of goods were purchased online – up 29 per cent from the previous year – as opposed to £9.4bn purchased in department stores (*The Guardian*, 13.2.06). ebay has undoubtedly contributed much to this trend, but more sustainably, perhaps, people's increased familiarity with making internet transactions has led to such cyber-mediated activities as 'freecycling', whereby people advertise their unwanted goods on the net as free to anyone who wants them and bothers to pick them up. www.freecycling.org is about recycling and reducing the amount of stuff that goes to landfill. It is an example of ICT affording possibilities for shopping without increasing material consumption, with people learning to rearticulate and reproduce one set of everyday lifestyle values (consumption) with another (reuse) (Child, 2006).

Two reports from Forum for the Future (Forum, 2004; Goodman, Alakeson and Jorgensen, 2004) on the contribution of new media technologies to the economy and society are positive. Small- and medium-sized enterprises (SMEs) are potentially the largest beneficiaries of broadband. Within the health sector, the future possibilities of teleconsulting will mean enhanced access for patients living in remote areas to specialist advice and guidance and, although the message is a little more mixed, there are indications that ICT and the internet can foster and multiply social capital. In *Making the Net Work*, Alakeson et al (2003) suggest that use of the internet over a long period led to more frequent socializing, with social contacts located geographically beyond the local community of the user. The internet acts as a social focus in many homes, with families watching film trailers together before collectively deciding what to watch. Families share online gaming experiences, 'cheat codes', shopping (dubious maybe in other respects) or simply help with children's homework. Broadband has also helped community centres be more operationally efficient. Of course, increased access to high-speed internet connections has a downside, with burgeoning online pornography businesses, terrorist and other hate sites, software pirating, and so on, but there are also benefits, particularly to the growth of global activism, political participation and free speech leading to individual and group empowerment.

Forum has also identified a number of negative environmental impacts of broadband and ICT, but many of these are possibly only short term, as people, businesses and communities upscale and upgrade. Processes of dematerialization will have a more positive and direct impact on our ecological footprint:

> *Broadband is being implemented primarily because of the obvious economic and social benefits that it brings. The environmental effects of broadband are more mixed. Take for example*

> *telework, largely enabled by broadband internet access. It is*
> *implemented first of all because it is economic at a company level,*
> *and second because there is employee demand, associated with*
> *quality of life and working efficiency. It is implemented because*
> *of the social and economic benefits. But from an environmental*
> *point of view the estimates of impacts vary widely from positive*
> *(less car travel, less office space required) to negative (extra car*
> *travel stimulated, more energy used in the home). At the direct*
> *primary level, rolling out broadband has an environmental cost:*
> *specialist equipment must be manufactured and disposed of at*
> *end of life, and small but significant amounts of electricity are*
> *consumed.* (Forum, 2004, p31)

Broadband encourages more internet usage and this will mean increases in electricity consumption, CO_2 emissions and climate change unless more power is generated from renewable sources. Online banking transactions are potentially more resource efficient than travelling to your local branch, but for this to occur there need to be significant organizational changes, perhaps involving the closure of high street banks and certainly totally secure and efficient computer applications. All this could conceivably impact negatively on some aspects of social and personal life, and there is also the problem of ICT hardware manufacture, usage, rapid obsolescence and waste. In the UK, mobile phone users tend to replace their models every 18 months, possibly more often. Smaller products are resource intensive, but if their useful life can be extended through easy upgrades then this need not be a problem. Mobile computing devices, including 'thin clients', are probably less energy intensive than desktop computers, and with increased teleworking there will be less need for hardware in the office, although it is quite possible that just as every member of many families has their own TV, they may also have their own computer. Some negative impacts are therefore dependent on user behaviour rather than design and manufacture, and this is where consumer learning about the consequences of lifestyle and technology on the environment is important. Learning can take place through the activities of environmental campaigners and government agencies and through corporate marketing and communications. Ecover, for example, has an open information policy. You can go to their website and see how their products are made. This free access to information is about corporate sharing – enabling customers to understand the nature of the product through learning about sustainable development. The net can be used to start dematerializing production, although success here will also depend on changes in social habits and expectations as well as technological affordances. Alakeson et al (2003, p80) note that downloading 56 minutes of music from the internet 'is twice as resource efficient as buying a CD online and more than two and half times as resource efficient than going to a shop to buy a CD'. However, this all depends on whether the music is then burnt onto a CD (or two) and what type of connection the user has. There is still a tendency for consumers to want to own a tangible product, but time may change this. Waage, Shah and Girshick (2003, p95) identify a number of points that could make ICT a key factor in sustainable development. These include creating new products free of persistent organic pollutants, heavy metals, and so forth; hardware that can be easily upgraded rather than replaced; energy-efficient hardware; designs deploying services that cycle materials through 'closed loop' processes; manufactures using renewable energy; ICT access for all people while respecting cultural differences and needs; and health and safety issues for individuals and communities.

William J. Mitchell, author of *City of Bits* (1996), *E-topia* (2000) and *Me++* (2003), sees immense potential in the future development and application of new media technologies to both public and private spheres. He suggests that intra-urban digital networking has the potential to provide a contemporary version of a public forum revitalizing democratic debate and participation. Online communities will complement physical ones, stimulating new social relationships, entrepreneurial opportunities, economic markets and informational connections in the process. As rural telecommunications infrastructure develops to deliver a range of services, from education and health to work and sustainable business practices, the classic distinctions between rural and urban living may gradually fade. With processes of virtualization and miniaturization continuing to shape our use of space, our understanding of place will inevitably alter. Digital sensors will enable us to accurately monitor our use of renewable and non-renewable resources. An electronically managed vehicle rental and distribution service might lead to the decline of the two- and three-car household – after all, most of the time the car is just sitting there doing nothing – and this would reduce costs, resource use and, if people travel less, pollution too. As noted above, with laptops, notebooks, datasticks, and wireless or broadband connections, it may well be possible to work from virtually anywhere. If this is so, then it is likely people will choose to live and work where it is nice, where work can be done effectively and a healthy life can be lived. Mitchell writes:

> We will also need to re-examine traditional approaches to land use zoning, which presume that workplaces generate noise, traffic and pollution and hence must be rigorously separated from residential areas. Telecommunications-based work has few of these undesirable effects, and so affords the possibility of inter-weaving living and working spaces in a much finer-grained way – a matter of floor plans rather than land-use maps. (Mitchell, 2000, p74)

Mitchell recognizes that many properties may not be able to accommodate digital workspaces and that some poor communities will not attract the necessary investment while some of the wealthier ones may remain firmly within the gated enclaves; planners, architects, business people, community groups and others will need to work together to realize a vision of 'the laptop at the pizza café table instead of the PC in the gated condo'. There is a lot of professional learning still to do.

Forum for the Future recommends that, among other things, 'telework technology packages should be sold with training on adapting processes, awareness of social and environmental impacts ... consumer awareness of the environmental impact of the always-on culture could be built into marketing communications' (Goodman, Alakeson and Jorgensen, 2004, p49). There seems to be increasing evidence that work processes are being transformed by the application of ICT and that, if this occurs with some environmental sensitivity, new media technologies could render businesses more efficient, cyclical in resource consumption, networked and sustainable. Telework is growing and, although there may be feelings of isolation and an increase in working hours for some teleworkers, it does seem to enable people to strike a better work–life balance than perhaps they could have secured with more traditional work and commuting patterns. Unfortunately, miles not driven commuting to work may partially be made up by miles driven on social trips. The companionship of the office may be missed and career opportunities may be lost by simply not being seen when you should be. Alakeson et al (2003) further suggest that the informal learning opportunities afforded by regular face-to-face contact with colleagues and clients may hamper the development of soft skills like interpersonal communication and networking. Additionally, home may no longer be that refuge from work and, just as the pager or cell phone means you are always potentially contactable, working from home means you are always potentially at work. New routines, work practices, protocols and disciplines will need to develop and it may be that the home is only one of the many places mobile workers use. Wireless connectivity makes many diverse sites potential workspaces. Public transport is more amenable to mobile computing than travelling by car. You can't look at a computer screen and through the windscreen at the same time and safely stay on the road. Wireless internet facilities are increasingly being made available on many mainline trains. A hotel room can, and frequently does, serve as an office. So does a laptop on a café table or a park bench, rearticulating public space and leading to new 'real' as well as virtual relationships and connections with people who do likewise. In this way ICT may create a greater degree of urban hetereogeneity, replacing experiences of separation with new opportunities for encounter, gatherings, meetings and diversification. (Lefebvre would be pleased.) Theoretically at least, time would seem to have been freed up by teleworking, enabling greater attention to be given to domestic and even community activities. Studies by Penny Gurstein (2001) suggest, however, that changes in people's ways of living and their domestic arrangements may not necessarily be smooth or conflict free. Those who telework from home may find their work lives impinging upon their home lives. Hours are often long and irregular, with domestic schedules having to fit in around work priorities. Women with full-time family responsibilities experience this the most, and the best way to cope seems to be a rigid compartmentalization of work life, work time and work space, apart from other activities. This requires learning good self-discipline and time management skills and, although there may be a blurring of boundaries between work and home, this need not necessarily be negative. If a personally effective and culturally productive integration of private and public spheres can be fashioned, the flexibility of these new work–domestic arrangements may be particularly attractive to those wishing to be free of corporate constraints.

Not all work with ICT is equally or intrinsically rewarding, of course. Gurstein distinguishes between people who work with computers and people who work for them. The crucial factor here is the control a person has over the nature of the work, the nature of the employment contract and the social setting in which the work takes place. Call centres are not the most exciting places to be, but then neither is processing data at home, working in a factory or doing the ironing especially exciting. The real imperative is to make the technology work for people, and this can be achieved by making technology that affords this possibility and for people to be willing to learn to do new things or to do familiar things differently.

ICT in Community Development

ICT is a very important element in the MCTi initiative, which has benefited immensely from the talents and energy of a local businessman who enthusiastically drives it forward by encouraging others to learn about ICT's potential in promoting community regeneration and development and the skills necessary to make this happen. What looks like rocket science initially soon becomes a familiar part of a person's everyday experience. David, the leader of the ICT focus group, strongly believes ICT will 'drive the economic sustainability' of the largely rural locality of Tiverton and the Exe Valley. Before the end of 2005, he and his team had developed and marketed the Exe Valley Plan's first quick-win project, the 'Virtual Office', and then immediately concentrated on a systems development to strip away unnecessary duplication and dated procedures to 'get optimum outcomes'. David continues:

> For the Exe Valley Plan, this could maximise the benefits of the MCTi 'healthcheck' process, enabling a comprehensive database of the area to be built up and regularly updated. In the longer term, not only could it ensure that all projects put forward in the Exe Valley Plan were thoroughly analysed in terms of their future sustainability, but it could also significantly help to generate funding for these projects. Suggestions contributed at the Community Event and launch included a 'web net' with the potential to link with all local services. This could lift the area's agricultural economy; create a virtual pannier market by linking village shops and allowing specialisations; and provide an advisory arm, linked to the voluntary and community sector and to the statutory sector. (interview with author)

Huggins and Izushi (2002) have shown how businesses in rural areas have far fewer opportunities to interact with one another than their counterparts in urban areas. Transport problems aside, there are also fewer opportunities to access ICT learning opportunities, even when these are perceived as relevant or useful. David recognizes this, because he has seen 'people's eyes glaze over' when he talks about computers, dynamic search engines, algorithms, microsites, anchor tags and the like. As a passionate entrepreneur, David sometimes feels like the lone ranger. For many people ICT is still an alien world, a matrix of possibilities, fears and confusions. In addressing the possibility of resistance, reluctance or trepidation, David and his colleagues have designed a visually attractive website with an emphasis on simplicity and interactivity. Anyone with basic computer skills and the ability to write a document in Word will be able to create their own web-page, with images. A simple facility will exist whereby people can write their own electronic business cards, 'microsites', or, for a small fee, phone in to dictate text to a community member who will do this for them. Accessible links to information on the local community, culture, economy, property, sport, leisure, health, politics and voluntary sector is part of the conception. 'This is a way of giving people power, which is what it's all about, really', David told me. But for ICT to work most effectively it has to operate within a 'wired culture', with sufficient community members networked and willing to exploit the resource and facilitate the learning required by others to join in. It is possible to use the metaphor of a digital ladder rather than a digital divide, with individuals and groups having differential access, capacity or inclination to use the technology. For example, ICT offers opportunities to people who are disabled or have hearing difficulties to communicate with a wide and geographically distributed range of individuals, groups and organizations.

In the Tiverton and Exe Valley MCTi, ICT is envisioned as a key component of developing a sustainable community and local economy. ICT is one important means through which this could happen, something which came out quite clearly at the launch Community Event in September 2005. Its realization will entail a series of significant learning experiences and activities. For MCTi coordinator Fern, sustainable development is crucial and people's understanding of this notion will become firmly rooted in their own practice, their changing living and working environments, and, ultimately, their everyday lives if the current level of awareness, connectivity and achievement is maintained. Fern notes:

> *I do think ICT is very important, because one of the things about a rural area is that you have a lot of isolated people, particularly people who have come from the agricultural sector, which is shrinking and changing dramatically. They have to adapt and one way they can do this readily and find niche markets for their products is by being familiar with web developments, portals and so forth, or else having somebody on hand who could do that for them, and I think a huge area of activity for us will be education*

*in IT – setting up systems perhaps whereby marketing can reach
a much wider proportion of the population. It could be with
global economics and the reduction of the oil capacity globally
that local produce becomes more economic again, but they need
to prepare for that now. They can't wait for that to change as
individual businesses. They need to build up markets now.* (interview with author)

If ICT development can nurture the idea, and practice, of an 'electronic forum',
with people selling goods, seeking markets and discussing matters of interest
and significance to them and their locality, then democratic participation and
dialogue will occur publicly beyond the enclosed spaces of committee rooms,
council chambers, AGMs and invitation-only conferences, where observers
may have the right to listen but not to speak. It is conceivable that future
disagreements and differences may be resolved, and priorities established,
through discussion in virtual as well as real spaces.

However, it should be remembered that around 50 per cent of adults in
the UK do not have basic computer skills and do not engage with the internet
in any form. Many do not want to and many others have not had the opportunity to do so. There is also potential for new media technologies to be of
benefit only so long as the (social) 'digital divide' is overcome. A study,
Connecting People: Tackling Exclusion?, published by the Greater London
Authority in November 2003 found there was a high level of curiosity about
the internet among socially excluded groups, ie people with low incomes, poor
health, low-level skills, bad housing, living in degraded environments. This
curiosity was matched by an equally high sense of achievement once these
groups had learnt the requisite basic computer skills needed to use the net. An
important factor impeding access was groups' and individuals' over-estimation
of the cost of computer hardware and internet usage. The study also found
that socially excluded groups, even for those with home computers, often used
online facilities at community centres and other public access facilities because
this spread the cost. Even when in employment, these groups had little or no
opportunity to use the net at work and therefore accessed public facilities.
Much informal support, advice and guidance was provided by individuals who
had previously learnt what was necessary and were willing to share their learning with others. Many older people may not have a friendship network
including many ICT users and sometimes a public access centre acted as a focal
point for people of all ages and backgrounds to learn. Neighbourhood support
also has the advantage of being able to articulate and understand local needs
and of providing useful social role models for others to aspire towards or
emulate. The GLA study showed that for those who had problems with basic
literacy and numeracy, the desire to use the internet stimulated a wish to learn
other skills. New socially excluded users made most use of the net to discover
the availability of education, training and job opportunities or to seek health-
care information or advice. Of course, lacking access to ICT, or not having
basic ICT skills, is not a cause of exclusion in itself, but it does certainly exacer-

bate the experience of exclusion. The Danish experience of Information and Community Service Centres in the 1980s was positive in that they strengthened social networks and social dialogue among many disadvantaged groups, and it is hoped the Tiverton MCTi process similarly succeeds.

COMPUTER GAMES AND LEARNING

A certain degree of computer literacy, ability and confidence to communicate effectively is required for social dialogue and interaction via the web to be more than a dream, but people learn from each other through participation, by simply doing, getting involved, defending or promoting an interest, from attending short training courses at a local college, school or adult education centre, or informally from friends, family members and neighbours. Brian Loader and Leigh Keeble's (2004) *Challenging the Digital Divide?* is a thorough review of the literature on community informatics initiatives in which they bring together a wide range of studies showing how the nature of the learning environment, placing computers in non-threatening locations, can be used for a variety of social, recreational and cultural purposes and be far more attractive to technophobes and people with low confidence or poor records of formal educational achievement than those found in more formal and sometimes quite daunting learning environments where the learning of ICT skills may occur outside the sphere of everyday life experience. The authors note that the successful learning of ICT skills must resonate with, and be relevant to, everyday life experiences and concerns – work, health, leisure, and maybe even playing a game or doing an online quiz. Maybe this could relate to lifestyle choices, waste reduction and calculating a household's ecological footprint – how many baths, how much water used, how many black bin bags, how much processed food, how many food miles, how many trips in the car, and so on. Plenty of these online quizzes exist, and when these activities are tied to existing social networks and community activities, learning becomes fun and productive. Casapulla et al (2001) write of working with the Milan Community Network to devise and implement a game, Scopri il Tesoro (Discover the Treasure), that married real life and virtual worlds, the idea being that the best way to learn about the internet is through the internet itself. In this game people got to know each other in the real world and then communicated, met, played or cooperated virtually. Or they might do it the other way round, ensuring that activities in one dimension would affect activities in the other. The game was first rolled out in 1996, and by the time of its last edition in 2000 over 5000 people had played. A children's version was developed in 1998–1999. Casapulla et al write:

> To win the game, people spontaneously assume a provocative approach. In that way they learn the fundamental principles of the appropriate use of network technologies while enjoying themselves, according to the well-known pedagogical principle

> *that you will retain longer and understand better what you have learned while playing. Moreover, in a treasure hunt, you are also spurred both to cooperate (with members of your team) and to compete (among teams) thus learning to use the net as a platform for both cooperation and competition.* (Casapulla et al, 2001, p95)

Many writers have looked to new computer technology, cyberspace, virtual realities and virtual communities as means to enhance standards and quality of life and living (Rheingold, 2000, 2002; Levy, 2000). There are also educational benefits with online learning, the development of virtual learning communities with the use of new media technologies, that may impact favourably upon achieving more sustainable and effective learning environments on and off the school, college and university campus (Laurillard, 2002). Roy Hawkey of the Natural History Museum in London argues that ICT has significant potential to enlarge the scope of informal learning – learning that is 'differentiated by learner choice rather than by the imposition of the governing body or the expert referee' (Hawkey, 2002, p5). Virtual visitors to the Natural History Museum outnumber physical ones, and, for Hawkey, in the fast changing world of scientific uncertainty, innovation and controversy, it is not the transmission of 'facts' but the learning of general principles and values, enquiry skills and the ability to critically evaluate evidence and to ask questions – more and better questions, relevant and substantial questions – that is truly important. ICT can offer pathways and signposts, can facilitate an ecology of learning that empowers and enables groups and individuals. This is the museum policy and it is one that complements the views of many sustainability practitioners and educators (Sterling, 2001; Scott and Gough, 2003). One internet resource developed by Hawkey enables users to virtually handle, and so learn from, museum objects. QUEST (Questioning, Understanding and Exploring Simulated Things), writes Hawkey:

> *enables learners to measure, weigh, magnify, touch, examine under UV light and even date the objects. The aim is to collect data first hand and to try to interpret it. Most significantly, QUEST enables learners to share their ideas in the online notebook. The ensuing discussions are fascinating, many cross-age, cross-culture, even transatlantic.* (Hawkey, 2002, p17)

Video games also offer learning opportunities that are useful in promoting forms of learning, activities and experiences that may foster more sustainable habits of mind, awareness and conduct. 'Serious games' and 'advergames' are becoming seriously important. UNICEF has attracted around 11,000 web visitors a day to play its Becoming a UNICEF World Hero. Food Force, based on the UN World Food Programme, had over two million subscribers and more than ten million plays by October 2005. Designed for 8–13 year olds and translated into five languages, by the end of that year Food Force was also available in Chinese and Japanese versions. The game provides information about geographical areas in need of relief, and virtual tasks such as organizing air drops and distributing food within a city. Lesson plans for teachers and fundraising ideas are also provided and players may post comments on the web. Stokes (2005) sees immense potential for games in promoting and realizing development education. More than books, video games have the capacity to immerse the player for hours in a challenging learning environment. Players inhabit a space that is outside their personal or professional experience. They may organize a disaster relief convoy or plan a sustainable city, and this can offer profound insights and develop virtual on-the-job knowledge and understanding, perhaps triggering potentially long-term changes to attitudes, values and behaviour. Shaffer et al highlight the significance of video games:

> *These rich virtual worlds are what make games such powerful contexts for learning. In game worlds, learning no longer means confronting words and symbols separated from the things those words and symbols are about in the first place. The inverse square law of gravity is no longer something understood solely through an equation; students can gain virtual experience walking on worlds with smaller mass than the Earth, or plan manned space flights that require understanding the changing effects of gravitational forces in different parts of the solar system. In virtual worlds, learners experience the concrete realities that words and symbols describe. Through such experiences, across multiple contexts, learners can understand complex concepts without losing the connection between abstract ideas and the real problems they can be used to solve. In other words, the virtual worlds of games are powerful because they make it possible to develop situated understanding. (Shaffer et al, 2004, p4)*

Games can integrate ways of knowing, doing, caring and being by situating virtual/professional identities within a specific framework of knowledge, socio-cultural identity, values and activities. In order to learn to operate within a professional world, one needs to be able to think and act as if one were a member of that particular professional community. A game developed by the University of Wisconsin enables learners to understand urban ecology by engaging in an imaginary urban planning process. Shaffer et al again:

> *Data shows that in Madison 2200, players form – or start to form – an epistemic frame of urban planning. But they also develop their understanding of ecology and are able to apply it to urban issues. As one player commented, 'I really noticed how [urban planners] have to think about building things like urban planners also have to think about how the crime rate might go up, or pollution or waste, depending on choices.' Another said about walking on the same streets she had traversed before the*

> workshop, *'You notice things, like that's why they build a house there, or that's why they build a park there.'* (Shaffer et al, 2004, p13)

Although not professionally focused, commercial games such as SimCity or Civilization have important learning potential. They now incorporate elements that could conceivably nurture a greater awareness of sustainability issues. Both games are highly interactive and offer opportunities for complex social or historical modelling, although certainly in Civilization, nationalism and imperialism seem particularly prominent domain assumptions. Interestingly, with Civilization IV the designers have ensured each city has a health value (instead of pollution) relating to its happiness. 'Just as luxuries help happiness, certain foods will help health. Factories will decrease health, while certain structures will improve it. So instead of cleaning up black dots, you manage the concept of pollution at the city level' (Chick, 2005).

In the 1990s critics noted that the designers of SimCity assumed that low taxes would encourage growth and high taxes cause recessions, and that the game discourages nuclear power and supports investment in public transport. 'And most fundamentally, it rests on the empiricist, technophilic fantasy that the complex dynamics of city development can be abstracted, quantified, simulated and micromanaged' (Friedman, 1995). In offering a technocratic approach to urban development, SimCity articulates hegemonic social and political values, but these too can be criticized if players are made aware of how and why these elements operate in the way they do. Discussion, virtual or actual, can criticize a game's domain assumptions, alternative values and conceptions applied if these are made available through immersion in a broader (sustainable) learning environment. The Sim game has been used in many urban studies classes in colleges and universities in the US and probably the UK too.

Personally I am interested in the potential computer games have in developing new learning opportunities around sustainability and, as a professional educator, I have become increasingly involved in developing formal online learning programmes for existing, and future, sustainability practitioners. There are many opportunities to both resocialize society and reschool formal institutions of learning. Computer facilities, online resources and learning methods offer amazing, almost overwhelming possibilities, but it is necessary to prevent oneself from being seduced by the technology. Learning aims, however fluid or heuristic, must be the basis of any substantive engagement with sustainability issues, debates and practices, and a healthy scepticism combined with enthusiasm are central ingredients of active, critical and reflective learning.

I spoke with a group of mature full- and part-time Master's students currently on a sustainable development programme about this very issue. They all share common values but these range from the deeply ecological to the quite technocentric and the students' previous experiences span from working in business and finance, local government, the media and community development to full-time education and bringing up a family. It was clear that many of James P. Gee's ideas – that we can learn a lot about learning and literacy from video games (Gee, 2003) – were widely accepted, but it was the experience of everyday life, work and family that framed their understanding of this new media's potential to foster learning for sustainability. One thing: learning to play a game and indeed the game itself can take considerable time, and this is something busy mothers, fathers, workers and students do not have in abundance.

For Dennis:

> *There is a time element to it, to get involved in learning how a game really works. There is a lot of repetition, time invested in it. My kids play SimCity and we have been trying to build a sustainable city, and the version I've got you can cover the whole place in wind farms but you can't seem to generate enough electricity to keep the place going. The algorithms are biased against it, but what is good about it is that it introduces them to think about these sorts of things and it becomes part of their normal values. They don't question it in a way. They kind of accept that they have got to think about those types of things – pollution and waste and what happens to the crime level.*
>
> *There is always a problem of building in the complexity of the real world into a simulation, but a problem for me is the idea that there is a best way of doing things, of building a SimCity or becoming a football manager, and that conflicts with reality, where there are many ways of doing things and different ways can lead to different solutions. It depends on the place, the community, the situation and which is right for that community, in that situation at that time.* (interview with author)

For Anne:

> *It is very much dependent on the technology building in those types of parameters. Is it accurate about when you position a wind farm in that sort of environment, say with a simulated wind speed? Is it generating that amount of electricity? Are the facts right? You are so dependent on the model. I would query that... It might be possible to transfer what you've learnt in a game, but is there a market for it?* (interview with author)

For Linda:

> *I think there is a role and there is obviously something there that needs to be embraced, developed and used as a tool; but I would also say that dialogue and discussion is where real change will happen. My thought on it is when you do community consulta-*

tion and planning it would be great to have something that would give you visuals. So if people did say 'OK, so if the future is wind farms how would it work?' then you could click buttons, show images and calculate and it would still be part of a discussion. I think if people are just plugged in on their own they are only getting the information that the software programmer has put in there. You are not getting a dialogue of values. (interview with author)

For Lucy:

You learn better by physically doing something or seeing something than through reading about something or hearing about something. Particularly children – if kids get on the computer and do alphabet games they pick that up really, really quickly compared to if they sit down and do it from a book. If you try to teach something using a computer you actually get the information in far more quickly. They say that's more mechanical, that we're more like computers, but if they take things in better with computers or with pictures surely that's a good thing.

I'd like my kids to sit down and make planets, and wind farms and ecocities. My six-year-old went onto a computer on this thing where you start off with a hundred rabbits and you've got to say how much food they get, how much water they get and see what happens. He sat there, he played that and he killed all the rabbits and then made billions of rabbits but he knew exactly what he was doing. When he came off of that he could tell me by altering the water or the food or the temperature of the accommodation the rabbits would either thrive or die, and that was really an extremely simple game. If you can learn that much from something so simple then what can you learn from something more complicated. (interview with author)

If computers are perceived as a tool in the service of promoting a more sustainable world, then surely the benefits far outweigh the potential dangers (Monke, 2005). The 36 learning principles Gee (2003) has identified as informing the structure and experience of many games are both positive and constructive. For Gee, learning has to be critical learning. It has to recognize semiotic domains like video games as design spaces that do manipulate us in certain ways and which we too can manipulate in certain ways, because ultimately they are human creations. The very fact that SimCity has been perceived as technocentric shows that other experiences and values (of the non-game world) can lead to critical thinking and reflection. Certainly both the internal design of the game and the social network players inhabit are crucial to games stimulating active learning. The design of many games ensures that they reward players who upgrade their skills and expertise and penalize those who do not.

This is a very valuable principle not always followed effectively in formal learning institutions. It is possible to acquire a level of skill and knowledge that articulates and requires a form of intuitive engagement that Dreyfus and Dreyfus (1986) associate with high-level expertise. There is an inherent principle in many games pushing the player/learner forward to the limits of his/her regime of competence. To appreciate a semiotic domain one has to think like a designer; maybe this is God-like but it is also highly creative and exploratory. Games articulate certain cultural models according to the task or narrative, and critical and active learning enables players to perceive the implications of values and action frameworks that may be unfamiliar or even alien to them. Gee writes of a game called Under Ash, developed by a Syrian publishing house, which has a young Palestinian boy confronting Israeli soldiers and settlers. The player is deeply immersed in Palestinian meaning perspectives, just as players of US military games may see Arabs from US meaning schemes and perspectives. For Gee, the potential of video games is both immense and still largely unmet. He writes:

> *Video games have an unmet potential to create complexity by letting people experience the world from different perspectives. Part of this potential is that, in a video, you yourself have to act as a given character... You must live in a virtual world and make sense of it. This making sense of the virtual world amid not just thought but also action in the world amounts to experiencing new and different cultural models. Furthermore, you may experience these models much more consciously than is typical of our daily lives in the real world.* (Gee, 2003, p151)

Friedman argues that games, like other media, have the power to alter perception. They teach structures of thought by teaching the player to internalize the programme's logic. Players have to learn what the computer will allow and respond rapidly to it, although it is quite possible for players to cheat and subvert the rules of the programme by hacking into its internal structure and altering its internal logic (Gee, 2003). Bowers goes one step further, perhaps, by saying the root metaphor at the base of the digital industrial revolution shapes a cultural mindset that enables us to speak glibly of building ecosystems or communities, of designing frogs, or of the human brain processing information. In thinking of human culture as increasingly sophisticated machines we lose touch with communal memory, of sensory ways of knowing, of the joys of inter-species communication, of knowledge and understanding rooted in the experience of place and the wisdom of previous generations. For Bowers, subjectivity and cyberspace reinforces an anthropocentric engagement with the world that hinders the emergence of a more ecological and sustainable way of being, meaning-making and knowing. Bowers writes:

> *Computer-mediated thought and communication amplifies other characteristics of individual subjectivity. Unlike the subjectivity*

in ecologically centred cultures, where the self is integral to a larger moral/spiritual ecology that includes other forms of life and creates strict norms governing reciprocal relationships, the subjectivity reinforced in cyberspace is anthropocentric. Humans can view the environment from a variety of self-interested perspectives: as a natural resource, as an object of natural beauty, as an engineering challenge in improving natural systems, as a source of leisure, and so forth. With varying degrees of realism, cyberspace accommodates all of these perspectives. But the mediation process cannot be altered to eliminate anthropocentrism from the subjectivity intrinsic to cyberspace. If the natural environment is represented on screen as a simulation, or as a technical problem to be solved, it is inherently understood from a technocentric perspective. (Bowers, 2000, pp36–37)

Bowers has a point here, but it is possible to reflect on our digitalized experiences, to recognize the implications of our actions and the technological affordances that shape them. After all, it is people and people's social, political and historical values that have designed games and game play. Computers and the internet are compelling, seductive and immersive tools. We are not yet in the world of *The Matrix* and hopefully never will be if we recognize the technology's possibilities and limitations – their affordances. Smith (2004) has examined the potential of new media technologies in reducing the environmental footprint of higher education in sustainable urban design. He looks at the ecological impacts of computer manufacture and use, of students travelling to study abroad and of the application of these new information and communication technologies in a specific case – transmitting a webcast about Poundbury, while personally in Devon, to his students back home in Indiana. Smith suggests that computer technology can enhance learning experiences and reduce ecological impacts, although he is the first to admit that more work is needed in this area: 'It can be argued that sustainable education offers rich opportunities for us to explore the complex links between human systems and natural systems, and in this context an exploration of issues related to use of computers in sustainable education would be a very rewarding journey' (Smith, 2004, p8).

The telecommunications company BT has produced a Better Business Game (http://www.btplc.com/Societyandenvironment/Businessgame) as part of its 'Betterworld' corporate social responsibility strategy. The game, which can be played online and lasts in the region of 30 minutes, aims to familiarize business people with some techniques, procedures and ideas whereby they can manage social and environmental issues more effectively and sensitively. The game starts with the player logging on and becoming the 'charismatic CEO' of a new company. I did this and quickly found myself confronted with problems to which I invariably had a choice of three responses. Should I invest in a more sustainable product line, pull a loss-making subsidiary out of a town, causing a huge increase in unemployment, and so on? The effect of my decision on shareholder confidence and other stakeholder interests was calculated and represented for me graphically. Occasionally, a decision would prompt the appearance of a little TV screen and a news headline demonstrating the public relations fallout of a decision. The scenarios were interesting and realistic, but when I played it seemed that the more ethical I was in my decision-making and the more sensitive I was to social, environmental, fair-trade or labour issues, the less viable my business became – at least in the eyes of my share-holders and to an extent my employees. In real life this may well also be true, as a CEO's duty is to make money for his or her shareholders, and it certainly shows the difficult waters ethical businesses have to navigate to maintain both their values and their profitability. Sometimes I thought, 'why bother – better stick to education and community work', especially when comments from the AGM appeared on screen. The verdict from my shareholders was damning ('you'd be better off burning your money than investing in this company'), whereas pressure group campaigners said, 'this company is a beacon of respon-sibility in the business world' and, although a selection of my employees thought I was the 'worst boss ever', my customers remarked that 'if caring about customers was a competition, they [the company] would get first prize'. My company's public profile was low too – it isn't easy being both green and recognized as a going concern. For the record, my approval ratings were 17 per cent from shareholders, 18 per cent from employees, 41 per cent from neighbours, 92 per cent from customers and 85 per cent from campaigners. In many ways, this game confirmed the view that the business of business is business and Peter Drucker's and Milton Friedman's ideas that the triple bottom line and CSR ought to be avoided if you are to concentrate on making money for your shareholders (Bakan, 2004). But this flies in the face of the evidence of those increasingly well-publicized ethical businesses who do seem to be doing well and all those, particularly those working with The Natural Step (Nattrass and Altomare, 1999), suggesting that sustainable businesses are good businesses, profitable businesses and businesses of the future. The game certainly brought many things home to me, but perhaps a more sophisticated and nuanced process lasting hours rather than minutes would factor in more complex responses, giving the ethical business person some opportunity to develop a market for sustainable goods and services. After all, it has been done. Maybe I'll try it again sometime.

LEARNING TO BE SUSTAINABLE: BUSINESS AND EDUCATION

The Natural Step (TNS) is an approach that may be seen as part of a social learning process set within clearly defined first-order principles based on desired outcomes (ie sustainability of the whole ecosphere) – the 'Four System Conditions'. Thus, in a sustainable society, as Cook (2004) explains, nature is not subject to systematically increasing:

- Concentrations of substances extracted from the Earth's crust;
- Concentrations of substances produced by society; or
- Degradation by physical means.

Further, in a sustainable society, people are not subject to conditions that systematically undermine their capacity to meet their needs (Cook, 2004).

When I spoke with Victor, a business strategy consultant in Ireland, I asked how he was currently fashioning his consultancy around sustainability and environmental issues. Working from a small cottage in the county of Limerick he shares with two other businesses, one involved with the creative arts, the other engaged in developing sustainability profiles, much of his work is under-taken via email and the net – teleworking – and his approach struck a chord with my own personal values. A reflective person, he told me that he needs to do something that is important, worthwhile, focal, and that for him sustain-ability is a 'focal practice'. The most important capacity business people need to acquire, he said, is 'critical self-reflection and the desire to make a change'. It is not always easy and certainly not always possible, but the ability to work with others in a social learning partnership is key. For 15 years or more, partnership has been an important principle in public and private sector activ-ities, but Victor detects a certain fatigue in the policy rhetoric as outcomes do not always match expectations. 'There needs to be some leadership too,' Victor told me as he discussed the merits of backcasting, the value of the Natural Step framework and the possibility of applying this tried-and-tested approach to greening a cluster of private businesses and social enterprises in Ireland. 'If I just advertised this service, I'd go hungry, but there is a need, the Celtic tiger, 13 per cent growth per annum...'. The seed for sustainability learning has to be sown and, not for the first time, cost savings are the hook, but the wider problem, particularly with small- and medium-size enterprises (SMEs), is the lack of strategic thinking. 'SMEs over here just fire-fight – deal with one daily crisis after another. It's fire-fighting.' So the learning needed has to do with time, with thinking into the long term, of making this approach an element of mainstream everyday business practice, and this requires shifts in perspectives, meaning schemes, values, procedures and dispositions. It is a cumulative process, but one that may conceivably be hastened by the shock of a rapid and permanent increase in oil prices that will affect not only costs and bottom lines but also the economic workings of the globalized economy. A serious hike in costs may function as a disorientating dilemma to an individual and maybe even to a system, stimulating a greater interest in sustainable lifestyles and sustainable learning.

In the south-west of England, help is available for SMEs interested in becoming more environmentally responsible. 'Envision', funded by the European Union and the Learning and Skills Council, offers support and guidance, often in the form of mentoring, discussions, opportunities to observe others, attending short courses and learning informally within emerging communities of practice. The Devon-based printing company Colour Works was the 2005 overall award winner of the Devon Environmental Business

Initiative (DEBI) and is just one example of a business modelling pro-sustainable and economically profitable behaviour. Not a big company by any means, Colour Works is a business in an industry that is rarely regarded as a leader of sustainable development, but within two years the company has reduced its waste by 90 per cent, filling just four 100-litre rubbish bins every week instead of 27. It has switched to using vegetable inks and has reduced the amount of chemicals used in the process from 13 per cent to 5 per cent. The intention, with new presses being installed, is to reduce this further to 2 per cent. With the help of Envision, the staff and business have gone through stage three of the BS8555 environmental management system and the aim is to achieve the more demanding ISO14001 standard, which if achieved will be mean Colour Works will be the only 'jobbing printer' south of Bristol with this accreditation. 'It would give us a huge marketing edge,' company director Paul Hall told me. The environmental and ethical commitment of the company's owners makes good business sense. Its client base includes a number of organizations with environmental interests (including Tamar Valley, Paignton Zoo, Torbay Coast and Countryside, and Dartmoor National Park) and has expanded as a result of developing a green profile and, in developing and maintaining a competitive advantage, Colour Works's success means that the company is taken seriously by other SMEs which may otherwise have seen the operation as idealistic, impractical or just too risky. Paul Hall believes that environmental SMEs are in a good position to influence attitudes and behaviour in their interaction with customers and suppliers and in a world where people are becoming increasingly aware of environmental change and rebranding – Beyond Petroleum, for example – and that there are business opportunities to be had:

> *The challenge in the printing market, and I guess in quite a few other markets, is that there are a lot of people around who are printers and we all use very much the same sort of machinery and to an extent the same sort of processes. We deliver products. Clients may say there are these companies, they all do more or less the same thing, what's marking them out? I'll go for the cheapest. What we are able to do is go back to the client base and say, 'OK, look, environmental printing doesn't cost the earth. It is not an expensive process. In costs no more in reality than ordinary printing, but it does bring with it the benefit that you are contributing, in a small way, to the environmental beauty that is Devon.' This has given us the opportunity to quote for a wider range of business and we have picked up a few more clients on the back of winning the DEBI award. We have to be a little careful in how we target our customers. We have about 120–200 regular customers and, of these, only one has got back to me and said 'please stop sending me the environmental material – I don't care'. All the others have been very positive, very enthusiastic.*
> (interview with author)

It is through modelling sound business practice, marketing and nurturing customer interest that other SMEs will recognize the advantages of adopting a resource-efficient and sustainable practice. It requires a continual learning process involving some formal learning as well as informal learning. It also requires changes in working habits that can be facilitated by changing the working environment and its culture. Paul again:

> *The hardest bit is ensuring that the staff, at all times, follow the system. You have to make it easy for them. So you have to provide bins – one for recycling and one not-for-recycling. But the bins mustn't be too far for them to get to otherwise they won't use them. It's about changing the culture of people's lives. Like in any organization, some will take it on 100 per cent and roll it out at home. Others will just say 'OK, I'll chuck in that bin because it's close'. It's continual education of the staff, day in and day out. It's a continual ongoing training. Envision have been in a couple of times over the last few months to give the staff half-hour refresher courses to keep their enthusiasm going. It's like anything else – health and safety, for example – it's got to be part and parcel of their everyday working environment and working life.*
> (interview with author)

The formal education sector has a role to play too in encouraging multi-faceted knowledge and skills-based learning for sustainability. There is a need to prepare for the future rather than train for the present. In the UK many professional bodies are insisting that sustainability and not just environmental issues are addressed in vocational and continuing professional development (CPD) education. Progress is still slow, as the House of Commons Environment Audit Committee (EAC) noted in 2005: 'It is clear to us that, for far too many schools, ESD is either not known about or is judged to be a low priority.' With many universities seeing sustainable development as simply another subject area to be marketed, and an awkward one too; given its need for trans-disciplinary collaboration on research and teaching (Blewitt and Cullingford, 2004), sustainability has yet to be mainstreamed in academe. There are issues of academic freedom involved, but is not supporting at least a dialogue on sustainable development a responsible exercise of academic freedom? Unfortunately, the paradigm shift Stephen Sterling (2001) calls for in his *Sustainable Education* is still a long way off. One interesting new development is the £4.5m recently awarded to the University of Plymouth by the Higher Education Funding Council for England to integrate sustainability throughout the institution's activities – from curriculum to estates. This could be a sign of things to come, but formal education tends to follow rather than lead, and it is the wider society and our wider cultural environment that need to change if the learning within formal educational institutions is to follow suit. This is not to deny the important responsibility formal education has. As the EAC noted:

Ignorance of an individual's role in contributing damage to the environment, such as negative bio-diversity impacts, unsustainable use of natural resources and climate change, is inexcusable and frankly dangerous. The longer the status quo prevails the more frightening the message becomes and the more threatening, to the modern Western way of life, the solutions will appear. Already there is the danger that the 'problem' of climate change is perceived as just too big for one person, or even one nation, to do anything about, thereby providing an alibi for those unwilling to consider alternatives. Education for sustainable development therefore is essential if people are, firstly, to understand and accept why the government might have to agree to what may be significant changes to the way the country operates on an international and business level and, secondly, to understand and agree to make, as individuals, the kinds of behavioural changes necessary on a personal level to make the whole thing work. Informed choices can only be made by people who understand the options and the issues and know the cost of whichever course of action is decided upon. (House of Commons Environment Audit Committee, 2005, paragraph 10)

It is about time learning organizations took the lead, and one example of such leadership is the Genesis Project – a £2.5m educational resource funded by the South West of England Regional Development Agency (SWRDA) and the Learning and Skills Council and housed in the Somerset College of Arts and Technology (SCAT). The largely 16–19 college offers a range of formal and informal learning opportunities, including a foundation degree in sustainable development, mainstream further education courses, learning activities for primary and secondary school children, and programmes for disadvantaged young people and adults. In 2003 the college was a member of the 'Learning to Last' project, again funded by the Learning and Skills Council (Blewitt, 2005), and the aspirations and ambitions of the college's small Genesis team is finally being realized. The project is attracting considerable interest from educators, businesses, particularly construction businesses, the media and, most importantly, students.

SCAT is also one of the government's centres of vocational excellence (CoVE), the only one in the country which has received the award with 'sustainability' in its title. The main feature of the college's commitment to sustainable construction is the Genesis Centre and Genesis Project, which (according to their website, www.somerset.webhoster.co.uk/quickstart/index.php?id=227)

- *will explore, explain and evaluate cutting-edge thinking in sustainable construction by introducing the use of sustainable practices and materials into mainstream construction industry;*

- *consists of a series of pavilions constructed of earth, straw, clay and timber, with living roofs, and a water pavilion demonstrating the latest water-saving devices;*
- *promotes energy saving and utilize both solar and biomass forms of energy;*
- *serves as a facility enabling people from throughout the South West to access information on sustainable construction and have the opportunity to see high quality buildings which have been constructed using sustainable methods;*
- *demonstrates the benefits of sustainable urban drainage systems designed to regulate the flow of water into our rivers;*
- *serves as a hub for wider sustainability activities involving the community working with our partners, the Somerset Trust for Sustainable Development; and*
- *provides a wide range of resources and learning opportunities for schoolchildren, college students, the public, architects and builders.*

Ian Moore, Genesis Operations Director, told me:

'*The primary aim of the Genesis Project is to demonstrate that you can integrate sustainable materials into mainstream construction. There are now 500 CoVEs covering all vocational areas, but we are the only one with sustainability in the title. We realized there was a need to promote sustainable construction methods and materials.*' (interview with author)

At the time of my visit, early in 2006, the construction of the Genesis Centre was nearing completion. Designed by a South West architectural practice, Archetype, this structure is more than a demonstration green building. It is a 'promotion building' and platform for the sustainable learning project, which, as Ian said, is 'an on-going thing to address the skills and updating that is required so that we have the appropriate workforce out there to see that we can effectively work with sustainable materials'. During the construction process the college has hosted CPD events for the Royal Institute of British Architects and has had community and business groups and members of the public looking around, all showing great interest in the unusual materials used in an otherwise mainstream construction on a college campus. These materials include straw bales, baked earth, recycled yoghurt cartons and other low-carbon materials. One aim of Genesis is to show construction companies that these materials work and that by using them they will be able to gain or maintain a competitive advantage over businesses that do not, but the theme of sustainability is also being integrated throughout the college curriculum. Yvonne Mackeson, another Genesis team member, is also mapping where sustainability fits with the school-based National Curriculum – science, citizenship, textile design, catering and so on. Most encouragingly for SCAT and for

Figure 7.1 *The Genesis Project at Somerset College of Arts and Technology, Taunton*

those wishing to promote sustainability is the response of mainstream builders, who have seen Genesis under construction. Tim, another team member, told me:

> *I can honestly say there has not been a single what you could term 'mainstream contractor' or builder who has not recognized the potential of what we have got in there. Nobody has ever walked in there and said 'blimey, what's this?' People can see it for what it is – an application of materials that they previously believed had no place in modern construction. They appear pretty won over by the whole thing. We are not trying to tell anybody we have the solution to sustainable construction. We are saying, 'Here is a demonstration of what you could do; here are some possibilities and materials you might care to use.'* (interview with author)

The interior design is flexible, with four pavilions and open areas for networking and discussion. It is light and airy. The earth wall in one part of the building is polished with beeswax and is incredibly tactile; the straw bale is still visible in another, giving the visitor a glimpse of the materials used. One part of the roof is made from living cedar, another of recycled rubble; a 37-kilowatt biomass boiler, which can take off-cuts from SCAT's carpentry shop, has been installed to heat the building; and solar panels provide additional energy from a renewable source. The recyclable carpeting in the lecture theatre has been provided by Renewal, a company previously hired by the Welsh Assembly. The seating is made from wood from sustainably managed forests. 'Genesis is working,' I was told, 'interest from a number of big housing developers is increasing.' These developers either viewed the environmental ideas as a commercial opportunity or, as Ian said, had genuinely 'fallen in love with the Genesis agenda'. Local companies will need to visit Genesis to update their knowledge, gain the requisite practical skills and understand the wider context of sustainability. 'CPD,' said Tim, 'opens the door wonderfully to the wider issues of sustainability, sustainable development and sustainable construction. If you had advertised it in its own right they wouldn't have been interested.' The project has also introduced professional builders, engineers and architects to existing specialists in sustainable construction, and one important transformative learning experience has been the overturning of professional prejudice. At first, these green specialists were assumed by ordinary builders to be just 'open-toe-sandal-wearing tree huggers, not professionals in their own right. They soon changed their minds when they learnt they had worked with McAlpine on the Eden Project.'

Informal and formal learning about sustainability is central to the college as a whole – not just confined to Genesis. There are fair-trade notices in the student refectory. Retail students will gain work experience in the Genesis Centre shop; marketing students have already been involved in the shop's design and have suggested products; textile students are currently using the centre as a assignment on the use of sustainable fabrics; and the Genesis team is talking with a local artist who uses crushed recycled glass and ostrich eggs to work with the art students on a mosaic. The list goes on. Genesis is potentially a base for a wide range of learning, but existing qualification frameworks and externally decided programme content is restrictive. The curriculum authorities still have a lot to learn. Ian enthusiastically recalled SCAT's environment day in 2005 as an example of how sustainability is pervading the entire ethos of the institution:

> *On 8 June last year we had our own Environment Day. We had a pledging station in the atrium, presentations by energy savings people, CO₂ Balance doing presentations and stalls set out for all of the SCAT community. The pledging station had strings hanging down and staff and students were encouraged at the end of the day to write on little notelets what they would do differently as a result of Environment Day. We collected them all but what will*

stick with me is that next morning I went for my coffee and standing in queue in front of me was a very Goth young lady, extremely black and white, and as she got to the front of the queue she said to the lady serving, 'Excuse me, would it be alright in future if I brought my own cup?' The canteen lady answered, 'Yes, of course, but why?' 'Well, yesterday, we learnt that it would be more sustainable...' (interview with author)

The Genesis patron is Kevin McCloud, the presenter of the television series *Grand Designs*, who very much believes in the project and has asked no fee for his public endorsement. This popular media link can only help to further promote the project. It is a grand design come true.

Many more are needed.

SUSTAINABILITY AND THE CULTURE OF EVERYDAY LIFE

This book has not been a how-to manual, a how to live a greener, more ethical, more playful, more sustainable life guide. There are plenty of those around and plenty of magazines and professional journals which will advise you on how to live slower, eat healthier, build your ecohome, shop more ethically, garden organically, learn more effectively and live more simply. Leo Hickman's *A Good Life: A Guide to Ethical Living* (2005a) is an impressive guide to just that, including lists of addresses, contacts and extremely sensible advice. His *A Life Stripped Bare* (Hickman, 2005b) is a wonderful, honest account of how he and his partner's lifestyle was audited and dissected by experts, according to ecological, social justice and other ethical criteria. The political implications of a fridge-freezer's contents, the health implications of that bag of supermarket salad, the environmental implications of using disposable nappies, driving to work and developing new modes of behaviour are reflected upon with humour and some anxiety. It is a human story, not a political pamphlet, and resonates with everyday worries, questions, doubts and tensions. It is fun to read and makes sense. The intention is to live a greener but normal life. Lucy Siegle's *Green Living in the Urban Jungle* (2001) is also a sparky guide to living more sustainably. She offers a mix of personal stories, tips, case studies, funny observations, useful addresses, websites and phone numbers. Donnachadh McCarthy's *Saving the Planet Without Costing the Earth* (2004) starts from the base of our Western habits and patterns of living, advising how greening our lifestyles can be cost-effective, common sense and easy. OK, so using a natural toothpaste will cost more, but if you cut out one bag of crisps you make up the financial loss and become slightly healthier too. There are also plenty of guides to campaigning (Rose, 2005), social marketing (McKenzie-Mohr and Smith, 1999) and culture jamming (Lasn, 2000). These can be bought easily online or ordered from any bookstore. There are also compelling books of travel writing that do more than skim the surface of a global tourist trail (Kaplan, 1997) and novels that tell entertaining stories with a difference, showing that popular culture too is open to environmentally sensitive and culturally creative interventions. Carl Hiaasen's eco-thrillers like *Tourist Season* (1986) and *Sick Puppy* (1999) have wonderful comedic touches, enabling his more socially and ecologically critical takes on tourism, property development and human greed to show these aspects of life to be really quite absurd, often stupid and totally irrational. We can learn a lot about the three ecologies, particularly our own subjectivities, from both fiction and non fiction (Coles, 1989). As de Certeau would say, they are utopian (cultural) spaces.

Juliet Schor (1998) has written eloquently of the out-of-control consumerism of American culture. How the desire for more and better can never be satisfied if more and better are perceived as one and the same thing. Americans work more and spend more. Debt is increasing as consumer aspirations rise, homes increase in size, domestic garages multiply in number and personal debt expands. Britain is in a very similar situation, with competitive consumerism determining lifestyle, long working hours and unhealthy and unsustainable living habits. Long working hours cause stress and illness, correlating directly with poor business practices, business performance and work relations and no improvement in productivity. As Madeline Bunting (2005) says, with 26 per cent of working Britons putting in more than 48 hours a week and about 16 per cent in excess of 60 hours, we are becoming 'willing slaves', all in an attempt to offset economic or job insecurity, buy that foreign holiday, maintain our consumer lifestyle and service our financial debts. In a lead article in *The Independent*, Martin Hickman (2006) reported that 66,000 individuals would become insolvent before 2006 ends; that, excluding mortgages, the average household debt in Britain is £7650; and that two-thirds of all credit card debt in the EU is British. Apart from opting for bankruptcy, one choice is simply to consume less. And, why not choose more ethically too?

Schor writes of the voluntary simplicity movement populated mainly by educated middle-class whites with pots of cultural capital, social and personal confidence that has enabled them to downshift and live slower. Pressures of work and time, matched by declining job satisfaction, have led some people to review their lives and careers, saying enough is enough. Better to have more quality time instead of that new mobile. 'Simple livers' may cut the clutter from their lives, live without the latest material trappings and find happiness: function is more important than cultural symbolism; personal identity is not tied to goods and chattels; social status is based on positive and deliberate choices to fashion a low spending, eco-sensitive lifestyle. This may sound a little counter-cultural, but so what? Subvert a lesson from Apple: 'Think Different', be different. As Schor notes, most consumers associate brand status with quality but are not able to distinguish between branded goods without looking at the labels. They are pretty much stuck when the labels are taken off. We often buy, give and receive goods we don't want, then quickly cast them aside. And this occurs not only at Christmas. Living differently is a way of finding happiness, meaning and comfort in work, rest and play. It is possible to bank with an ethical bank or contribute to an ethical pension, spend less and spend wisely, cut down or cut out those holiday flights, share and maintain older goods rather than continuously buy new, buy organic or local foodstuffs, garden organically, purchase fairly traded products, car share, telework more or live nearer the workplace, reduce household waste, energy and water consumption, and refurbish (or even build) an environmentally sound home. With the food eaten in Britain travelling 30 billion kilometres before it ends up on the plate, with each of us travelling on average nearly 200 kilometres a year to fetch it from the supermarkets, the photograph I took of the squash store on Phil's farm, for me, sums up many things. This is seasonal food grown two miles from where I live, organically produced, purchased and consumed locally, tasty and reasonably priced. It is one aspect of living a more sustainable and more pleasant lifestyle and, although it's true that I live in Devon, a green county, it is also possible for many of us to source food locally or grow it in our gardens, however small they may be, as Leo Hickman and the residents on Oak Meadow prove. That is a start, but you might also want to check whether your local supermarket has deliberately marked up the price on fair-trade or organic niche goods (*The Money Programme*, BBC2, 10 March 2006). If they have, take the cue from Kalle Lasn – challenge the company, have a go.

To live and enjoy a more sustainable life we can start with the everyday, but it is always important to remember that everyday life is not something isolated or separable from wider social, economic, political and environmental forces. We need only to pause for a second to consider the reasoning behind the fair-trade movement to realize that social equity and globalization are concerns that directly impinge on all of us. We don't have to rehearse the now almost clichéd slogan of 'Think Global, Act Local' either, but it is sometimes good to do so if only to remind ourselves, and others, of what is truly important. Learning is not a solitary activity; it is inherently social and inherently practical. We learn with our whole being – our emotions, bodies and minds all rolled into one. We learn from others, from our social and ecological environment, from the TV, from everyday life, from buying fair trade or a squash from Phil; even in schools, colleges and universities. We may also learn from books and websites, but it is up to us to make sense of it all, to apply and to reflect on it. We do this best with others, but we do this in context too with our friends, relatives, colleagues. They will see us, form opinions of us, accept or seek to understand the choices we make or do not make. Laugh maybe. Admire maybe. Check out freecycling or fair trade coffee too, because *we* have.

Our material possessions carry cultural meanings, and our lifestyles, aesthetic tastes, ethical judgements and social practices will say something to others, interpreted through shared meaning schemes and perspectives. You may wish to fashion your subjectivity through driving a brand new gas-guzzling SUV, wearing the latest fashion spectacles, reading *The New York Times*, shopping at the deli, eating organic, or quietly and intentionally living a less consumer-orientated, less wasteful, less materialist, more environmentally aware and thoughtful life. You don't have to live in an alternative community to tread more lightly on the earth or to be as passionate and principled as Laura (see Chapter 2). It might help, though. The point is that perhaps you do have to reflect upon your life, your habits of mind and behaviour, your wants and needs, priorities and luxuries, hopes and values. Marketers recognize that for many people a brand fills an absence of meaning in their lives, that value is frequently derived from image, that marketing is about addressing personal aspiration through the flow of media culture (Arvidsson, 2005). A sustainable lifestyle ought to be able to fill that meaning gap, since no one wants a degraded, conflict-ridden, intolerant, irrelevant, profligate and irresponsible world. We can learn to create a sustainable world by learning to live more meaningful lives, engaging in 'focal practices', watching and making more meaningful cultural products. Listening to our elders or learning from other, indigenous, peoples. Let's talk about it but let's just do it too. Haven't I heard that somewhere before?

We can learn from our unsustainable everyday lives too if we ask ourselves questions and search out answers. If you go into a newsagent's selling a wide range of popular magazines and journals, very few will address environmental or sustainability issues directly, and those that do are inevitably targeted at specialist niche readerships. Some specialist eco-magazines can only be purchased through subscription, as with the attractively designed house journal of Forum for the Future, *Green Futures*, or CAT's *Clean Slate* or *Sustain*, focusing on the built environment. Some eco-magazines have broadened their appeal by combining attractive photography, good journalism, lifestyle guidance and invitations to join an organic wine club. *The Ecologist* is doing this without losing its critical edge, and new environmentally sensitive journals are beginning to appear on the shelves, suggesting going green is an increasingly popular and acceptable lifestyle choice. *Organic Life*, launched in November 2005, is one such publication, with articles, photos and advertisements on food, health, gardening, childrearing, books, eating out and entertainment. Printed on high-quality recycled paper, its design, like that of *The Ecologist*, suggests that design and good communication facilitates learning. *The Green Parent* can be found in Waitrose (as you might expect), and there are many local or regional journals addressing a wider audience through a value-based commitment, good design and writing, and possibly free distribution. *Connect* is my local green freebie, supported by advertising revenue and offering more and more people opportunities to learn about sustainable living, global warming, pollution, environmental justice, renewable energy, complementary medicine, green businesses and other issues affecting everyday living. Some mainstream publications are recognizing the significance of sustainability issues too. *Grand Designs*, the journal accompanying the television series of the same name, will occasionally publish features on eco-building techniques, renewables, recycling and the need to reuse materials. This too is becoming common sense. Quality national and regional newspapers across the political spectrum in the UK are reporting more directly on a broad range of environment and sustainability issues, particularly now the full implications of global warming are generally accepted. *The Daily Telegraph* (Lonsdale, 2006) ran a report on the environmental irresponsibility of builders ignoring environmental construction regulations and on 25 March 2006 the whole of the

Saturday Property section was devoted to eco-homes; *The Guardian* (Belloe, 2005) reported on business and pressure groups collaborating on CSR activities; *The Independent* commissioned research suggesting the tipping point for irreversible climate change has already passed; *The Observer* ran a poll on ethical business initiatives (Siegle, 2006); and BBC Radio broadcast and later podcast the green edition of its *In Business* programme. Thanks to the public communication and marketing expertise of the Eden Project, environmental issues pop up quite regularly in local and regional papers in the South West and nationally. The Eden Project is always newsworthy, always worth a good picture. In the US, the reluctance of the corporate press and broadcasting media to engage with sustainability and political controversy has led to the emergence of various indymedia networks, blog sites, and environmental and human rights film festivals and a growth in radical documentary film-making and distribution (often on DVD). Some interventions are particularly feted, for example Al Gore's *An Inconvenient Truth*, screened at the Sundance Film Festival in 2006 and those by Robert Greenwald, whose reputation as a Michael Moore with attitude is justly deserved. You can buy, or rent, his DVDs too. They are just a mouse click away.

What I am suggesting here is my take on the social world as it is and as it could be. There is a discernible shift in public attitude as parts of the media are helping to cultivate an awareness, a desire, a need for people to live, work and consume more ethically. There are even academic articles to prove this, but as always 'more research is needed', more funding, more discussion. The world has changed. Make Poverty History's media campaign in 2005, in part owing to its use of celebrities, generated considerable media interest and a public responsiveness that has in turn influenced consumer behaviour. As Jemma Kidd told the London *Evening Standard*, 'Live 8 and the Make Poverty History campaign proved how much we all want to make a difference to people's lives, and I hope now that cotton has been certified [fair trade], the fashion industry will take note of this incredibly fast-growth movement' (Mayhew, 2006). Well-known brands such as Gap, Next and Zara are signing up to the Ethical Trading Initiative. In March 2006 Marks and Spencer's launched its own range of fair trade cotton T-shirts and socks as part of its Red project, which donates 50 per cent of proceeds to African charities. This followed a poll suggesting that 90 per cent of its customers wanted retailers to sell goods produced in a fair and humane manner. In 2005 the UK's eco-fashion industry was worth £43m and leading labels such as People Tree reported a 70 per cent increase in sales (Robson, 2006). In March/April 2006 Top Shop started stocking baby clothes from three fair trade suppliers and London's Craft Council dedicated a touring show to eco-fashion, with the express aim of demonstrating how outfits made from sustainable sources, such as bamboo, can fit neatly into modern lifestyles. The CEO of Wal-Mart, Lee Scott, announced in 2005 that the company would be 'aggressively investing approximately US$500m annually in technologies and innovation' to reduce greenhouse gas emissions in its existing stores, increase its fleet efficiency, sharing 'all learnings with the world', including competitors, and assisting in the design and support of a green company programme in China (www.walmartstores.com). Is this just PR? In 2005 Nestlé secured a fair-trade designation for one of its coffees ('Partners Blend'). Is this just PR? And there are now a large number of enterprising green businesses producing or selling pretty much everything – organic wine, green knickers, toiletries, building supplies, insurance and financial services, fine art prints, magazines and books, fuel-efficient cars. Many demonstrate the possibilities of further developing the market for green manufactures and ethically traded goods. The Blackspot Anticorporation, set up by activists associated with *Adbusters* magazine, launched what *The Ecologist* magazine called 'the most ethical shoe in the world', the Unswoosher, made from 100 per cent organic hemp in Portugal by workers earning between 420 and 700 euros a month (the Portuguese minimum wage is 365 euros). Is this reproducing consumerism or fashioning a new form of sustainable consumption?

We may also read or see reports of local community developments that also aim at nurturing more sustainable lifestyles. The village of Chew Magna, just outside Bristol, received national and local media coverage for its project 'Go Zero' on waste and CO_2. It promotes local food too. An open day in October 2005 attracted around 500 people and through a live broadcast by Radio Bristol and a feature on BBC Radio Four's *Changing Places* in January 2006 the village has generated interest in many other communities, with more Go Zero projects planned in the South West. John Pontin, a local businessman who has lived in the village for 40 years, leads the Chew project. His aim is to reduce, preferably eradicate, waste in all its forms – of money, people and energy. He has managed to lose about seven tonnes of carbon from his lifestyle by installing a wood pellet boiler in his home and heating his water when possible with a three-square-metre solar panel. For him it is certainly financially viable and, if others do it too, as a number of neighbours are considering, then it will be possible to 'feel better, to be richer and have a viable future; it should be a natural human sentiment to do this'. Pontin has also purchased an old mill and converted it into a community centre. By the end of 2005 the village recycling rate was around 37 per cent. With increased house building in the region, transport and energy issues to the fore, and climate change increasingly apparent, the global is certainly local. I have found it possible to learn a great deal about sustainability locally, in the home or garden, from local communities and businesses. It is not necessary to go far but it is frequently necessary to secure some advice and guidance from colleagues, colleges, non-governmental organizations (NGOs), local authorities, the internet and even from the television.

Educational and sustainability toolkits may be found on the web; although many of these are valuable, there is sometimes the feeling that all sustainability needs is a couple of technical fixes. Just think about the toolkit metaphor for a moment. Toolkit approaches to sustainability, often referred to as 'environmental modernization' downplay the idea that fashioning more sustainable living and working practices requires a deep understanding of complexity, creativity and a developmental reflexive learning capability that transcends simple technicist or managerial problem-solving (Blewitt, 2005).

But toolkits can help. In 2006 the United Nations Environment Programme (UNEP) and the Swedish Ministry of Sustainable Development embarked on the development of an education toolkit for undergraduates and professionals in marketing and communications. The development strategy, aimed at enabling marketers and advertisers to build consumer confidence in green brands, has three main elements:

1 Demonstrate and analyse the business case and the marketing and communications potential of sustainable development in the framework of corporate social and environmental responsibility;
2 Allow future marketing and communications professionals to become fully aware of the key role they can and should play in bringing together new consumer demands for sustainability and corresponding products and services; and
3 Hand them the tools to develop both effective corporate communications strategies that build confidence in greener brands and powerful marketing campaigns on specific green products and services.

As a foundation for this, in 2005 UNEP published 'Talk the Walk' as an interactive PDF with hyperlinks to commercials, advertisements, reports and articles. The aim is to promote sustainable consumption through green advertising and marketing, noting that some of the most heavily promoted products in Britain are highly resource intensive – foods, cars, many domestic appliances and so on – and that significant improvements can be made in terms of environmental impact if more sustainable lifestyles and production practices can be implemented. The cultivation of 'brand communities' around ethically produced and traded goods and services is a possible outcome, since brand communities share a consciousness in kind, a sense of moral responsibility, and exhibit varying degrees of solidarity, obligation and duty and construct and disseminate meaning to others. They are not bounded by geographical constraints either. Muniz and O'Guinn (2001) note that while members of a brand community feel a connection to the brand, interestingly the feeling of connectedness between members is stronger. The potential for social and informal learning about sustainability, for developing social solidarity and eco-social capital together with the cultivation of sustainable practices, products or services, is immense:

> Moreover, among less advertised spending categories, energy, water and construction account for a significant part of both the households' expenditure and their environmental footprint. In these categories, significant potential exists to reduce consumption and environmental impacts through green purchases (by a factor of two) or responsible behaviour (by a factor of four).
> This conclusion is also true for social impacts such as human rights: products selected in the British Ethical Purchasing Index on the grounds of clear ethical choice made available to

> *consumers are also heavily advertised ones such as food, banking, household goods and personal items. Considering these facts, and assuming that companies invest in advertising on product categories for which consumer behaviour is malleable, it appears that advertising and marketing could be significant levers to achieve reduction of negative environmental and social impacts on a global scale.* (UNEP, 2005, pp8–9)

UNEP argues for a combination of eco-efficiency measures and more sustainable consumption patterns. People in the West, particularly, seem wedded to the convenience, status and low cost of many goods once considered luxuries but now considered essentials. The same phenomenon is evident in the developing nations too, particularly in China and India. Many products from relatively minor ones like greetings cards and magazines to more significant ones like cars, boats and planes are part of the very fabric of our everyday lives. It is important to do something more than just consider how these things are produced, the nature of the materials used and the amount of waste we create.

It is time to go green and to recognize that the local and the global are connected just as the private and the public are. One place to start the long journey towards a more sustainable world is with our own everyday lives and the learning that inevitably follows from reflecting on them. But reflection and learning needs to translate into action, however small and seemingly trivial. It might not seem much to turn the thermostat down a degree, but remember the effect a butterfly's wings may eventually have.

References

Aberley, D. (ed) (1993) *Boundaries of Home*, New Society Publishers, Gabriola Island, Canada

Adam, B. (1998) *Timescapes of Modernity: The Environment and Invisible Hazards*, Routledge, London

Agents for Environmental Justice and Scandrett, E. (2003) *Voices from the Grassroots*, 'Redressing the Balance' handbooks, no 4, Friends of the earth, Edinburgh

Agrawal, A. (1995) 'Dismantling the divide between indigenous and scientific knowledge', *Development and Change*, vol 26, pp413–439

Agyeman, J., Bullard, R. and Evans, B. (2002) 'Exploring the nexus: Bringing together sustainability, environmental justice and equity', *Space and Polity*, vol 6, pp77–90

Alakeson, V., Aldrich, T., Goodman, J. and Jorgensen, B. (2003) *Making the Net Work: Sustainable Development in a Digital Society*, Xeris Publishing, Teddington, UK

Alexander, D. (1996) 'Bioregionalism: The need for a firmer theoretical foundation', *The Trumpeter*, vol 13, no 3, available at: http://trumpeter.athabascau.ca/content/v13.3/alexander.html

Allan, S., Adam, B. and Carter, C. (eds) (2000) *Environmental Risks and the Media*, Routledge, London

Appadurai, A. (1996) 'Disjuncture and difference in the global cultural economy' in Appadurai, A. (ed) *Modernity at Large*, University of Minnesota Press, Minneapolis

Arvidsson, A. (2005) 'Brands: A critical perspective', *Journal of Consumer Culture*, vol 5, no 2, pp235–258

Bagnall, G. (2003) 'Performance and performativity at heritage sites', *Museum and Society*, vol 1, no 2, pp87–103

Bakan, J. (2004) *The Corporation: The Pathological Pursuit of Profit and Power*, Constable, London

Ballantyne, R. (1998) 'Interpreting "visions": Addressing environmental education goals through interpretation' in D. Uzzell, and R. Ballantyne (eds) *Contemporary Issues in Heritage and Environmental Interpretation*, HMSO, London

Bandura, A. (1977) *Social Learning Theory*, Prentice Hall, Englewood Cliffs, NJ

Bandura, A. (2004) 'Social cognitive theory for personal and social change by enabling media' in A. Singhal, M. J. Cody, E. M. Rogers and M. Sabido (eds) *Entertainment-Education and Social Change: History, Research, Practice*, Lawrence Erlbaum, Mahwah, NJ

BARB 2005, available at: http://www.barb.co.uk/viewingsummary/weekreports.cfm?report=weeklyterrestrial&RequestTimeout=500

Barefoot College (2000) *The Barefoot Photographers: Tilona – Where Tradition and Vision Meet*, Lustre Press, New Delhi

Barr, S. (2003) 'Strategies for sustainability: Citizens and responsible environmental behaviour', *AREA*, vol 35, no 3, pp227–240

Barry, J. (1999) *Rethinking Green Politics*, Sage, London

Barton, H. (2000) 'The neighbourhood as ecosystem' in H. Barton (ed) *Sustainable Communities: The Potential for Eco-Neighbourhoods*, Earthscan, London

Bateson, G. (1972) *Steps to an Ecology of Mind*, University of Chicago Press, Chicago, IL

Baym, N. K. (2000) *Tune In, Log On: Soaps, Fandom and Online Community*, Sage, London

BBC (2004) *The BBC's Learning Impact*, available at: www.bbc.co.uk

Bedford, T., Jones, P. and Walker, H. (2004) *'Every little bit helps...' Overcoming the Challenges to Researching, Promoting and Implementing Sustainable Lifestyles*, Centre for Sustainable Development, University of Westminster, London

Beder, S. (2002) *Global Spin: the Corporate Assault on Environmentalism*, Green Books, Totnes

Belloe, S. (2005) 'Campaigners get into the business of business', *The Guardian*, 28 November 2005

Bennett, O. (2005) 'What's in the bag?', *The Independent*, 28 November

Bennett, T. (1995) *The Birth of the Museum: History, Theory, Politics*, Routledge, London

Bentley, G., Hallsworth, A. G. and Bryan, A. (2003) 'The countryside in the city – Situating a farmers' market in Birmingham', *Local Economy*, vol 18, no 2, pp109–120

Benyus, J. M. (2002) *Biomimicry*, Perennial, New York

Berg, P. (2002) 'Bioregionalism', available at: http://www.columbiana.org/feature4-2002.htm

Berry, H. and McEachern, M. (2005) 'Informing ethical consumers' in R. Harrison, T. Newholm and D. Shaw (eds) *The Ethical Consumer*, Sage, London

Bird, S. E. (2003) *The Audience in Everyday Life: Living in a Media World*, Routledge, London

Blewitt, J. (2004) 'The Eden Project – making a connection', *Museum and Society*, vol 2, no 3, pp175–189

Blewitt, J. (2005) 'Education for sustainable development, governmentality and "Learning to Last"', *Environmental Education Research*, vol 11, no 2, pp173–185

Blewitt, J. and Cullingford C. (ed) (2004) *The Sustainability Curriculum*, Earthscan, London

Blythman, J. (1996) *The Food We Eat*, Michael Joseph, London

Blythman, J. (2003) *Shopped: The Shocking Powers of British Supermarkets*, Fourth Estate, London

Booth, A. L. and Jacobs, H. M. (1990) 'Ties that bind: Native American beliefs as a foundation for environmental consciousness', *Environmental Ethics*, vol 12, pp27–43

Bordiga, E. et al (2002) 'Civic culture meets the digital divide: The role of community electronic networks', *Journal of Social Issues*, vol 58, no 1, pp125–141

Borgmann, A. (1984) *Technology and the Character of Contemporary Life*, University of Chicago Press, Chicago, IL

Borgmann, A. (1999) *Holding Onto Reality*, University of Chicago Press, Chicago, IL

Bourdieu, P. (1977) *Outline of a Theory of Practice*, Cambridge University Press, Cambridge

Bowers, C. (2000) *Let Them Eat Data*, University of Georgia Press, Athens, GA

Bragg, S. and Buckingham, D. (2003) *Young People, Media and Personal Relationships*, Broadcasting Standards Commission, London

Bridger, J. C. and Luloff, A. E. (1999) 'Toward an interactional approach to sustainable community development', *Journal of Rural Studies*, no 15, pp 377–387

Brookfield, S. D. (1986) *Understanding and Facilitating Adult Learning*, Open University Press, Buckingham

Bruner, J. (1990) *Acts of Meaning*, Harvard University Press, Cambridge, MA

Bruno, K. (2000) 'BP: Beyond Petroleum or Beyond Preposterous?' CorpWatch website, 14 December, available at www.corpwatch.org/article.php?id=219

Bryman, A. (1999) 'The Disneyization of society', *The Sociological Review*, vol 47, no 1, pp25–47

Buckingham, D. (2000) *The Making of Citizens: Young People, News and Politics*, Routledge, London

Buckingham, D. and Scanlon, M. (2003) *Education, Entertainment and Learning in the Home*, Open University Press, Buckingham

Budd, M., Craig, S. and Steinman, C. (1999) *Consuming Environments: Television and Commercial Culture*, Rutgers University Press, New Brunswick

Bullard, R. D. and Johnson, G. S. (2000) 'Environmental justice and its impact on public policy decision making', *Journal of Social Issues*, vol 56, no 3, pp555–578

Bullock, S. (2000) *The Economic Benefits of Farmers' Markets*, FOE, London

Bunting, M. (2005) *Willing Slaves: How the Overwork Culture is Ruling Our Lives*, Harper Collins, London

Burgess, J. (2003) 'Sustainable consumption: Is it really achievable?', *Consumer Policy Review*, vol 13, no 3, pp78–84

Burningham, K. and Thrush, D. (2001) *Rainforests Are a Long Way from Here*, JRF, York

Cajete, G. (1994) *Look to the Mountain: An Ecology of Indigenous Education*, Kivaki Press, Skyland

CARMA International (2006) 'Western media coverage of humanitarian disasters', available at: www.carma.com/research/

Carducci, V. (2006) 'Culture jamming: A sociological perspective', *Journal of Consumer Culture*, vol 6, no 1, pp116–138

Carley, M., Chapman, M., Hastings, A., Kirk, K. and Young R. (2000) *Urban Regeneration Through Partnership*, Policy Press, Bristol

Carmichael, J., Talwar, S., Tansey, J. and Robinson, J. (2005) 'Where do we want to be? Making sustainability indicators integrated, dynamic and participatory' in R. Phillips (ed) *Community Indicators Measuring Systems*, Ashgate, London

Carr, D. (1990) 'The adult learner in the museum' in J. Solinger (ed) *Museums and Universities: New Paths to Continuing Education*, American Council on Education, MacMillan, New York

Carr, D. (2001) 'A museum is an open work', *International Journal of Heritage Studies*, vol 7, no 2, pp173–183

Carr, M. (2004) *Bioregionalism and Civil Society*, UBC Press, Vancouver

Casapulla, G., de Cindio, F and Ripamonti, L. A. (2001) 'Community networks and access for all in the era of the internet: "Discovering the treasure" of community' in L. Keeble and B. D. Loader (eds) *Community Informatics: Shaping Computer Mediated Social Relations*, Routledge, London

Caughey, J. L. (1984) *Imagining Social Worlds: A Cultural Approach*, University of Nebraska Press, Lincoln

CEC (2000) 'Memorandum on lifelong learning', Commission of the European Communities, Brussels

Chambers, R. (1997) *Whose Reality Counts?*, ITDG, London

Chambers, R. (2002) *Participatory Workshops*, Earthscan, London

Chaney, D. (1996) *Lifestyles*, Routledge, London

Cherrier, H. (2005) 'Using existential–phenomenological interviewing to explore meanings of consumption', in R. Harrison, T. Newholm, and D. Shaw (eds) *The Ethical Consumer*, Sage, London

Chick, T. (2005) Review of Civilization IV computer game on *GameSpy* website, 19 May, available at http://uk.pc.gamespy.com/pc/civilization-iv/617487p1.html

Child, B. (2006) 'One man's rubbish ...', *The Guardian*, 8 March 2006

Clifford, S. (no date) 'People, places and parish maps', available at: http://www.common-ground.org.uk/parishmaps/m-ppp.html, accessed 5 June 2006

Clouder, S. and Harrison, R. (2005) 'The effectiveness of ethical consumer behaviour', in R. Harrison, T. Newholm, and D. Shaw (eds) *The Ethical Consumer*, Sage, London

Coffield, F. (1999) 'Breaking the consensus: Lifelong learning as social control', *British Educational Research Journal*, vol 25, no 4, pp479–499

Coffield, F. (2000) 'Lifelong learning as a lever on structural change? Evaluation of white paper: "Learning to succeed: A new framework for post-16 learning"', *Journal of Education Policy*, vol 15, no 2, pp237–246

Cohen, A. P. (1985) *The Symbolic Construction of Community*, Routledge, London

Cohen, L. (1996) 'From town center to shopping center: The reconfiguration of community market places in postwar America', *The American Historical Review*, vol 101, no 4, pp1050–1081

Coleman, J. A. (1990) *Foundations of Social Theory*, Harvard University Press, Cambridge, MA

Coles, R. (1989) *The Call of Stories*, Houghton Mifflin, Boston, MA

Collins, J. et al (2003) 'Carrots, sticks and sermons: Influencing public behaviour for environmental goals', Demos/Green Alliance report produced for DEFRA, available at: wwwgreen-alliance.org.uk

Collinson, N. (2005) 'BBC *Springwatch* "end of term" final report', available at: www.bbc.co.uk/nature/animals/wildbritain/springwatch/results/index.shtml

Cook, D. (2004) *The Natural Step: Towards a Sustainable Society*, Green Books, Totnes

Cottle, S. (2004) 'Producing natures(s): On the changing production ecology of natural history TV', *Media, Culture and Society*, vol 26, no 1, pp81–101

Couldry, N. and Curran, J. (eds) (2003) *Contesting Media Power: Alternative Media in a Networked World*, Rowman & Littlefield, Lanham, MD

Cresswell, T. (1998) 'Night discourse: Consuming/producing meaning on the street', in N. R. Fyfe (ed) *Images of the Street: planning, identity an control in public space*, Routledge, London

Critser, G. (2003) *Fat Land: How Americans Became the Fattest People in the World*, Penguin, London

Crook, S. (1998) 'Minotaurs and other monsters: "Everyday life" in recent social theory', *Sociology*, vol 32, no 3, pp523–540

Csikszentmihalyi, M. and Hermanson, K. (1995) 'Intrinsic motivation in museums: Why does one want to learn?', in J. H. Falk and L. D. Dierking (eds) *Public Institutions for Personal Learning: Establishing a Research Agenda*, AMA, Washington DC

Curtis, F. (2003) 'Eco-localism and sustainability', *Ecological Economics*, no 46, pp83–102

Dach, C. (2006) 'The medium of the century', *Adbusters*, vol 14, no 1

Damasio, A. (2000) *The Feeling of What Happens: Body, Emotion and the Making of Consciousness*, Vintage, London

Davis, S. G. (1997) *Spectacular Nature. Corporate Culture and the Sea World Experience*, University of California Press, Berkeley

Davis, S. G. (2001) 'Shopping', in R. Maxwell (ed) *Culture Works: The Political Economy of Culture*, University of Minnesota Press, Minneapolis

DCMS (2005) Review of the BBC's Royal Charter – 'A strong BBC, independent of government', TSO, London

DCMS (2006) 'A public service for all: The BBC in the digital age', TSO, London

Debord, G. (1995) *The Society of the Spectacle*, Zone Books, New York

de Certeau, M. (1984) *The Practice of Everyday Life*, California University Press, Berkeley

DEFRA (2001) 'Survey of public attitudes to quality of life and to the environment', TSO, London

DEFRA (2005) 'Securing the future: Delivering UK sustainable development policy', TSO, London

Delgado, C. (2001) 'The eco-museum in Fresne: Against exclusion', *Museum International*, vol 53, no 1, pp37–41

de Zengotita, T. 2005 *Mediated: How the Media Shape Your World*, Bloomsbury, London

DfES (2004) 'Putting the world into world class education', TSO, London

Douglas, M. and Isherwood, B. (1996) *The World of Goods: Towards an Anthropology of Consumption*, Routledge, London

Dover, C. and Barnett, S. (2004) 'World on the box: International issues in news and factual programmes on UK television 1975–2003', available at www.ibt.org.uk/3WE

Downing, J. D. H. (2001) *Radical Media: Rebellious Communication and Social Movements*, Sage, London

Dreborg, K. H. (1996) 'Essence of backcasting', *Futures*, vol 28, no 9, pp813–828

Dreyfus, H. L. and Dreyfus, S. E. (1986) *Mind Over Machine: The Power of Human Intuition and Expertise in the Era of the Computer*, The Free Press, New York

Driskell, R. B. and Lyon, L. (2002) 'Are virtual communities true communities? Examining the environments and elements of community', *City and Community*, vol 1, no 4, pp373–390

Durning, A. T. (1992) *How Much is Enough? The Consumer Society and the Future of the Earth*, Earthscan, London

Eco, U. (1979) 'Can television teach?', *Screen Education*, no 31, pp15–24

Edelman, G. M. and Tononi, G. (2000) *Consciousness. How Matter Becomes Imagination*, Penguin, London

Eden Project (2003) *Eden Project: The Guide, 2003/4*, Eden Books/Transworld, London

Edghill, S. (2005) 'Sweet dreams turn sour in Ashley Vale', *Daily Telegraph*, 19 March

Edwards, A. (2001) 'Researching pedagogy: A sociocultural agenda', *Pedagogy, Culture and Society*, vol 9, no 2, pp161–186

Eliasoph, N. (1998) *Avoiding Politics: How Americans Produce Apathy in Everyday Life*, Cambridge University Press, Cambridge

Ellul, J. (1964) *The Technological Society*, Vintage Books, New York

Etzioni, A. (1995) *The Spirit of Community*, Fontana Press, London

Ewen, S. (1999) *All Consuming Images*, Basic Books, New York

Falk, J. H. and Dierking, L. D. (1992) *The Museum Experience*, Whalesback Books, Washington, DC

Falk, J. H. and Dierking, L. D. (2000) *Learning from Museums: Visitor Experiences and the Making of Meaning*, AltaMira Press, Walnut Creek, CA

Falk, J. H. and Dierking, L. D. (2002) *Lessons Without Limit: How Free-Choice Learning is Transforming Education*, AltaMira Press, Walnut Creek, CA

Falk, J. H., Moussouri, T. and Coulson, D. (1998) 'The effect of visitors' agendas on museum learning', *Curator*, vol 41, no 2, pp106–120

Farhi, P. (2005) 'Public broadcasting targeted by House', *Washington Post*, 10 June

Ferris, J., Norman, C. and Sempik, J. (2001) 'People, land and sustainability: Community gardens and the social dimension of sustainable development', *Social Policy and Administration*, vol 35, no 5, pp559–568

Field, J. (2000) *Lifelong Learning and the New Social Order*, Trentham Books, Stoke-on-Trent

Fisch, S. M. (2004) *Children's Learning from Educational Television*, Lawrence Erlbaum, Mahwah, NJ

Fiske, J. (1987) *Television Culture*, Routledge, London

Flyvbjerg, B. (1998) *Rationality and Power: Democracy in Practice*, University of Chicago Press, Chicago, IL

Foley, M. and McPherson, G. (2000) 'Museums as leisure', *International Journal of Heritage Studies*, vol 6, no 2, pp161–174

Forester, J. (1999) *The Deliberative Practitioner: Encouraging Participatory Planning Process*, MIT Press, Cambridge, MA

Forum for the Future (2004) 'Sustainable development in broadband Britain', available at: www.bt.com

Foster, J. (2001) 'Education as sustainability', *Environmental Education Research*, vol 7, no 2, pp153–165

Frey, B. S. (1998) 'Superstar museums: An economic analysis', *Journal of Cultural Economics*, no 22, pp113–125

Friedman, T. (1995) 'Making sense of software: Computer games and interactive textuality', available at www.duke.edu/~tlove/simcity.htm

Friends of the Earth (2001) *Pollution and Poverty - Breaking the Link*, Friends of the Earth, London

Frosh, P. (2003) *The Image Factory: Consumer Culture, Photography and the Visual Content Industry*, Berg, Oxford

Fuller, N. J. (1992) 'The museum as vehicle for community empowerment: The Ak-Chin Indian community eco-museum project', in I. Karp, C. M. Kraemer and S. D. Lavine (eds) *Museums and Communities: The Politics of Public Culture*, Smithsonian Institution, Washington, DC

Futerra (2006) 'Climate fear v climate change', Futerra Sustainability Communications, available at: www.futerra.org

Gabriel, Y. and Lang, T. (1995) *The Unmanageable Consumer: Contemporary Consumption and its Fragmentations*, Sage, London

Gauthier, J. L. (2004) 'Indigenous feature films: A new hope for national cinemas?' *CineAction*, no 64, pp63–71

Gee, J. P. (2003) *What Video Games Have to Teach Us about Learning and Literacy*, Palgrave/Macmillan, New York

Geertz, C. (1973) *The Interpretation of Cultures*, Fontana, London

Gelpi, E. (1979) *A Future for Lifelong Learning*, Dept of Adult and Higher Education, Manchester University, Manchester, UK

Gerbner, G. et al (2002) 'Growing up with television: Cultivation processes' in J. Bryant and D. Zillmann (eds) *Media Effects: Advances in Theory and Research*, Lawrence Erlbaum, Mahwah, NJ

Gibson, J. J. (1979) *The Ecological Approach to Visual Perception*, Houghton Mifflin, Boston, MA

Giddens, A. (1984) *The Constitution of Society*, Polity Press, Cambridge

Giddens, A. (1991) *The Consequences of Modernity*, Polity Press, Cambridge

Gilg, A., Barr, S. and Ford, N. (2004) 'Green consumption or sustainable lifestyles? Identifying the sustainable consumer', *Futures*, no 37, pp481–504

Gillmor, D. (2006) *We the Media: Grassroots Journalism, by the people, for the People*, O'Reilly, Sebastopol, CA

Gitlin, T. (2002) *Media Unlimited: How the Torrent of Images and Sounds Overwhelms our Lives*, Owl Books, New York

Gladwell, M. (2000) *The Tipping Point*, Abacus, London

Glover, T. D. (2003) 'The story of the Queen Anne Memorial Garden: Resisting a dominant cultural narrative', *Journal of Leisure Research*, vol 35, no 2, pp190–212

Godfaurd, J., Clements-Croome, D. and Jeronimidis, G. (2005) 'Sustainable building solutions: A review of lessons from the natural world', *Building and Environment*, no 40, pp319–328

Godin, S. (2002) *Unleashing the Idea Virus*, Simon & Schuster, New York

Goldfarb, B. (2002) *Visual Pedagogy: Media Cultures in and Beyond the Classroom*, Duke University Press, Durham

Goldman, R. and Papson, S. (1998) *Nike Culture*, Sage, London

Goodman, J., Alakeson, V. and Jorgensen, B. (2004) *Encouraging Green Telework*, Forum for the Future, Cheltenham, UK

Gordon, W. (2002) *Brand Green: Mainstream or Forever Niche?*, Green Alliance, London

Greater London Authority (2003) *Connecting People: Tackling Exclusion?*, GLA, London

Greenblatt, S. (1991) 'Resonance and wonder', in I. Karp and S. D. Levine (eds) *Exhibiting Cultures: The Poetics and Politics of Museum Display*, Smithsonian Institution Press, Washington DC

Griggs, G. (2001) *Reinventing Eden: The Past, the Present and the Future of our Fragile Earth*, Quadrille Publishing, London

Groenfeldt, D. (2003) 'The future of indigenous values: Cultural relativism in the face of economic development', *Futures*, no 35, pp917–929

Guattari, F. (2000) *The Three Ecologies*, Athlone Press, London

Gunter, B. and McAleer, J. (1997) *Children and Television*, Routledge, London

Gurstein, P. (2001) *Wired to the World, Chained to the Home: Telework in Daily Life*, UBC Press, Vancouver

Hardy, D. (2000) *Utopian England: Community Experiments 1900–1945*, E & FN Spon, London

Hargreaves, I., Lewis, J. and Speers, T. (2003) *Towards a Better Map: Science, the Public and the Media*, ESRC, Swindon

Harre, R. (1984) *Personal Being: A Theory for Individual Psychology*, Harvard University Press, Cambridge, MA

Hartley, J. (1999) *Uses of Television*, Routledge, London

Hastings, G. et al (2003) 'Review of research on the effects of food promotion to children', Food Standards Agency, London

Hawken, P., Lovins, A. B. and Lovins, L. H. (1999) *Natural Capitalism: The Next Industrial Revolution*, Earthscan, London

Hawkey, R. (2002) 'The lifelong learning game: Season ticket or free transfer?', *Computers and Education*, no 38, pp5–20

Heath, J. and Potter, A. (2005) *The Rebel Sell: How the Counterculture Became Consumer Culture*, Capstone, Chichester

Hein, G. (1998) *Learning in the Museum*, Routledge, London

Hiaasen, C. (1986) *Tourist Season*, Warner Books, New York

Hiaasen, C. (1999) *Sick Puppy*, Warner Books, New York

Hickman, L. (2005a) *A Good Life: A Guide to Ethical Living*, Transworld, London

Hickman, L. (2005b) *A Life Stripped Bare*, Transworld, London

Hickman, M. (2006) 'Britons in debt', *The Independent*, 3 January, pp1–2

Higgs, E. (2003) *Nature by Design*, MIT Press, Cambridge, MA

Hines, C. (2004) Introducing speech at launch party for the Eden Project's Waste Neutral initiative. See also www.edenproject.com/foundation/177.html

Hobson, K. (2003) 'Thinking habits into action: The role of knowledge and process in questioning household consumption practices', *Local Environment*, vol 8, no 1, pp95–112

Holland, L. (2004) 'Diversity and connections in community gardens: A contribution to local sustainability', *Local Environment*, vol 9, no 3, pp285–305

Holloway, L. and Kneafsey, M. (2000) 'Reading the space of the farmers' market: A preliminary investigation from the UK', *Sociologia Ruralis*, vol 40, no 1, pp285–299

Honore, C. (2005) *In Praise of Slow*, Orion, London

Hooper-Greenhill, E. (ed) (2000) *Museums and the Interpretation of Visual Culture*, Routledge, London

Hough, M. (1995) *Cities and Natural Process*, Routledge, London

House of Commons Environmental Audit Committee (2005) 'Environmental education: Follow–up to learning the sustainability lesson', fifth report of session 2004–05, available at www.publications.parliament.uk

Howard, P. and Ashworth, G. (1999) *European Heritage Planning and Management*, Intellect, Exeter

Howard, P. (2002) 'The eco-museum: Innovation that risks the future', *International Journal of Heritage Studies*, vol 8, no 1, pp63–72

Hoynes, W. (2003) 'Branding public service: The "New PBS" and the privatisation of public television', *Television and New Media*, vol 4, no 2, pp117–130

Huggins, R and Izushi, H. (2002) 'The digital divide and ICT learning in rural communities: Examples of good practice service delivery', *Local Economy*, vol 17, no 2, pp111–122

Huizinga, J. (1953) *Homo Ludens*, Beacon Press, Boston, MA

Hutchby, I. (2001) 'Technologies, texts and affordances', *Sociology*, vol 35, no 2, pp441–456

Illeris, K. (2002) *The Three Dimensions of Learning*, Roskilde University Press, Frederiksberg, Denmark

Illich, I. (1975) *Tools for Conviviality*, Fontana, London

Ingold, T. (1992) 'Culture and the perception of the environment' in E. Croll and D. Parkin (eds) *Bush Base: Forest Farm: Culture, Environment and Development*, Routledge, London

Ingold, T. (2000) *The Perception of the Environment*, Routledge, London

Jackson, A. (2000) 'Inter-acting with the past – The use of participatory theatre at museums and heritage sites', *Research in Drama Education*, vol 5, no 2, pp199–215

Jackson, T. (2005) *Motivating Sustainable Consumption*, ESRC Sustainable Technologies Programme, University of Surrey, Guildford, UK

Jasper, A. (2002) 'Planting stories', Eden Project (internal document)

Jasper, A. (2005) 'Visitor evaluation report', Eden Project (internal document)

Kaikati, A. M. and Kaikati, J. G. (2004) 'Stealth marketing: How to reach consumers surreptitiously', *California Management Review*, vol 46, no 4, pp6–22

Kane, P. (2004) *The Play Ethic*, Pan Books, London

Kaplan, R. D. (1997) *The Ends of the Earth*, Vintage Books, New York

Kaplan, R. and Kaplan, S. (1995) *The Experience of Nature: A Psychological Perspective*, Ulrich's Bookstore, Ann Arbor, MI

Karp, I. (1991) 'Culture and representation', in I. Karp and S. D. Levine (eds) *Exhibiting Cultures: The Poetics and Politics of Museum Display*, Smithsonian Institution Press, Washington, DC

Keen, M. and Mahanty, S. (2005) 'Collaborative learning: Bridging scales and interests', in M. Keen, V. A. Brown and R. Dyball, (eds) *Social Learning in Environmental Management: Towards a Sustainable Future*, Earthscan, London

Kemmis, D. (1990) 'Community and the politics of place', University of Oklahoma Press, Norman, OK

Kilpatrick, S., Field, J. and Falk, I. (2003) 'Social capital: An analytical tool for exploring lifelong learning and community development', *British Educational Research Journal*, vol 29, no 3, pp417–433

Klein, N. (2000) *No Logo*, Flamingo, London

Knowles, M. (1983) 'Andragogy: An emerging technology for adult learning', in M. Tight (ed) *Adult Learning and Education*, Routledge, London

Kollmuss, A. and Agyeman, J. (2002) 'Mind the gap: Why do people act environmentally and what are the barriers to pro-environmental behaviour?', *Environmental Education Research*, vol 8, no 3, pp239–260

Kozinets, R. V. and Handelman, J. (1998) 'Ensouling consumption: A netnographic exploration of the meaning of boycotting behavior', *Advances in Consumer Research*, no 25, pp475–480

Kress, G. (2003) *Literacy in the New Media Age*, Routledge, London

Lakoff, G. and Johnson, M. (1980) *Metaphors We Live By*, University of Chicago Press, Chicago, IL

Langhelle, O. (1999) 'Sustainable development: Exploring the ethics of our common future', *International Political Science Review*, vol 20, no 2, pp129–149

Lasn, K. (2000) *Culture Jam*, Quill, New York

Latour, B. (1993) *We Have Never Been Modern*, Harvard University Press, Cambridge, MA

La Trobe, H. (2001) 'Farmers' markets: Consuming local rural produce', *International Journal of Consumer Studies*, vol 25, no 3, pp181–192

Laurillard, D. (2002) *Rethinking University Teaching: A Framework for the Effective Use of Learning Technologies*, Routledge Falmer, London

Lawrence, F. (2004) *Not on the Label: What Really Goes into the Food on Your Plate*, Penguin, London

Lefebvre, H. (1991a) *Critique of Everyday Life*, vol 1, Verso, London

Lefebvre, H. (1991b) *The Production of Space*, Blackwell, Oxford

Lefebvre, H. (2002) *Critique of Everyday Life*, volume two, Verso, London

Lehtonen, T-K. and Maenpaa, P. (1997) 'Shopping in the East Centre Mall', in P. Falk and C. Campbell (eds) *The Shopping Experience*, Sage, London

Leonard, R. and Onyx, J. (2004) *Social Capital and Community Building: Spinning Straw into Gold*, Janus Publishing, London

Levy, P. (2000) *Collective Intelligence: Mankind's Emerging World in Cyberspace*, Perseus Books, New York

Lewin, K. (1951) *Field Theory in Social Science; Selected Theoretical Papers*, Harper & Row, New York

Lewington, A. (2003) *Plants for the People*, 2nd edition, Eden Books/Transworld, London

Liebes, T. and Katz, E. (1993) *The Export of Meaning: Cross-cultural Readings of Dallas*, Polity Press, Cambridge

Livesey, S. M. (2003) 'Organizing and Leading the Grassroots', *Organization and the Environment*, vol 16, no 4, pp488–503

Livingstone, S. (2004) 'Childhood obesity in food advertising in context', Ofcom, London, available at: www.ofcom.org.uk

Loader, B. D. and Keeble, L. (2004) 'Challenging the digital divide? A literature review of community informatics initiatives', Joseph Rowntree Foundation, York, available at: www.jrf.org.uk

Lonsdale, S. (2006) 'Blueprint for disaster', *Daily Telegraph*, 11 February 2006

Lury, C. (2004) *Brands: The Logos of the Global Economy*, Routledge, London

Lutz, C. A. and Collins, J. L. (1993) *Reading National Geographic*, University of Chicago Press, Chicago, IL

Lynch, K. (1981) *Good City Form*, MIT Press, Cambridge, MA

Macdonald, S. (2002) *Behind the Scenes at the Science Museum*, Berg, Oxford

Macnaghten, P. and Urry, J. (1998) *Contested Natures*, Sage, London

Maffesoli, M. (1996) *The Time of the Tribes: The Decline of Individualism in Mass Society*, Sage, London

Maiteny, P. T. (2002) 'Mind in the gap: Summary of research exploring "inner" influences on pro-sustainability learning and behaviour', *Environmental Education Research*, vol 8, no 3, pp209–306

Mander, J. (2002) *Four Arguments for the Elimination of Television*, Perennial, New York

Marcuse, H. (1972) *One Dimensional Man*, Abacus, London

Massey, D. (1994) *Space, Place Gender*, Polity Press, Cambridge

Max-Neef, M. (1991) *Human Scale Development: Conception, Application and Further Reflections*, Apex Press, New York

Max-Neef, M. (1992) 'Development and human needs', in P. Ekins and M. Max-Neef (eds) *Real-life Economics: Understanding Wealth Creation*, Routledge, London

Maxwell, S. (2001) 'Negotiations of car use in everyday life', in D. Miller (ed) *Car Cultures*, Berg, Oxford

Mayhew, L. (2006) 'How green are your jeans?', *Evening Standard*, 13 February, pp32–33

McCann-Erickson/UNEP (2002) 'Can sustainability sell?', available at: www.unep.org

McCarthy, D. (2004) *Saving the Planet Without Costing the Earth: 500 Simple Steps to a Greener Lifestyle*, Fusion Press, London

McDonough, W. and Braungart, M. (2002) *Cradle to Cradle*, North Point Press, New York

McGregor, D. (2004) 'Traditional ecological knowledge and sustainable development: Towards coexistence', in M. Blaser, H. A. Feit and G. McRae (eds) *In the Way of Development: Indigenous People' Life Projects and Globalization*, Zed Books, London

McKenzie-Mohr, D. and Smith, W. (1999) *Fostering Sustainable Behaviour: An Introduction to Community-Based Social Marketing*, New Society Publishers, Gabriola Island

McLuhan, M. (1994) *Understanding Media: The Extensions of Man*, MIT Press, Cambridge, MA

Mezirow, J. (1991) *Transformative Dimensions of Adult Learning*, Jossey-Bass, San Francisco, CA

Miles, M. (2000) *The Uses of Decoration: Essays in the Architectural Everyday*, John Wiley, Chichester

Miller, D., Kitzinger, J., Williams, K. and Beharrell, P. (1998) *The Circuit of Mass Communication*, Sage, London

Miller, D. (1998) *A Theory of Shopping*, Polity Press, Cambridge

Mitchell, W. J. (1996) *City of Bits*, MIT Press, Cambridge, MA

Mitchell, W. J. (2000) *E-topia: Urban Life, Jim – But Not As We Know It*, MIT Press, Cambridge, MA

Mitchell, W. J. (2003) *Me++: The Cyborg Self and the Networked City*, MIT Press, Cambridge, MA

Mol, A. P. J. and Spaargaren, G. (2000) 'Ecological modernization theory in debate', in A. P. J. Mol and D. A. Sonnenfeld (eds) *Ecological Modernization Around the World: Perspectives and Critical Debates*, Frank Cass, London

Monbiot, G. (2002) 'Planet of the fakes', *The Guardian*, 17 December 2002

Monke, L. (2005) 'Charlotte's webpage: Why children shouldn't have the world at their finger tips', *Orion*, September/October 2005, available at: http://www.oriononline.org/pages/om/05-5om/Monke_FT.html

Moon, J. A. (2004) *A Handbook of Reflective and Experiential Learning: Theory and Practice*, RoutledgeFalmer, London

Moores, S. (1993) *Interpreting Audiences: The Ethnography of Media Consumption*, Sage, London

Moores, S. (2000) *Media and Everyday Life in Modern Society*, University of Edinburgh Press, Edinburgh

Morito, B. (2002) *Thinking Ecologically: Environmental Thought, Values and Policy*, Fernwood Publishing, Black Point

Muniz, A. and O'Guinn, T. (2001) 'Brand community', *Journal of Consumer Research*, vol 27, no 4, pp412–432

Nattrass, B. and Altomare, M. (1999) *The Natural Step for Business: Wealth, Ecology and the Evolutionary Corporation*, New Society Publishers, Gabriola Island

Nilsson, B. and Rosen, B. (2001) 'Cultural history museums and human ecology – A challenge to integration', *Museum International*, vol 53, no 4, pp43–46

Nozick, M. (1999) 'Sustainable development begins at home: Community solutions to global problems', in J. Pierce and A. Dale (eds) *Communities, Development and Sustainability Across Canada*, UBC Press, Vancouver

ODPM (2004) *The Egan Review: Skills for Sustainable Communities*, ODPM, London

Oers, B. van. (1998) 'From context to contextualizing', *Learning and Instruction*, vol 8, no 6, pp473–488

Ofcom (2004a) *Ofcom's Strategy and Priorities for the Promotion of Media Literacy*, Ofcom, London

Ofcom (2004b) *Ofcom Review of Public Service Television Broadcasting: Phase 2 – Meeting the Digital Challenge*, Ofcom, London

Ofcom (2004c) *The Communications Market 2004*, Ofcom, London

Ofcom (2005) *The Communications Market 2005*, Ofcom, London

O'Guinn, T. and Shrum, L. J. (1997) 'The role of television in the construction of consumer identity', *Journal of Consumer Research*, vol 23, no 4, pp278–294

Paterson, M. (2000) 'Car culture and global environmental politics', *Review of International Studies*, no 26, pp253–270

Pearman, H. and Whalley, A. (2003) *The Architecture of Eden*, Eden Books/Transworld, London

Peck, J., Beloe, S., Muller, F. and Scott, F. (2004) *Through The Looking Glass*, SustainAbility/WWF-UK, London

Pepper, D. (1991) *Communes and the Green Vision*, Green Print, London

Petrini, C. (2004) 'Interview', *The Ecologist*, vol 34, no 3, pp50–53

Portes, A. (1998) 'Social capital: Its origins and applications in modern sociology', *Annual Review of Sociology*, no 24, pp1–24

Postman, N. (1987) *Amusing Ourselves to Death*, Methuen, London

Postman, N. (1993) *Technopoly: The Surrender of Culture to Technology*, Vintage Books, New York

Putnam, R. D. (1993) *Making Democracy Work*, Princeton University Press, Princeton

Putnam, R. D. (2000) *Bowling Alone: The Collapse and Revival of American Community*, Simon and Schuster, New York

Ratner, B. D. (2004) '"Sustainability" as a dialogue of values: Challenges to the sociology of development', *Sociological Inquiry*, vol 74, no 1, pp59–69

Reckwitz, A. (2002) 'Toward a theory of social practices: A development in culturalist theorizing', *European Journal of Social Theory*, vol 5, no 2, pp243–63

Reed, E. (1988) 'The affordances of the animate environment: Social science from the ecological point of view', in T. Ingold (ed) *What is an Animal?*, Unwin Hyman, London

Rheingold, H. (2000) *Tools for Thought*, MIT Press, Cambridge, MA, also available at www.rheingold.com/texts/tft/14.html

Rheingold, H. (2002) *Smart Mobs: The Next Social Revolution*, Basic Books, Cambridge, MA

Roberts, L. C. (1997) *From Knowledge to Narrative: Education and the Changing Museum*, Smithsonian Institution Press, Washington DC

Roberts, P. and Sykes, H. (eds) (2000) *Urban Regeneration: A Handbook*, Sage, London

Robinson, J. (2003) 'Future subjunctive: Backcasting as social learning', *Futures*, no 35, pp839–856

Robinson, J. (2004) 'Squaring the circle? Some thoughts on the idea of sustainable development', *Ecological Economics*, vol 48, pp369–384

Robson, J. (2006) 'Cred label', *The Daily Telegraph*, 18 March 2006

Roelofs, J. (1999) 'Building and designing with nature: Urban design', in D. Satterthwaite (ed) *The Earthscan Reader in Sustainable Cities*, Earthscan, London

Romig, K. (2005) 'The Upper Sonoran lifestyle: Gated communities in Scottsdale, Arizona', *City & Community*, vol 4, no 1, pp67–86

Rose, C. (2005) *How to Win Campaigns: 100 Steps to Success*, Earthscan, London

Roseland, M. (1998) *Toward Sustainable Communities: Resources for Citizens and their Governments*, New Society Publishers, Gabriola Island, BC

Rumbo, J. D. (2002) 'Consumer resistance in a world of advertising clutter: The case of *Adbusters*', *Psychology and Marketing*, vol 19, no 2, pp127–148

Sachatello-Sawyer, B. et al. (2002) *Adult Museum Programmes: Designing Meaningful Experiences*, AltaMira Press, Walnut Creek, CA

Sale, K. (1991) *Dwellers in the Land: The Bioregional Vision*, University of Georgia Press, Athens

Samuel, R. (1998) 'The lost gardens of Heligan', in A. Light (ed) *Raphael Samuel – Island Stories: Unravelling Britain*, Theatres of Memory, vol 2., Verso, London

Saunders, D., Wyn-Lewis, E ., Jones, A. and Watkins-Hughes, P. (2003) 'Public broadcasting and social action campaigns: A case study for informal learning', *Widening Participation and Lifelong Learning*, vol 5, no 1, pp8–24

Saunders, T. (2002) *The Boiled Frog Syndrome: Your Health and the Built Environment*, Wiley-Academy, Chichester

Savelson, A. (2005) 'Application of a health promotion model to community-based sustainability planning', *Local Environment*, vol 10, no 6, pp629–647

Scandrett, E., O'Leary, T. and Martinez, T. (2006) 'Speak, listen and learn', *Adults Learning*, February 2006, pp20–23

Schlosser, E. (2001) *Fast Food Nation*, Penguin, London

Schor, J. (1998) *The Overspent American*, HarperPerennial, New York

Schroeder, J. E. (2002) *Visual Consumption*, Routledge, London

Schumacher, F. (1974) *Small is Beautiful*, Abacus, London

Schutz, A. (1970) *On Phenomenology and Social Relations*, University of Chicago Press, Chicago

Schwarz, W. (2000) 'It's wonderland', *The Guardian*, 27 September 2000

Scott, W. and Gough, S. (2003) *Sustainable Development and Learning: Framing the Issues*, RoutledgeFalmer, London

Seyfang, G. (2005) 'Shopping for sustainability: Can sustainable consumption promote ecological citizenship?', *Environmental Politics*, vol 14, no 2, pp290–306

Shaffer, D. W., Squire, K., Halverson, R. and Gee, J. P. (2004) 'Video games and the future of learning', report published by the Academic ADL Co-Lab, Madison, WI

Shanahan, J. (1993) 'Television and the cultivation of environmental concern: 1988–92', in A. Hansen (ed) *The Mass Media and Environmental Issues*, University of Leicester Press, Leicester

Shattuc, J. M. (1997) *The Talking Cure: TV Talk Shows and Women*, Routledge, London

Shove, E. (2003) *Comfort, Cleanliness and Convenience: The Social Organisation of Normality*, Berg, Oxford

Sidaway, R. (2005) *Resolving Environmental Disputes: From Conflict to Consensus*, Earthscan, London

Siegle, L. (2001) *Green Living in the Urban Jungle*, Green Books, Totnes

Siegle, L. (2006) 'The Observer Ethical Awards 2006', *The Observer Magazine*, 12 February 2006

Singhal, A., Cody, M. J., Rogers, E. M. and Sabido, M. (eds) (2004) *Entertainment-Education and Social Change: History, Research, Practice*, Lawrence Erlbaum, New Jersey

Smales, J. (1999) 'How green is your valley?', *The Guardian*, 10 July 1999

Smit, T. (2001) *Eden*, Corgi Books, London

Smit, T. (2004) 'Interview with John Elkington', *Radar*, October 2004, available at: www.sustainability.com/insight/radar-article.asp?id=149

Smith, G. R. (2004) 'How green is technology? The paradox of online sustainable education', *International Journal of Sustainable Development and World Ecology*, no 11, pp1–9

Smith, J. (ed) (2000) *The Daily Globe: Environmental Change, the Public and the Media*, Earthscan, London

Sneed, C. (1997) 'The Garden Project: Creating urban communities', in H. Hannum (ed) *People, Land and Community*, Yale University Press, New Haven

Stagl, S. (2002) 'Local organic food markets: Potentials and limitations for contributing to sustainable development', *Empirica*, no 29, pp145–162

Sterling, S. (2001) *Sustainable Education: Re-visioning Learning and Change*, Green Books, Totnes

Sterling, S. (2004) 'An analysis of the development of sustainability education internationally', in J. Blewitt and C. Cullingford (ed) (2004) *The Sustainability Curriculum*, Earthscan, London

Stokes, B. (2005) 'Videogames have changed: Time to consider "serious games"', *Development Education Journal*, vol 11, no 3, available at www.netaid.org/documents/DEJ_article-Games_and_Development_Education-June05.pdf

Stokes, L. C. and Pankowski, M. (1988) 'Incidental learning of aging adults via television', *Adult Education Quarterly*, vol 38, no 2, pp88–99

Strasser, S. (1989) *Satisfaction Guaranteed: The Making of the American Mass Market*, Pantheon Books, New York

Strong, D. and Higgs, E. (2000) 'Borgmann's philosophy of technology', in E. Higgs, A. Light and D. Strong (eds) *Technology and the Good Life?*, University of Chicago Press, Chicago

Talbot, J. (1995) *Simply Build Green*, Findhorn Press, Findhorn

Taylor, R. (1996) 'Preserving the liberal tradition in "New Times"', in J. Wallis (ed) *Liberal Adult Education: The End of an Era*, Continuing Education Press, Nottingham

Taylor, R., Barr, J. and Steele, T. (2002) *For a Radical Higher Education: After Postmodernism*, Open University Press, Buckingham

Thompson, C. W. (2002) 'Urban open space in the 21st century', *Landscape and Urban Planning*, no 60, pp59–72

Thompson, J. B. (1996) *The Media and Modernity: A Social Theory of the Media*, Polity Press, Cambridge

Tilden, F. (1957) *Interpreting Our Heritage*, University of North Carolina Press, Chapel Hill, NC

Underhill, P. (2000) *Why We Buy: The Science of Shopping*, Thompson, Texere

UNEP (2005) 'Talk the Walk: Advancing sustainable lifestyles through marketing and communications', available at: www.talkthewalk.net

UNESCO (2005) 'United Nations Decade of Education for Sustainable Development (2005–2014)', available at: http://portal.unesco.org/education/en/ev.php

Urry, J. (1996) *The Tourist Gaze*, Sage, London

Uslaner, E. M. (1998) 'Social capital, television and the "mean world": Trust optimism and civic participation', *Political Psychology*, vol 19, no 3, pp441–467

Vanderstraeten, R. (2002), 'Dewey's transactional constructivism', *Journal of Philosophy of Education*, vol 36, no 2, pp233–246

Vergo, P. (ed) (1989) *The New Museology*, Reaktion Books, London

Vidal, J. (1999) 'Phoenix Park', *The Guardian*, 24 March

Waage, S., Shah, R. and Girshick, S. (2003) 'Information technology and sustainability: Enabling the future', *International Journal of Corporate Sustainability*, vol 10, no 4, pp81–96

Wackernagel, M. and Rees, W. (1996) *Our Ecological Footprint: Reducing Human Impact on the Earth*, New Society Publishers, Gabriola Island

Warde, A. (2004) 'Theories of practice as an approach to consumption', Cultures of Consumption working papers series, Centre for Research on Innovation and Competition & Department of Sociology, University of Manchester

Weaver, M. (2005) 'Rhythm and blues', *The Guardian*, 21 September

Wenger, E., McDermott, R. and Synder, W. M. (2002) *Cultivating Communities of Practice*, Harvard Business School Press, Boston, MA

Whittingham, J. (2005) 'Seed no evil', *The Garden*, vol 130, part 11, pp788–791

Williams, C. (ed) (1998) *Environmental Victims*, Earthscan, London

Wolverton, B. (1998) 'Sustainable Indoor Systems', *EcoDesign*, vol 6, no 3, pp14–16

Woolcock, M. and Narayan, D. (2000) 'Social capital: Implications for development theory, research and policy', *World Bank Research Observer*, vol 15, no 2, pp225–250

Worpole, K. (2000) 'Regaining an interior world', *Landscape Design*, no 289, pp20–22

Index